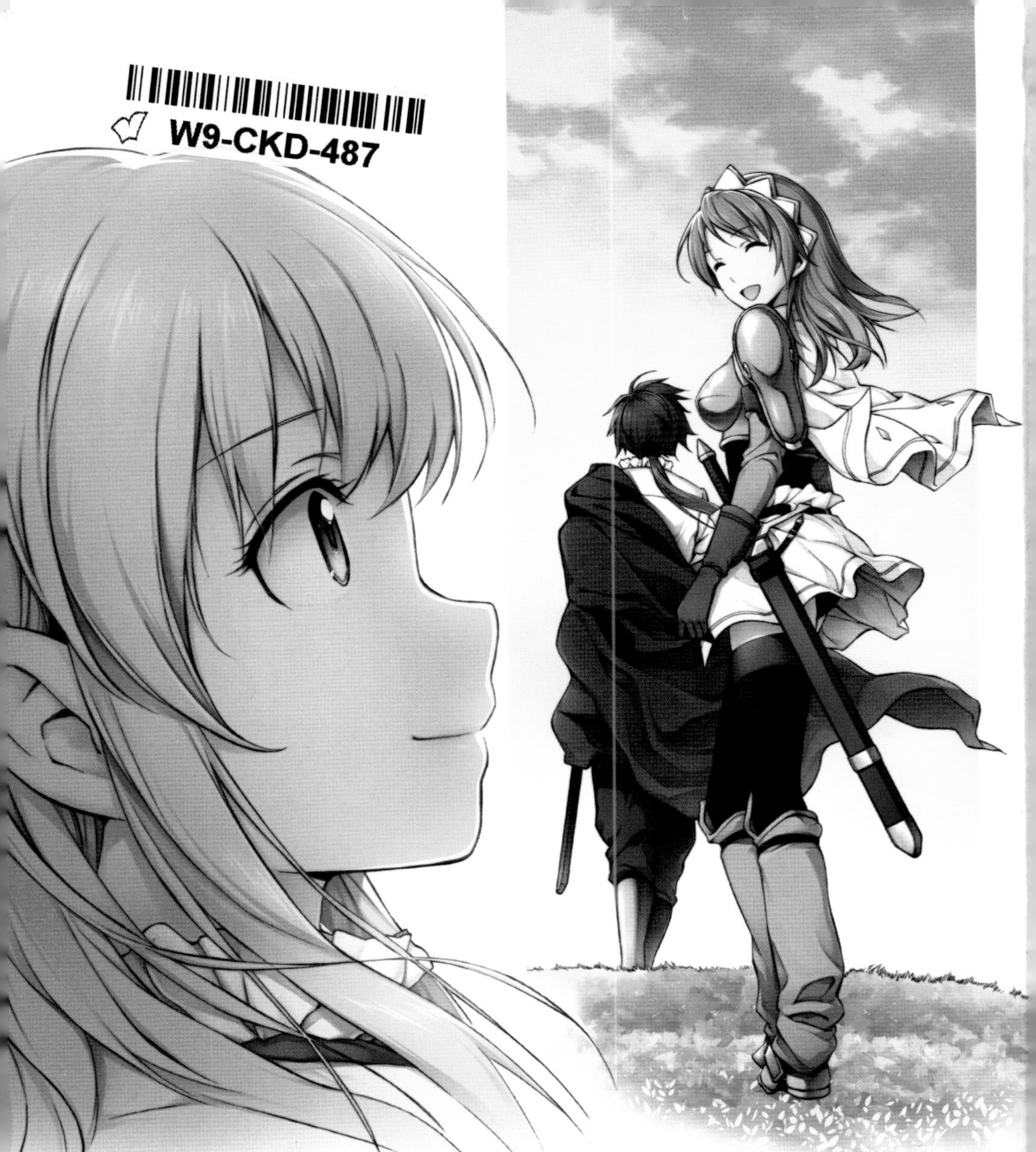

The Sacred Blacksmith

聖剣の刀鍛冶（ブラックスミス） 10

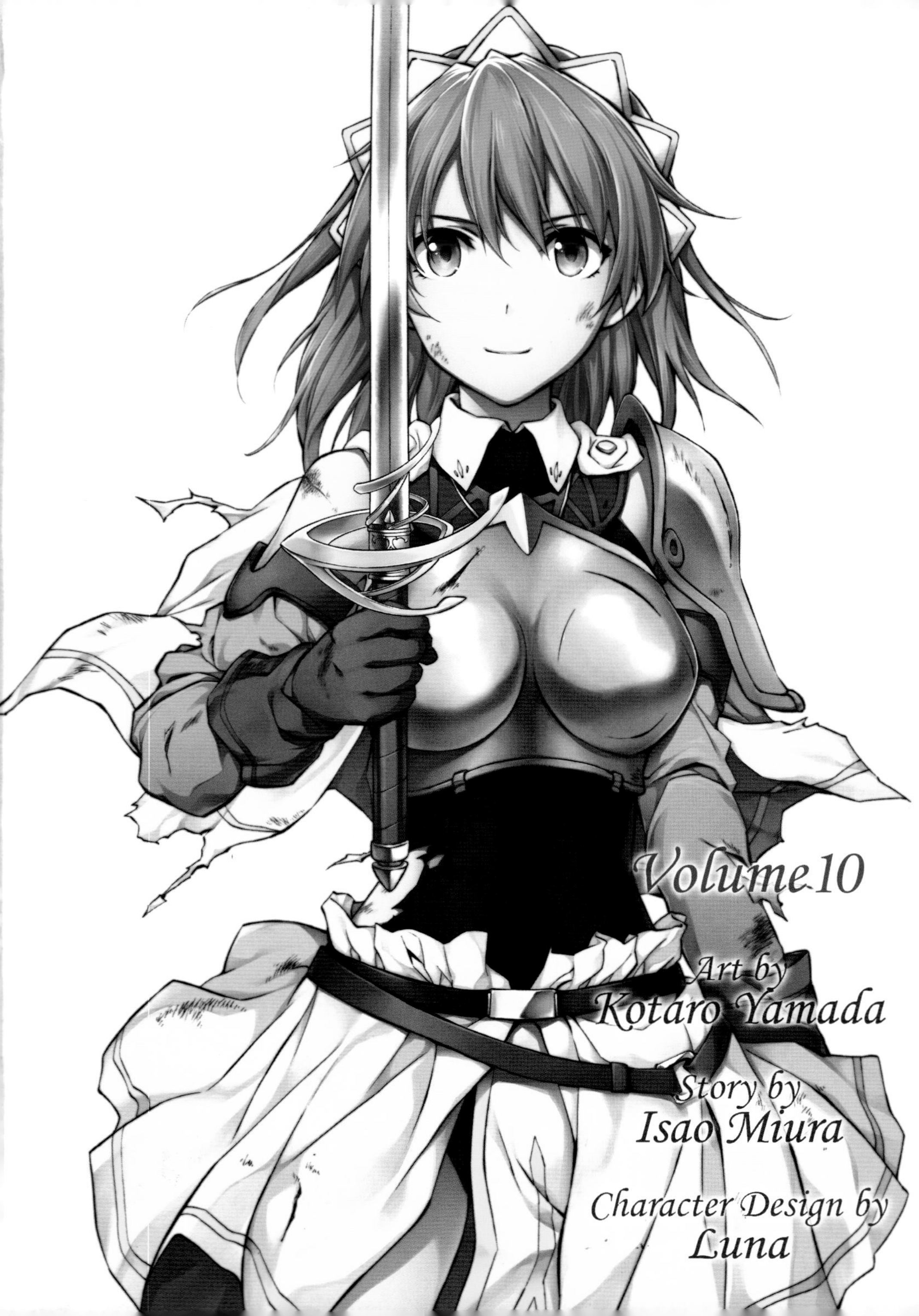

Volume 10

Art by
Kotaro Yamada

Story by
Isao Miura

Character Design by
Luna

Continent

Character

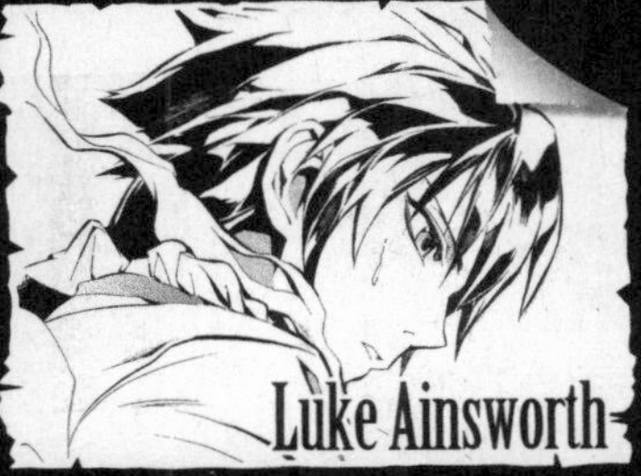

Luke Ainsworth

A proficient swordsman who uses an unusual blade called a "katana." Pessimistic and world-weary, he runs his own smithy.

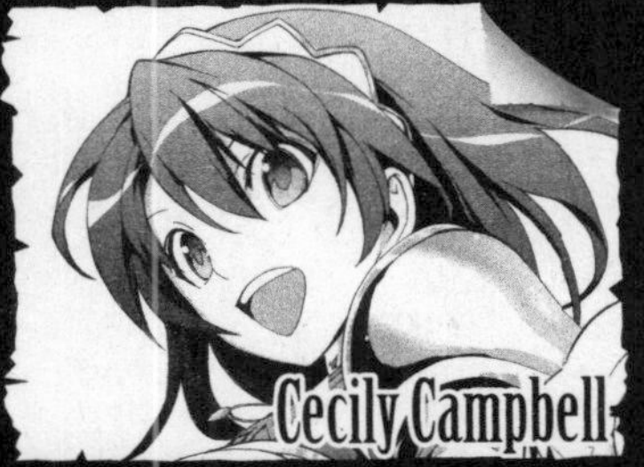

Cecily Campbell

A young lady knight who is part of the Knight Guard, charged with defending the Independent Trade City of Housman. Ex-nobility, she has a strong sense of justice.

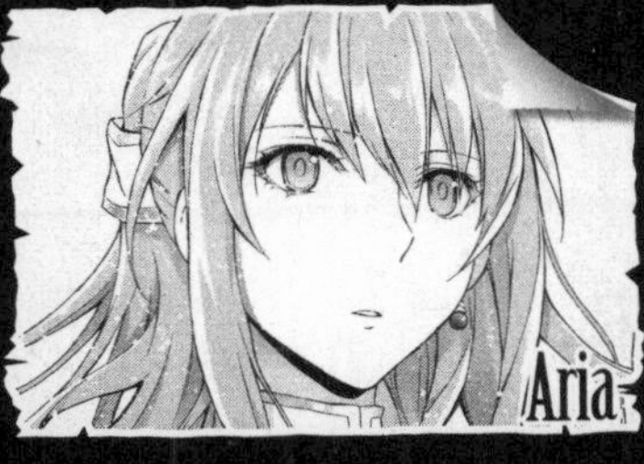

Aria

Though the original Aria gave her life to save Cecily in a moment of dire peril, she has been reforged into a new Sacred Blade. She has no memories of her past self, but she still serves as Cecily's partner.

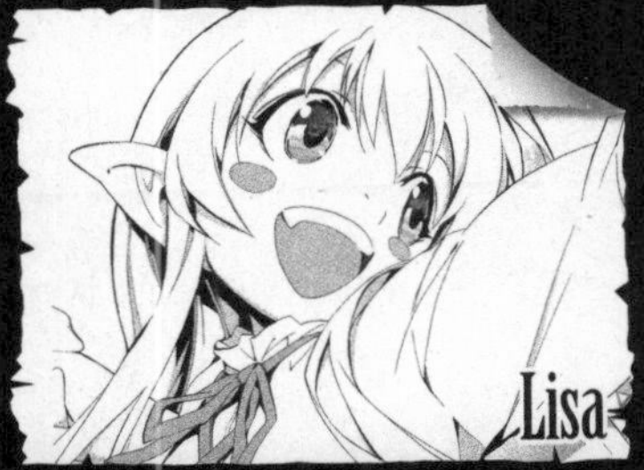

Lisa

The assistant who lives and works at Luke's smithy. Innocent and carefree, she loves talking with everyone. She says she is only three years old.

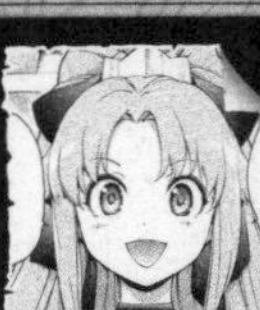

Zenobia Q. Lanchester

Ruler of the Militant Nation, she wants to see Valbanill destroyed. Her people call her the Little Queen.

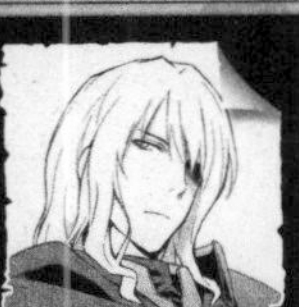

Siegfried

Knight Captain of the Empire. He uses Demon Pacts and keeps inhumans as pets.

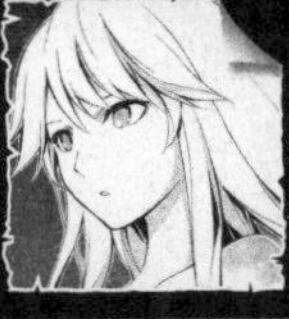

Nameless

A Demon Blade owned by the Imperial Crowd Powers. Created from rare "star metal," she became the base for the reborn Aria.

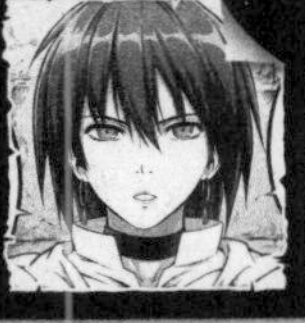

Sacred Blade

The original Sacred Blade holding the seal on Valbanill. However, she has reached the end of her power, which led her to leave Blair Volcano. She revealed to Luke the required materials for the forging of the Sacred Blade.

聖剣の刀鍛冶 *The Sacred Blacksmith*

Decades ago, a great war raged across the continent. Called the "Valbanill War," it saw the widespread use of powerful Demon Pacts. Forty-four years later, a young lady knight named Cecily Campbell meets a mysterious blacksmith named Luke Ainsworth and asks him to forge for her a sword.

THE INDEPENDENT TRADE CITY
THIRD DISTRICT KNIGHT CORPS CAPTAIN HANNIBAL QUASAR
INDEPENDENT TRADE CITY MAYOR HUGO HOUSMAN
THE MILITANT NATION
MILITANT NATION QUEEN ZENOBIA Q. LANCHESTER
MILITANT NATION TACTICIAN AREVIY IRVINE
THE IMPERIAL CROWD POWERS
IMPERIAL KNIGHT CAPTAIN SIEGFRIED
IMPERIAL KNIGHTS COMMANDER-IN-CHIEF AUGUSTUS ARTHUR

I AM THE ONE KNOWN AS THE SACRED BLADE.
DUE TO MY FAILING STRENGTH, I HAVE LOST THE POWER TO HOLD THE SEAL ON THE BEAST. THUS, I HAVE RETURNED TO CIVILIZATION.

The Imperial Crowd Powers has declared war on the Independent Trade City. Deciding that the safety of the citizens is paramount, the city council evacuates the city's entire population to the Militant Nation.

As the evacuation begins, a mysterious woman calling herself The Sacred Blade wanders into Luke's atelier. She speaks of how the Demon Katana forged by Luke has temporarily strengthened the seal on Valbanill, which has allowed her to relinquish her duty and spend her little remaining time amongst humanity.

KRA-THOOOOM
HN?!
NGH!!
GYA-AAH ...!!
AAA-AAH-HHH!
AAAH!!
AAH!!
AAAH!!
AAAH!!

NOW...
SPEAK THE DEATH PHRASE.

The Sacred Blade shares with Luke the materials needed for the forging of a true Sacred Blade: jewel steel, a demon blade, and star metal. Jewel steel, they have in plenty. For a Demon Blade, they had the remnants of Aria. As for the star metal--Nameless was made of it.

Meanwhile, Lisa performs a Demon Pact, sacrificing her own left eye to birth a new Demon Eye, so that Luke could regain his vision.

あらすじ Story

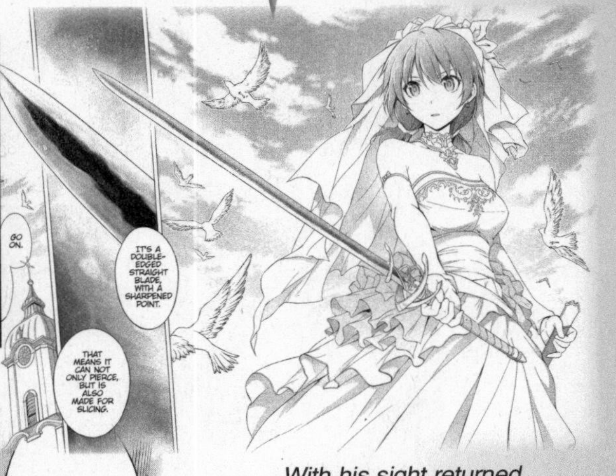
IT'S A DOUBLE-EDGED STRAIGHT BLADE, WITH A SHARPENED POINT.
GO ON.
THAT MEANS IT CAN NOT ONLY PIERCE, BUT IS ALSO MADE FOR SLICING.

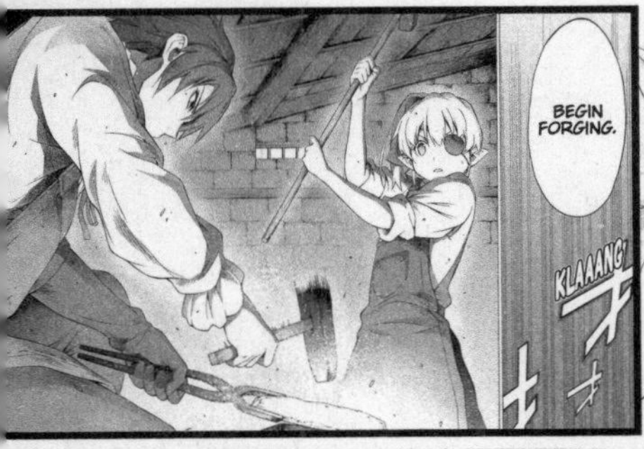
BEGIN FORGING.
KLAAANG

With his sight returned, Luke uses Nameless and the shattered fragments of Aria to begin forging a new Sacred Blade. After a fortnight of intense and back-breaking labor, the Sacred Blade Aria is born. Luke brings it to Cecily on the day of their wedding.

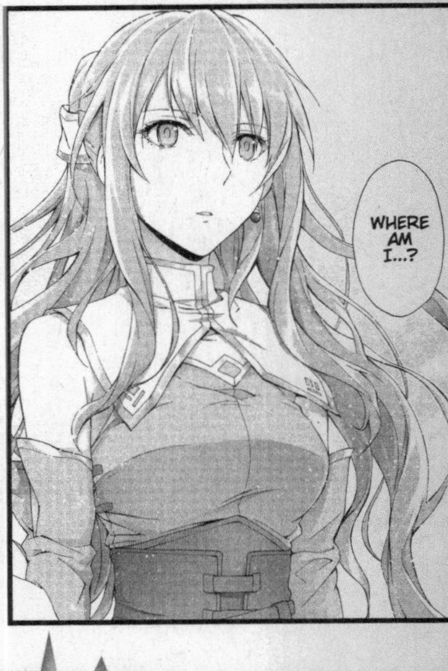
WHERE AM I...?

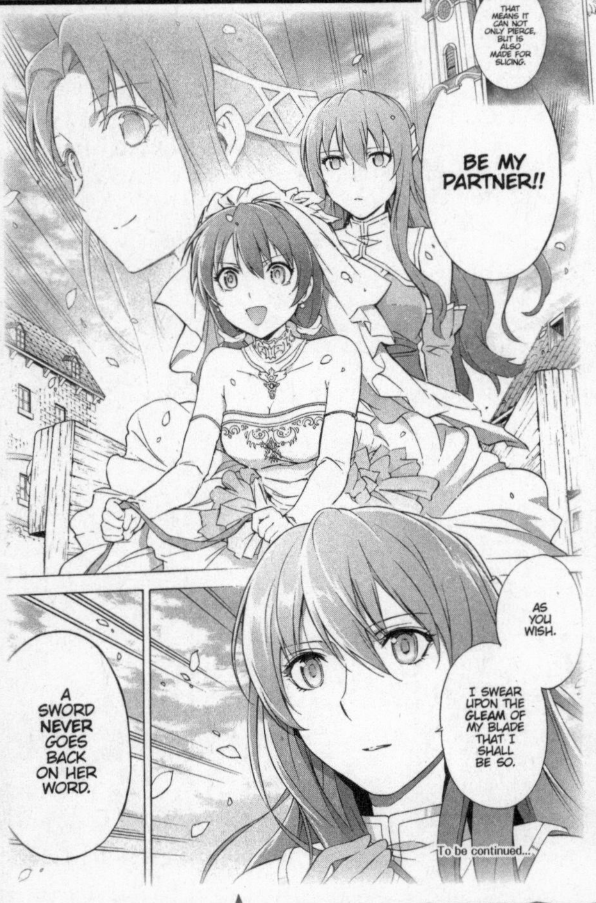
BE MY PARTNER!!
AS YOU WISH.
I SWEAR UPON THE GLEAM OF MY BLADE THAT I SHALL BE SO.
A SWORD NEVER GOES BACK ON HER WORD.
To be continued...

The Sacred Blacksmith

聖剣の刀鍛冶

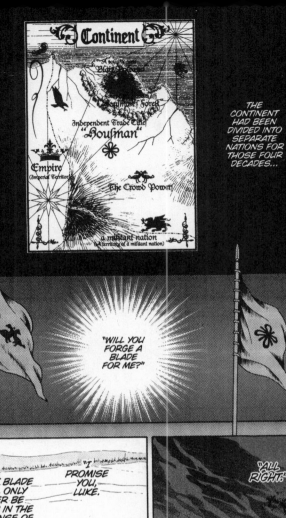

FORTY-FIVE YEARS HAVE PASSED SINCE THE END OF THE DESTRUCTIVE VALBANILL WAR.
THE CONTINENT HAD BEEN DIVIDED INTO SEPARATE NATIONS FOR THOSE FOUR DECADES...
Continent
Independent Trade Cities
"Housman"
Empire
(Imperial Territory)
The Crowd Powers
a militant nation
(a territory of a militant nation)
BUT NOW THOSE BORDERS WERE CRUMBLING.
"WILL YOU FORGE A BLADE FOR ME?"
"ALL RIGHT."
"LUKE, THANK YOU!"
Chapter 53 Valbanill (Part 1)
"I PROMISE YOU, LUKE.
"THAT BLADE WILL ONLY EVER BE USED IN THE DEFENSE OF THE CITY AND ITS PEOPLE.
"PLEASE! MAKE ME THE GREATEST SWORD IN THE WORLD!"
OUTSKIRTS OF THE INDEPENDENT TRADE CITY

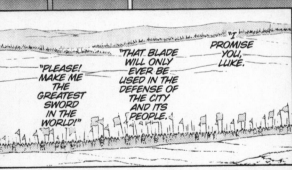

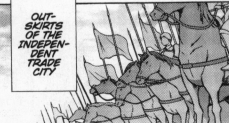

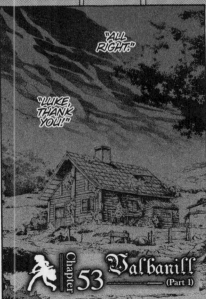

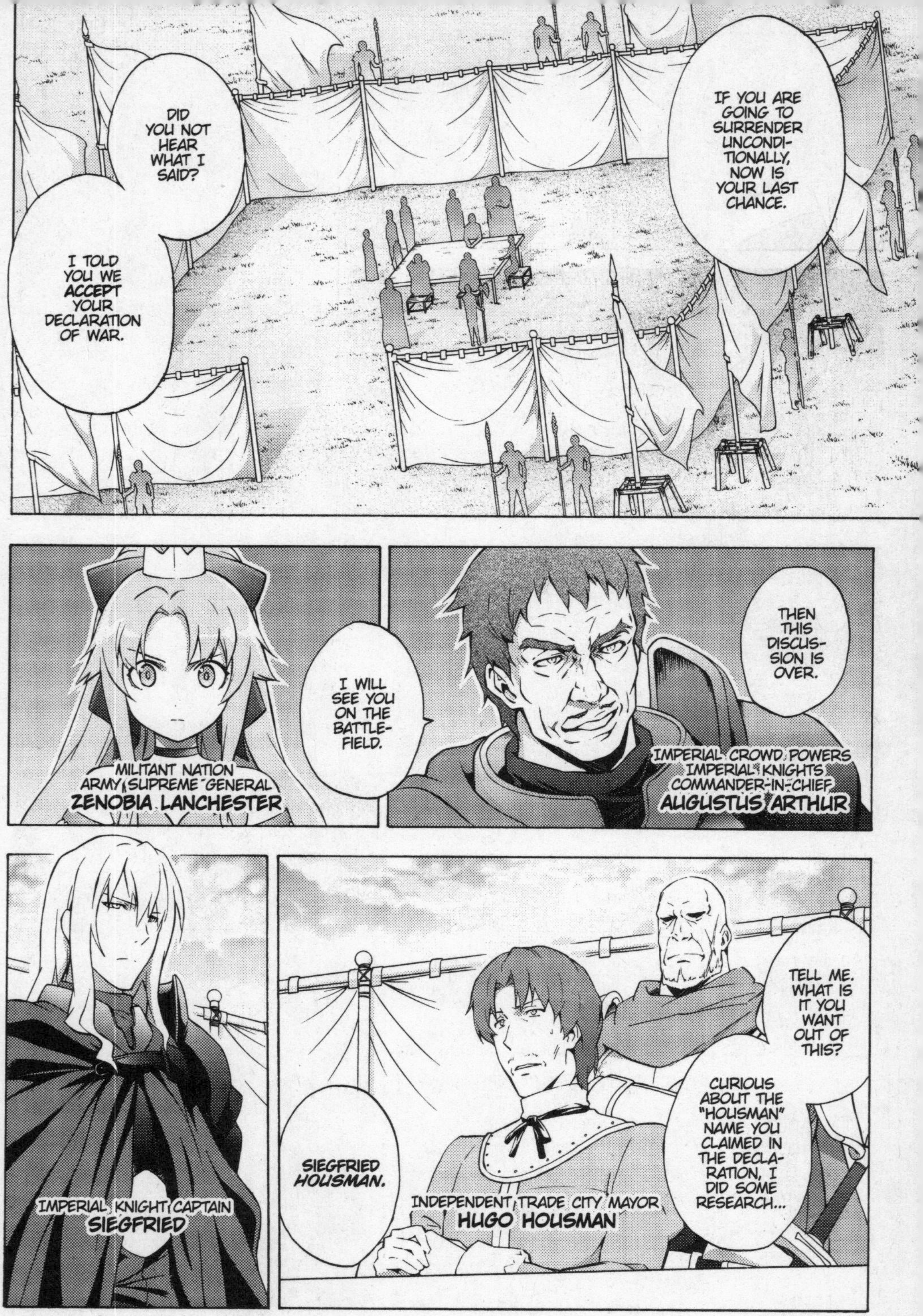
IF YOU ARE GOING TO SURRENDER UNCONDITIONALLY, NOW IS YOUR LAST CHANCE.
DID YOU NOT HEAR WHAT I SAID?
I TOLD YOU WE ACCEPT YOUR DECLARATION OF WAR.
THEN THIS DISCUSSION IS OVER.
IMPERIAL CROWD POWERS IMPERIAL KNIGHTS COMMANDER-IN-CHIEF
AUGUSTUS ARTHUR
I WILL SEE YOU ON THE BATTLEFIELD.
MILITANT NATION ARMY SUPREME GENERAL
ZENOBIA LANCHESTER
TELL ME. WHAT IS IT YOU WANT OUT OF THIS?
CURIOUS ABOUT THE "HOUSMAN" NAME YOU CLAIMED IN THE DECLARATION, I DID SOME RESEARCH...
SIEGFRIED HOUSMAN.
INDEPENDENT TRADE CITY MAYOR
HUGO HOUSMAN
IMPERIAL KNIGHT CAPTAIN
SIEGFRIED

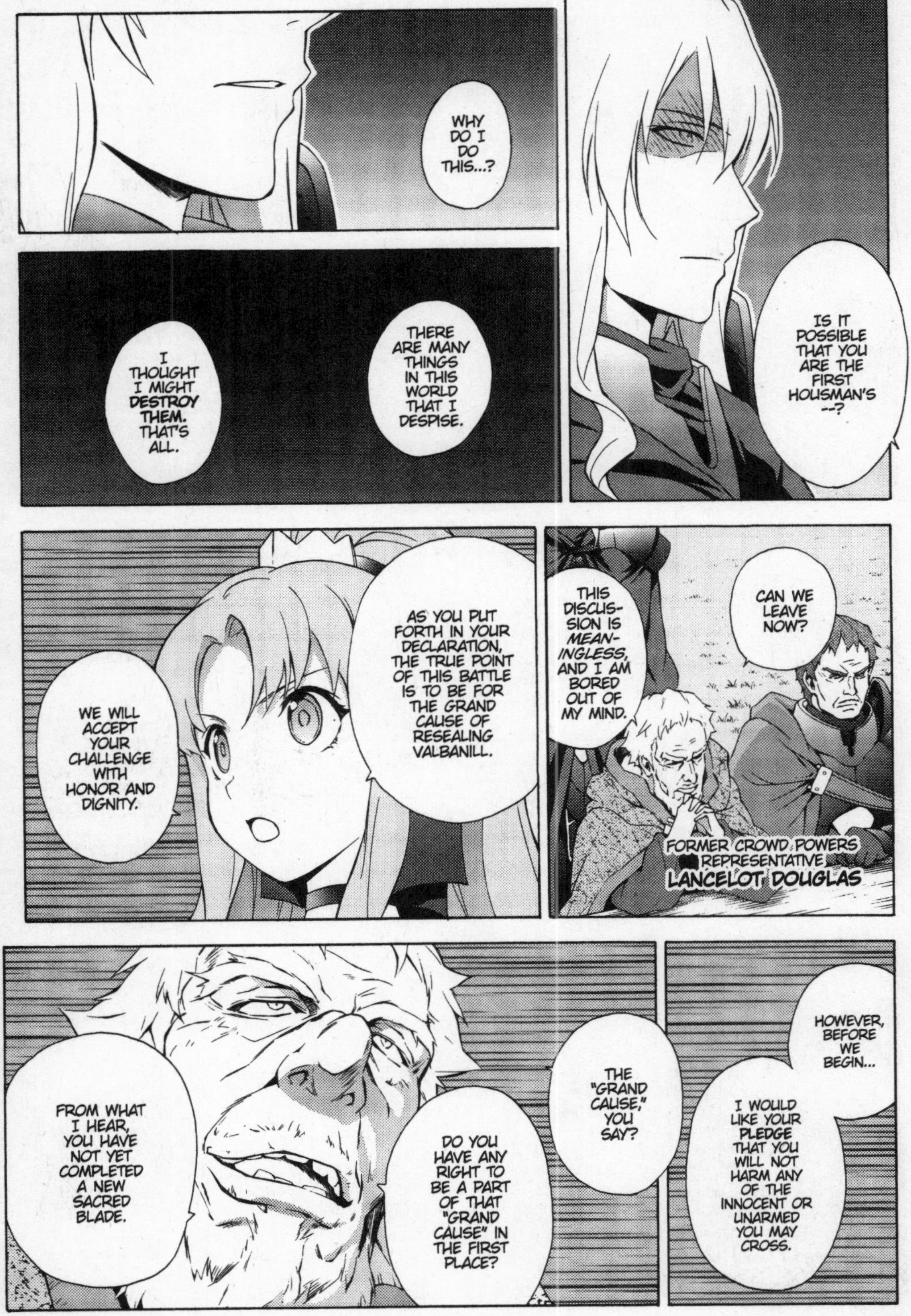
IS IT POSSIBLE THAT YOU ARE THE FIRST HOUSMAN'S --?
WHY DO I DO THIS...?
THERE ARE MANY THINGS IN THIS WORLD THAT I DESPISE.
I THOUGHT I MIGHT DESTROY THEM. THAT'S ALL.
CAN WE LEAVE NOW?
THIS DISCUSSION IS *MEANINGLESS*, AND I AM BORED OUT OF MY MIND.
FORMER CROWD POWERS REPRESENTATIVE LANCELOT DOUGLAS
AS YOU PUT FORTH IN YOUR DECLARATION, THE TRUE POINT OF THIS BATTLE IS TO BE FOR THE GRAND CAUSE OF RESEALING VALBANILL.
WE WILL ACCEPT YOUR CHALLENGE WITH HONOR AND DIGNITY.
HOWEVER, BEFORE WE BEGIN...
I WOULD LIKE YOUR PLEDGE THAT YOU WILL NOT HARM ANY OF THE INNOCENT OR UNARMED YOU MAY CROSS.
THE "GRAND CAUSE," YOU SAY?
DO YOU HAVE ANY RIGHT TO BE A PART OF THAT "GRAND CAUSE" IN THE FIRST PLACE?
FROM WHAT I HEAR, YOU HAVE NOT YET COMPLETED A NEW SACRED BLADE.

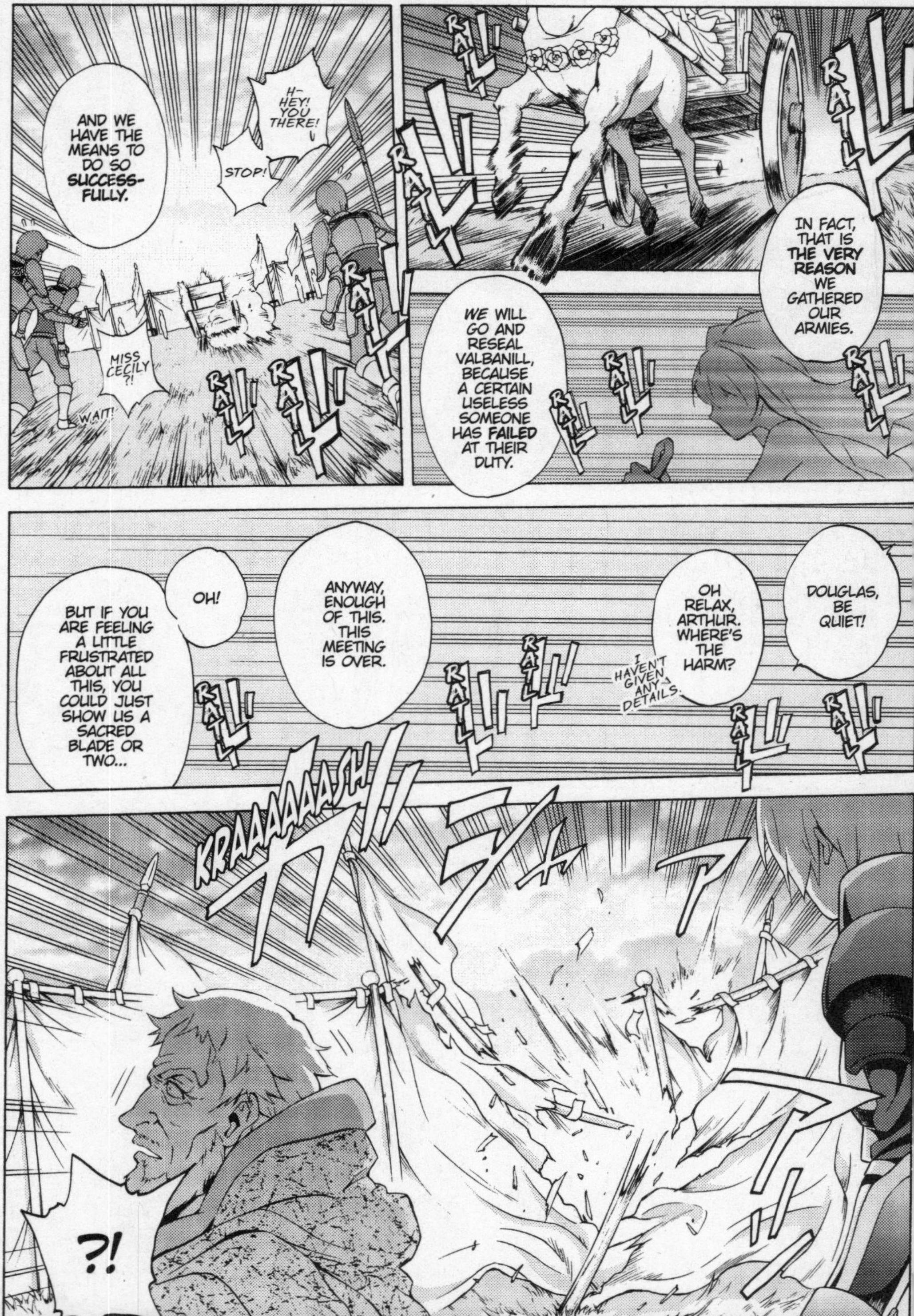
RATTL
RATTL
RATTL
IN FACT, THAT IS THE VERY REASON WE GATHERED OUR ARMIES.
RATTL
RATTL
WE WILL GO AND RESEAL VALBANILL, BECAUSE A CERTAIN USELESS SOMEONE HAS FAILED AT THEIR DUTY.
RATTL
H-HEY! YOU THERE!
AND WE HAVE THE MEANS TO DO SO SUCCESSFULLY.
STOP!
RATTL
MISS CECILY?!
RATTL
RATTL
WAIT!
DOUGLAS, BE QUIET!
RATTL
OH RELAX, ARTHUR. WHERE'S THE HARM?
I HAVEN'T GIVEN ANY DETAILS.
RATTL
RATTL
RATTL
ANYWAY, ENOUGH OF THIS. THIS MEETING IS OVER.
OH!
RATTL
BUT IF YOU ARE FEELING A LITTLE FRUSTRATED ABOUT ALL THIS, YOU COULD JUST SHOW US A SACRED BLADE OR TWO...
KRAAAAAASH!!
?!

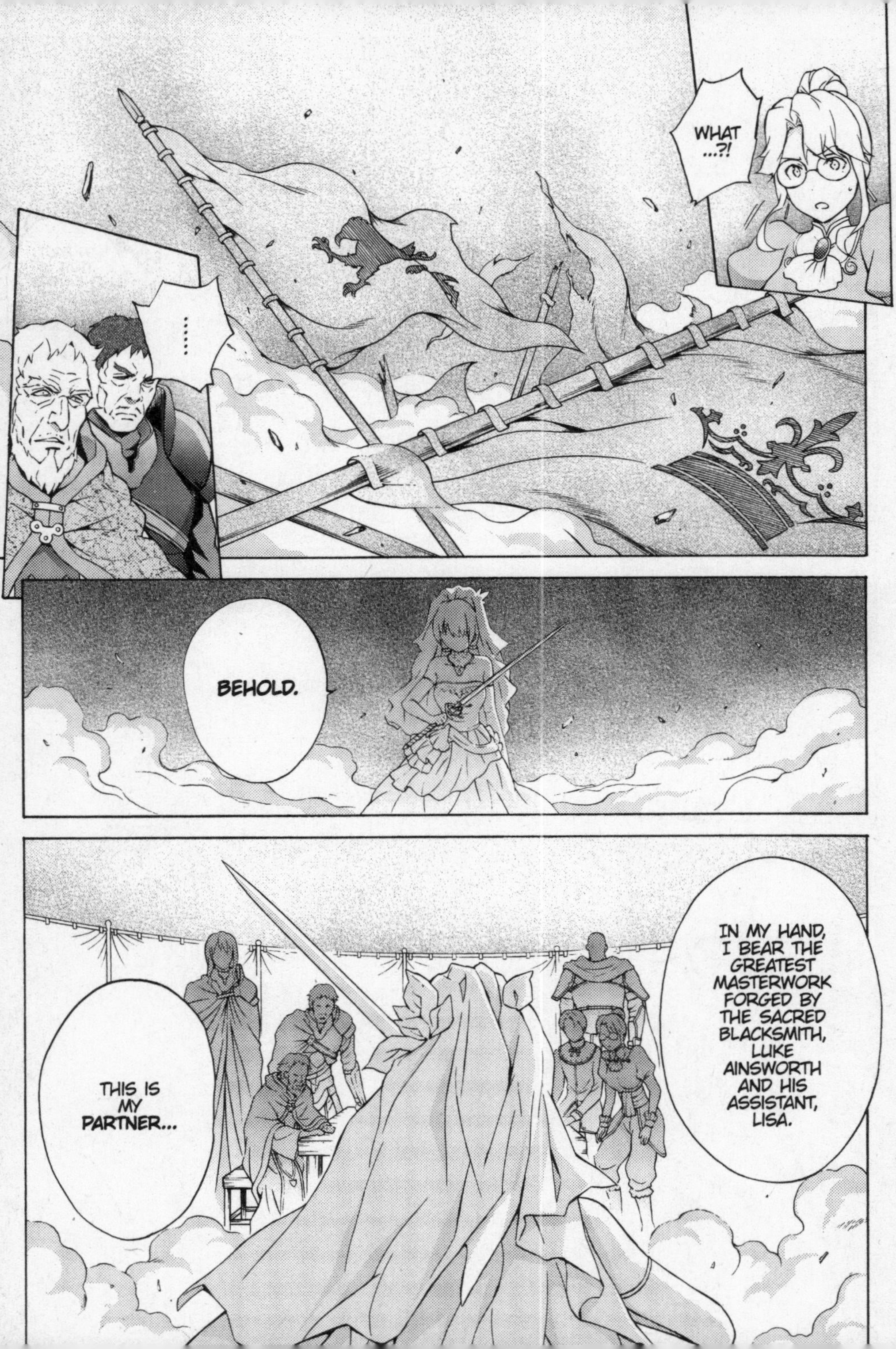
WHAT ...?!
......
BEHOLD.
IN MY HAND, I BEAR THE GREATEST MASTERWORK FORGED BY THE SACRED BLACKSMITH, LUKE AINSWORTH AND HIS ASSISTANT, LISA.
THIS IS MY PARTNER...

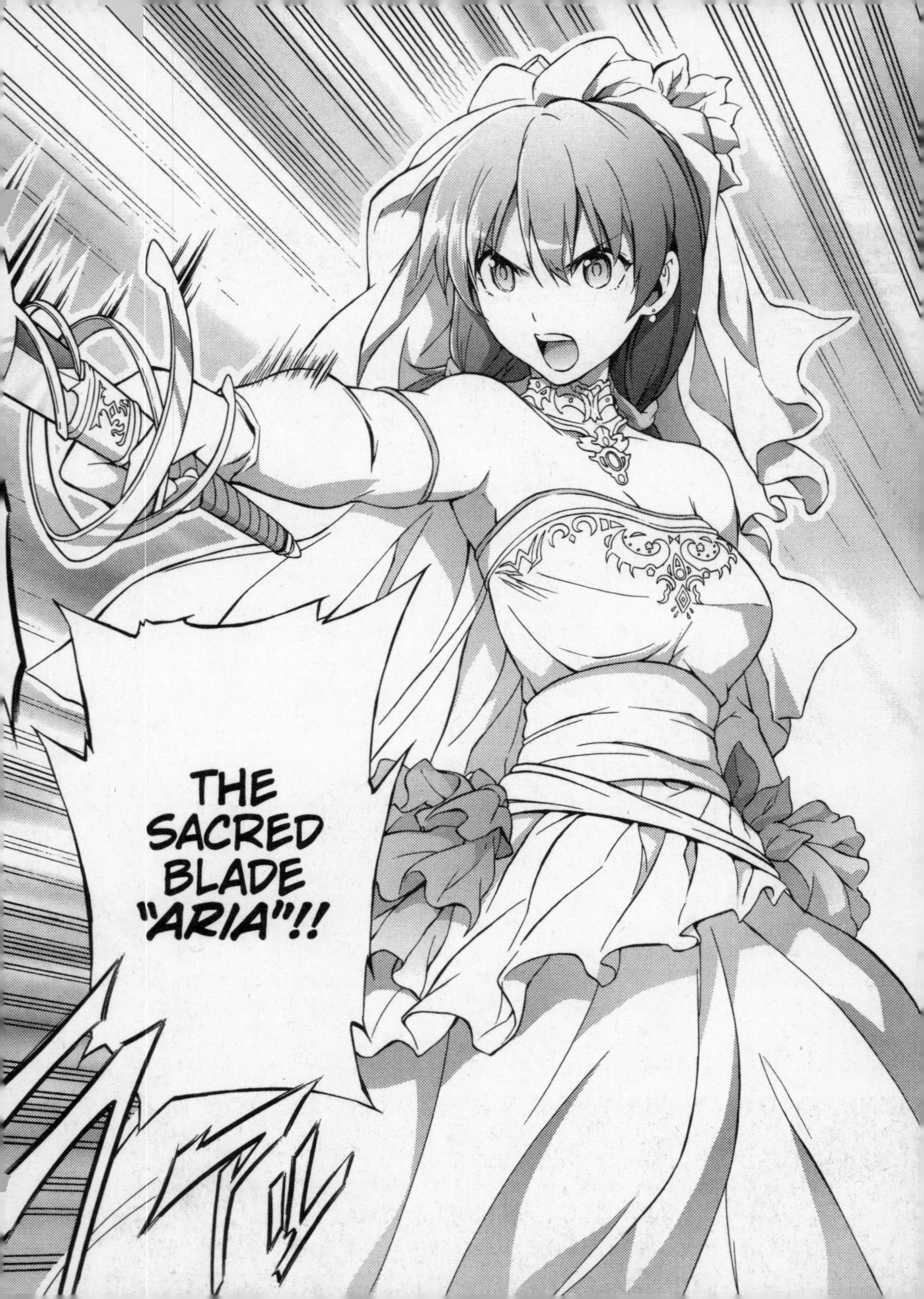
THE SACRED BLADE "ARIA"!!

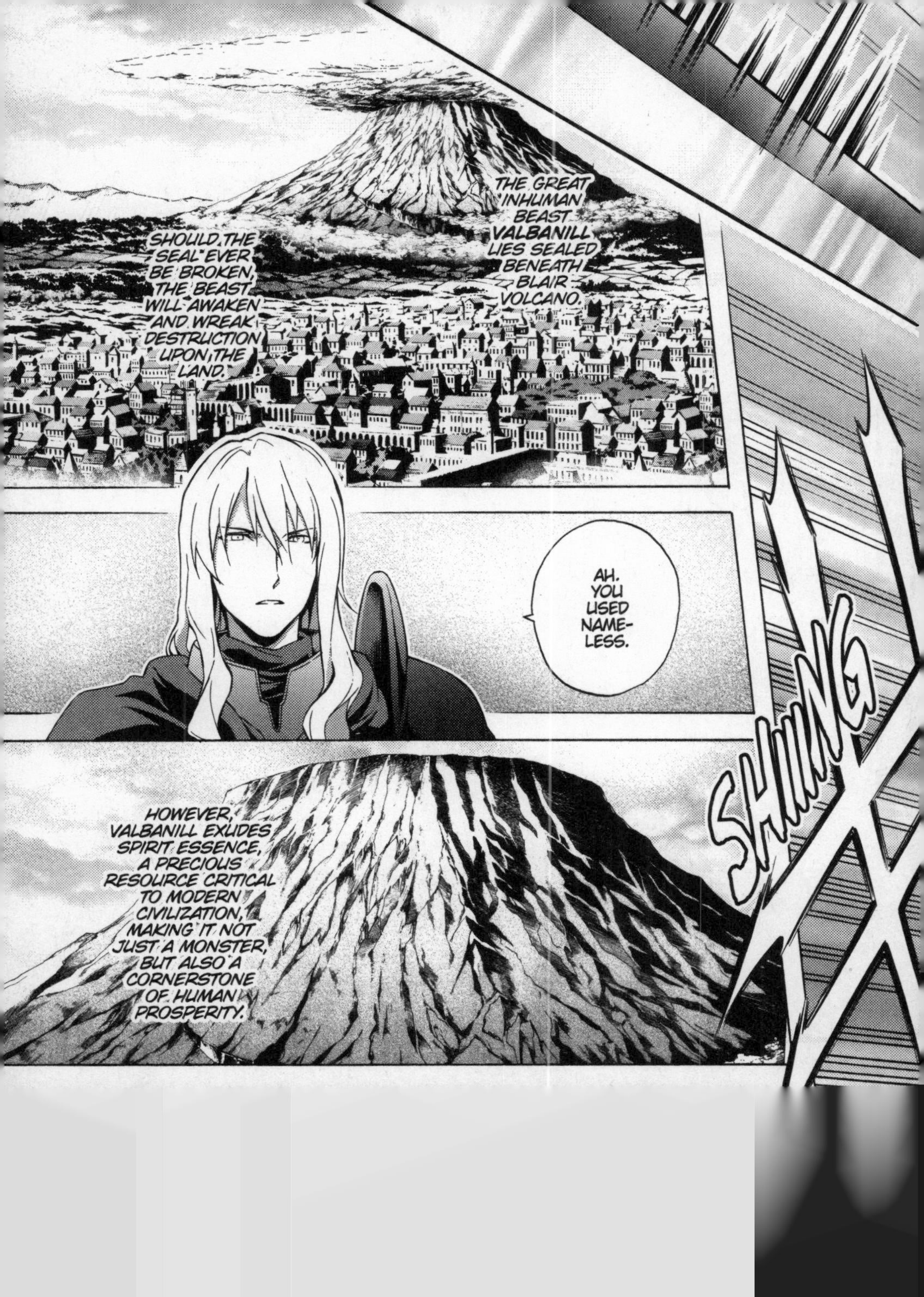
THE GREAT INHUMAN BEAST VALBANILL LIES SEALED BENEATH BLAIR VOLCANO.
SHOULD THE SEAL EVER BE BROKEN, THE BEAST WILL AWAKEN AND WREAK DESTRUCTION UPON THE LAND.
SHIING
AH. YOU USED NAME-LESS.
HOWEVER, VALBANILL EXUDES SPIRIT ESSENCE, A PRECIOUS RESOURCE CRITICAL TO MODERN CIVILIZATION, MAKING IT NOT JUST A MONSTER, BUT ALSO A CORNERSTONE OF HUMAN PROSPERITY.

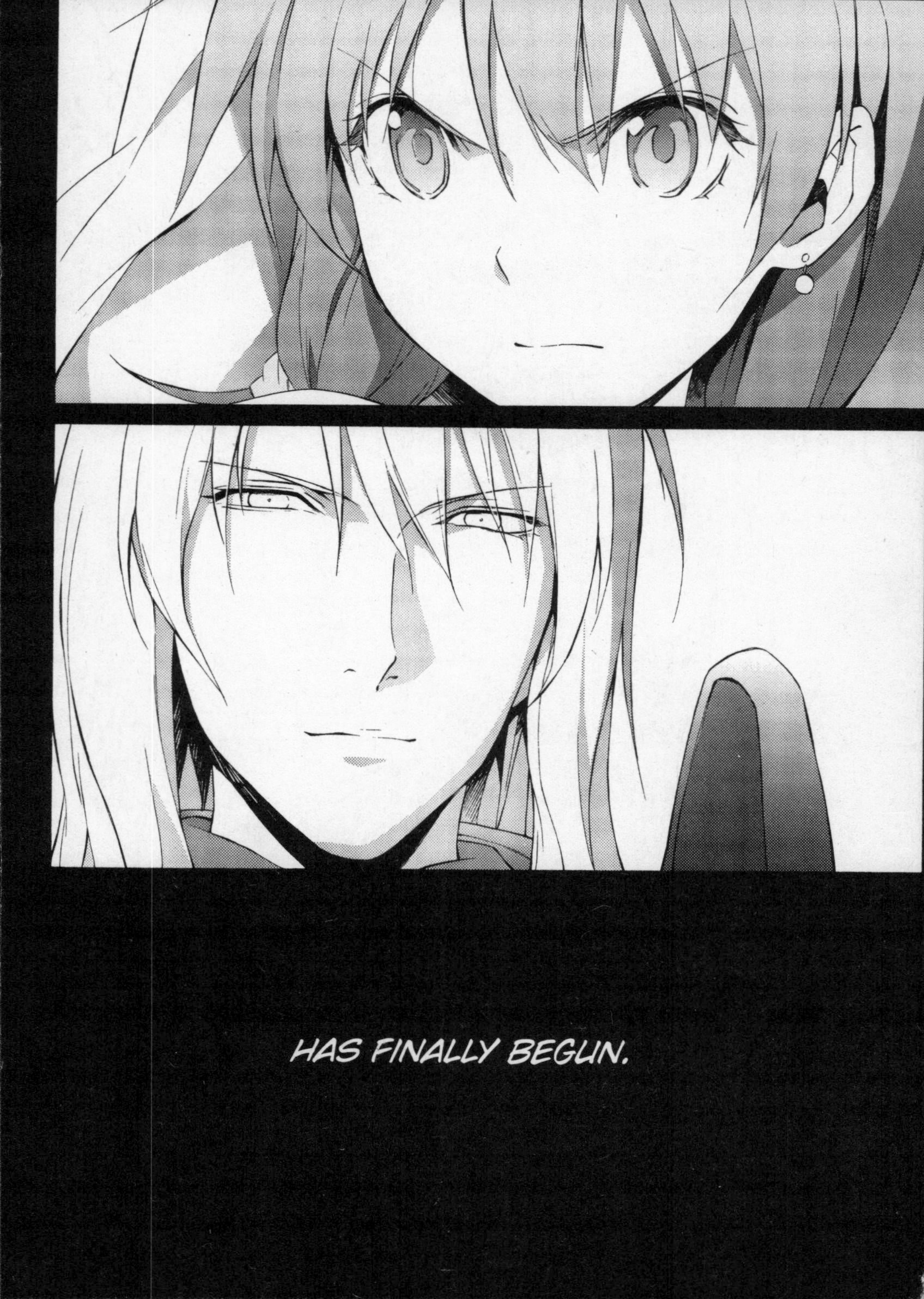
HAS FINALLY BEGUN.

The Sacred Blacksmith

聖剣の刀鍛冶

The Sacred Blacksmith

聖剣の刀鍛冶

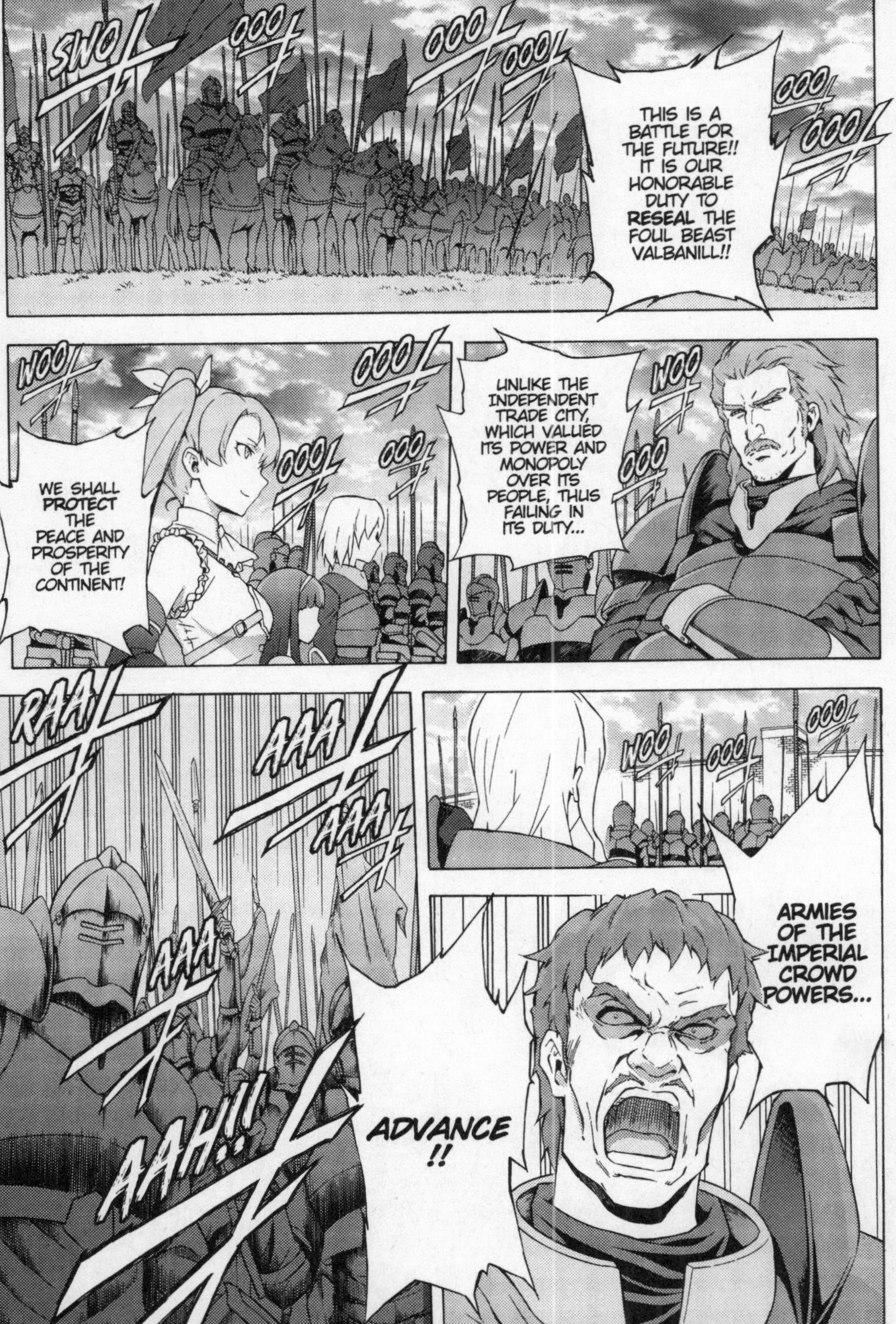

OOO
OOO
THIS IS A BATTLE FOR THE FUTURE!! IT IS OUR HONORABLE DUTY TO **RESEAL** THE FOUL BEAST VALBANILL!!
SWO
OOO
OOO
OOO
WOO
OOO
UNLIKE THE INDEPENDENT TRADE CITY, WHICH VALUED ITS POWER AND MONOPOLY OVER ITS PEOPLE, THUS FAILING IN ITS DUTY...
WOO
OOO
OOO
OOO
WE SHALL **PROTECT** THE PEACE AND PROSPERITY OF THE CONTINENT!
OOO
OOO
WOO
ARMIES OF THE IMPERIAL CROWD POWERS...
ADVANCE!!
RAA
AAA
AAA
AAA
AAH!!

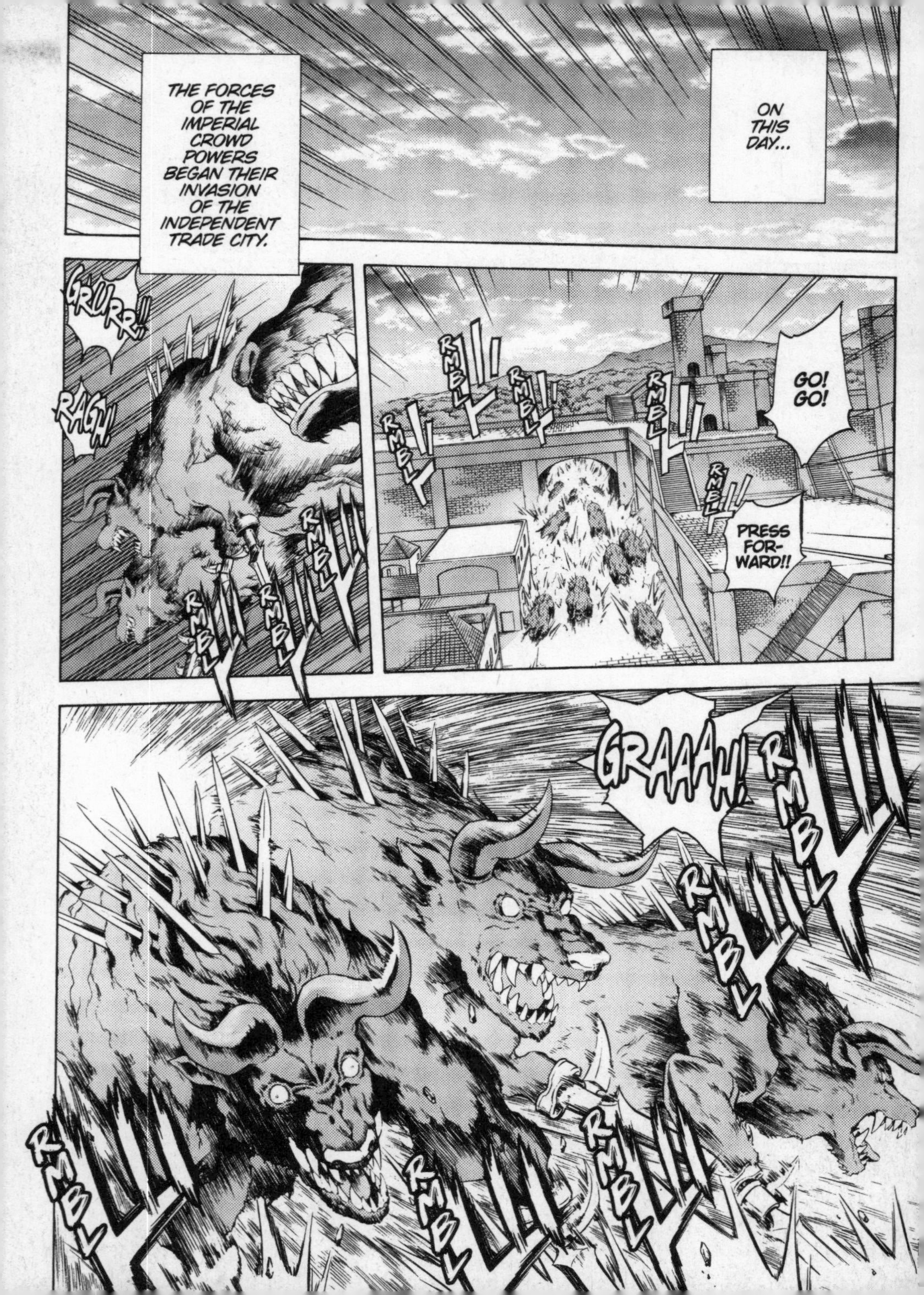
ON THIS DAY...
THE FORCES OF THE IMPERIAL CROWD POWERS BEGAN THEIR INVASION OF THE INDEPENDENT TRADE CITY.
GO! GO!
PRESS FOR-WARD!!
RMBL
RMBL
RMBL
RMBL
RMBL
GRURR!!
RAGH!
RMBL
RMBL
RMBL
GRAAAH!
RMBL
RMBL
RMBL
RMBL
RMBL

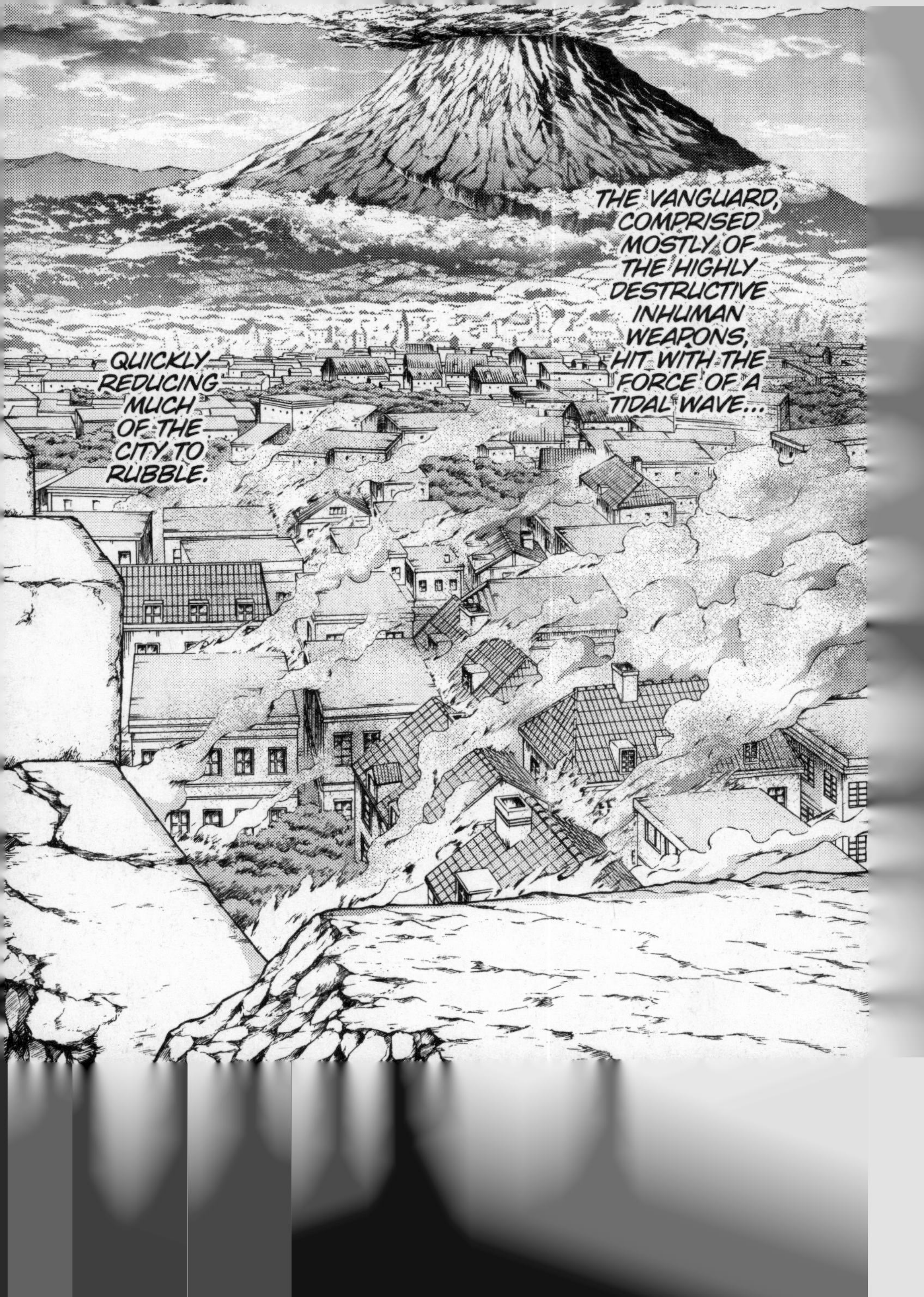
THE VANGUARD, COMPRISED MOSTLY OF THE HIGHLY DESTRUCTIVE INHUMAN WEAPONS, HIT WITH THE FORCE OF A TIDAL WAVE...
QUICKLY REDUCING MUCH OF THE CITY TO RUBBLE.

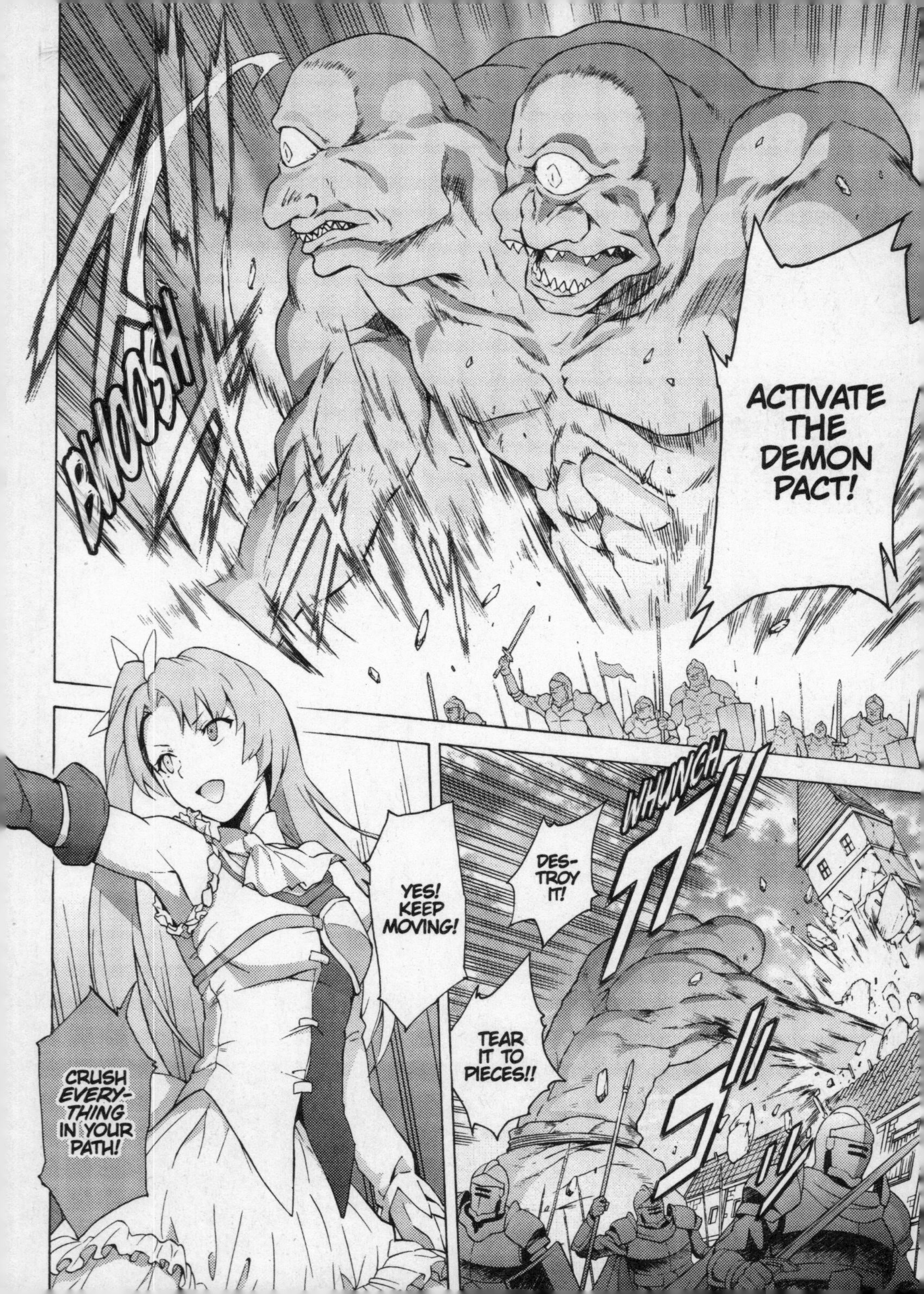
ACTIVATE THE DEMON PACT!
BWOOSH
WHUNCH
DES-TROY IT!
YES! KEEP MOVING!
TEAR IT TO PIECES!!
CRUSH EVERY-THING IN YOUR PATH!

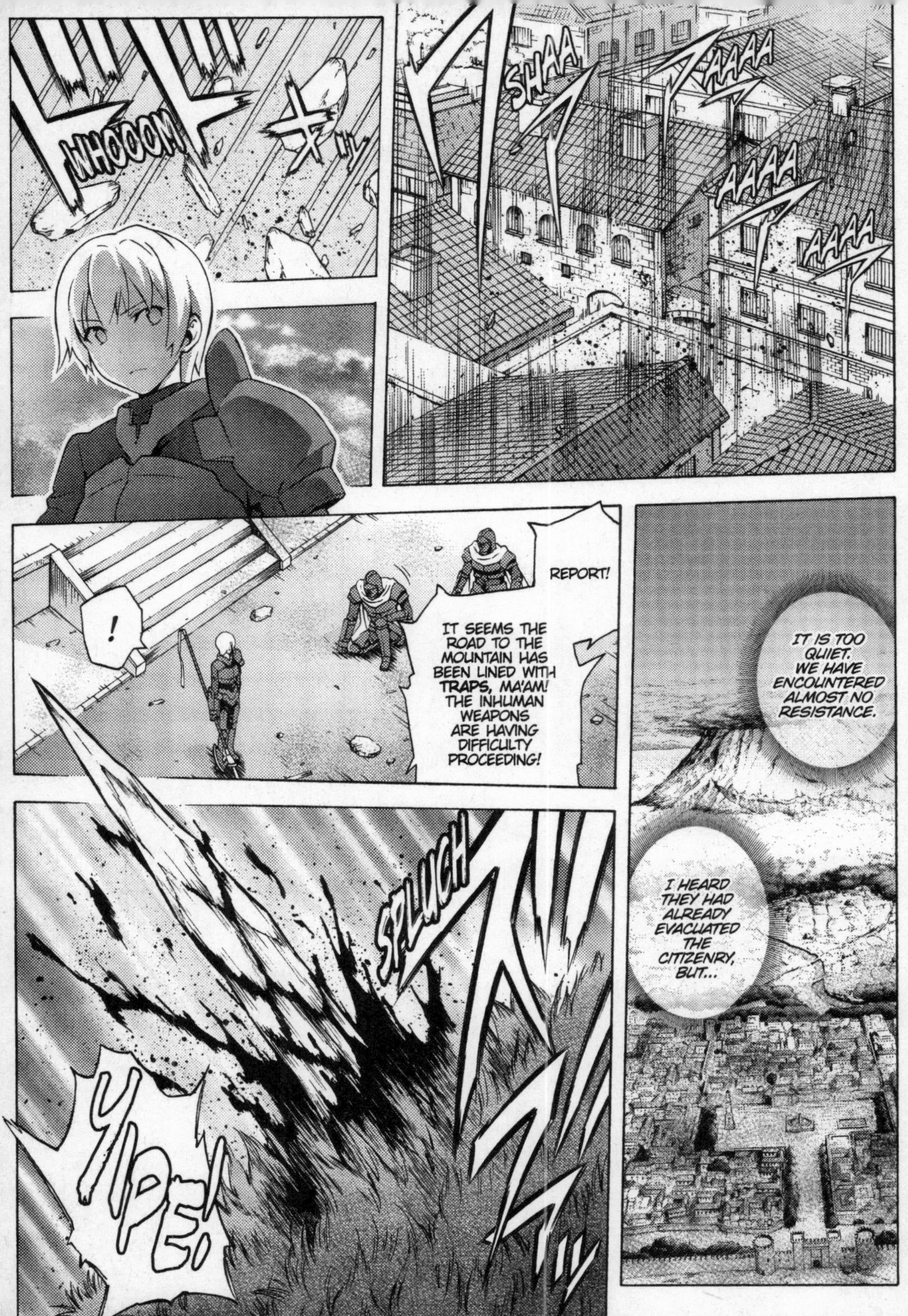
SHAA
AAAA
AAAA
AAAA
WHOOOM
IT IS TOO QUIET. WE HAVE ENCOUNTERED ALMOST NO RESISTANCE.
I HEARD THEY HAD ALREADY EVACUATED THE CITIZENRY, BUT...
REPORT!
IT SEEMS THE ROAD TO THE MOUNTAIN HAS BEEN LINED WITH TRAPS, MA'AM! THE INHUMAN WEAPONS ARE HAVING DIFFICULTY PROCEEDING!
!
SPLUCH
YIPE!

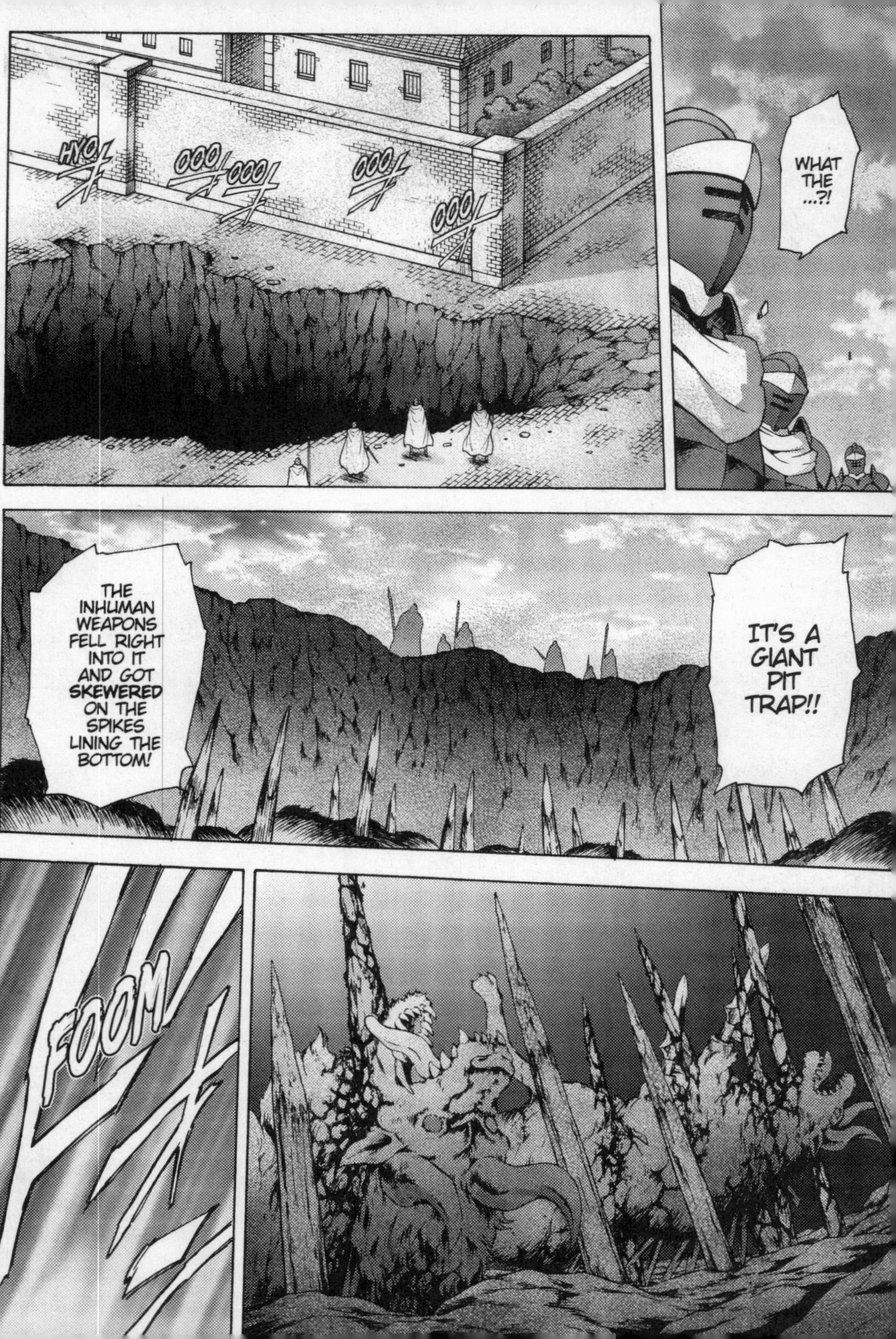
WHAT THE ...?!
HYO
OOO
OOO
OOO
OOO
IT'S A GIANT PIT TRAP!!
THE INHUMAN WEAPONS FELL RIGHT INTO IT AND GOT **SKEWERED** ON THE SPIKES LINING THE BOTTOM!
FOOM

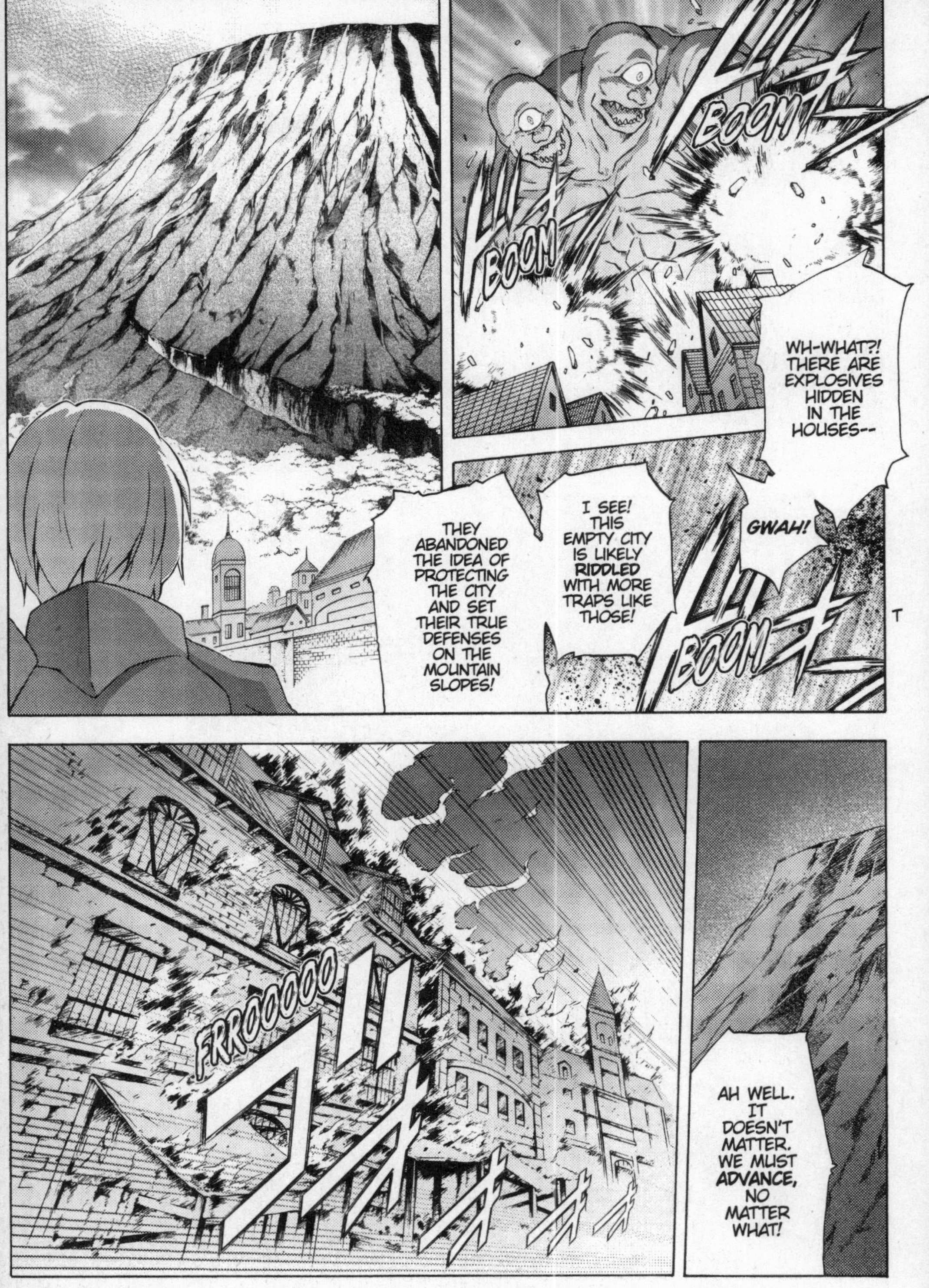
BOOM
BOOM
WH-WHAT?! THERE ARE EXPLOSIVES HIDDEN IN THE HOUSES--
GWAH!
BOOM
I SEE! THIS EMPTY CITY IS LIKELY RIDDLED WITH MORE TRAPS LIKE THOSE!
THEY ABANDONED THE IDEA OF PROTECTING THE CITY AND SET THEIR TRUE DEFENSES ON THE MOUNTAIN SLOPES!
AH WELL. IT DOESN'T MATTER. WE MUST ADVANCE, NO MATTER WHAT!
FRROOOOO

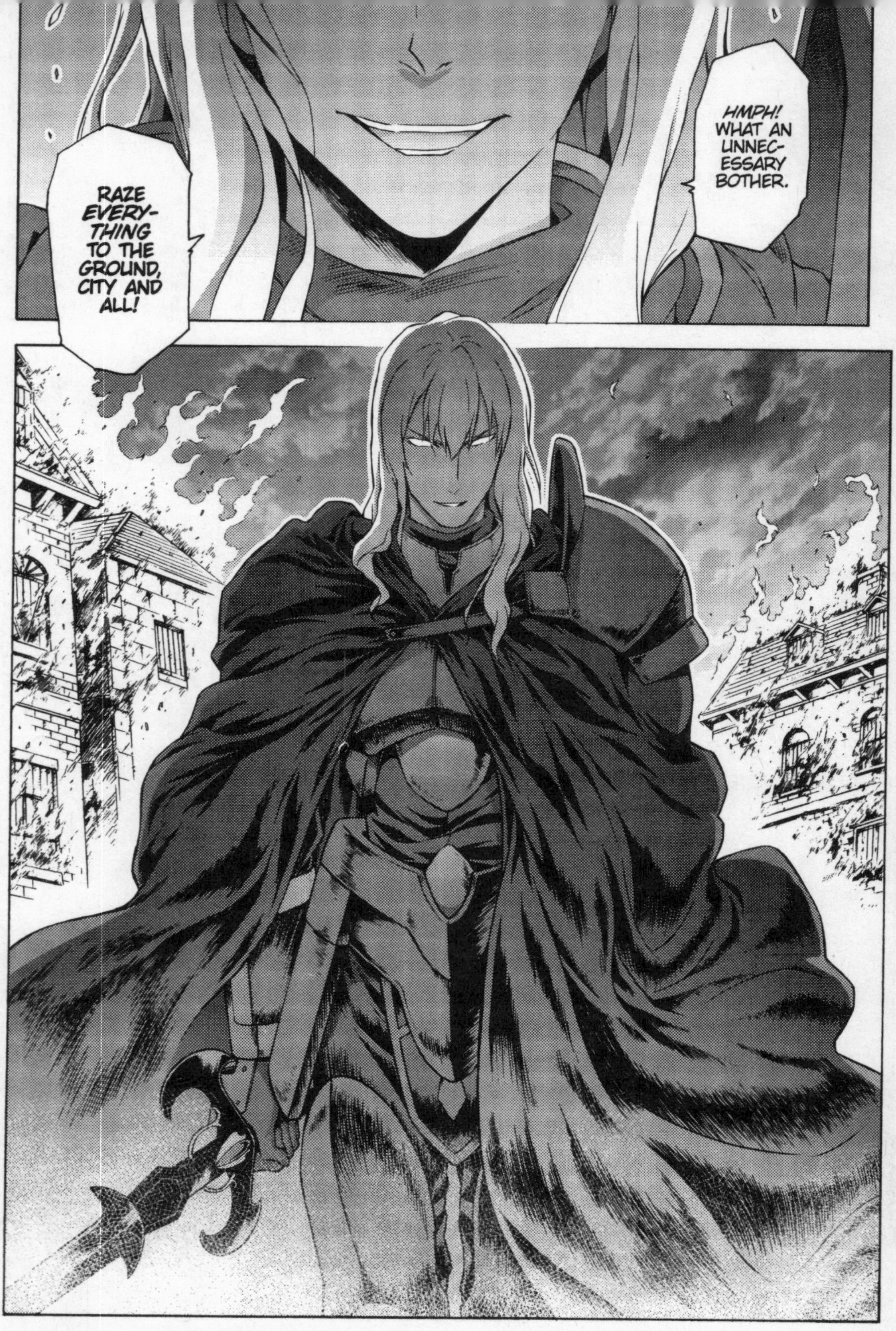
HMPH! WHAT AN UNNEC-ESSARY BOTHER.
RAZE EVERY-THING TO THE GROUND, CITY AND ALL!

The Sacred Blacksmith

聖剣の刀鍛治

The Sacred Blacksmith

聖剣の刀鍛治

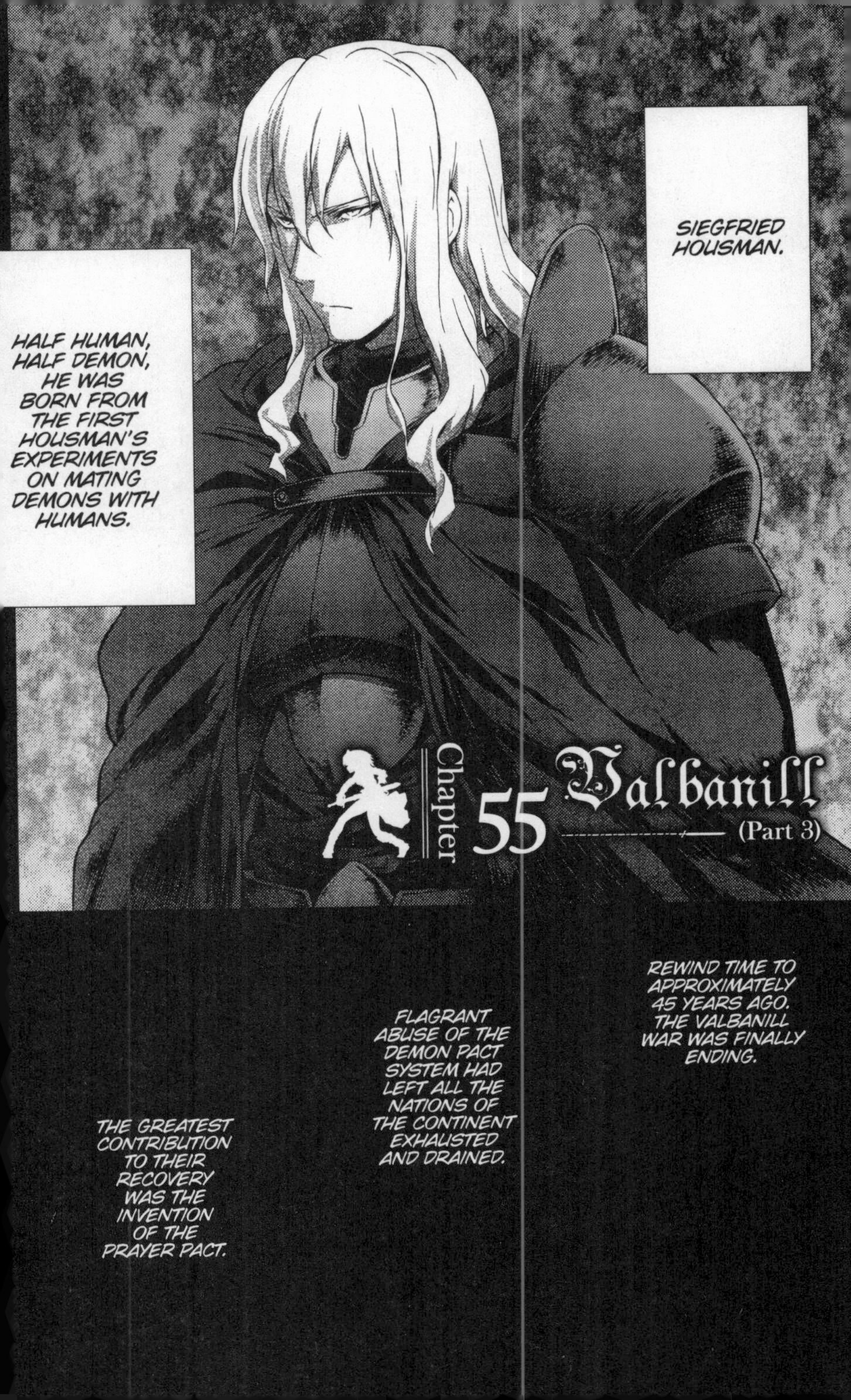
SIEGFRIED HOUSMAN.
HALF HUMAN, HALF DEMON, HE WAS BORN FROM THE FIRST HOUSMAN'S EXPERIMENTS ON MATING DEMONS WITH HUMANS.
Chapter 55 Valbanill (Part 3)
REWIND TIME TO APPROXIMATELY 45 YEARS AGO. THE VALBANILL WAR WAS FINALLY ENDING.
FLAGRANT ABUSE OF THE DEMON PACT SYSTEM HAD LEFT ALL THE NATIONS OF THE CONTINENT EXHAUSTED AND DRAINED.
THE GREATEST CONTRIBUTION TO THEIR RECOVERY WAS THE INVENTION OF THE PRAYER PACT.

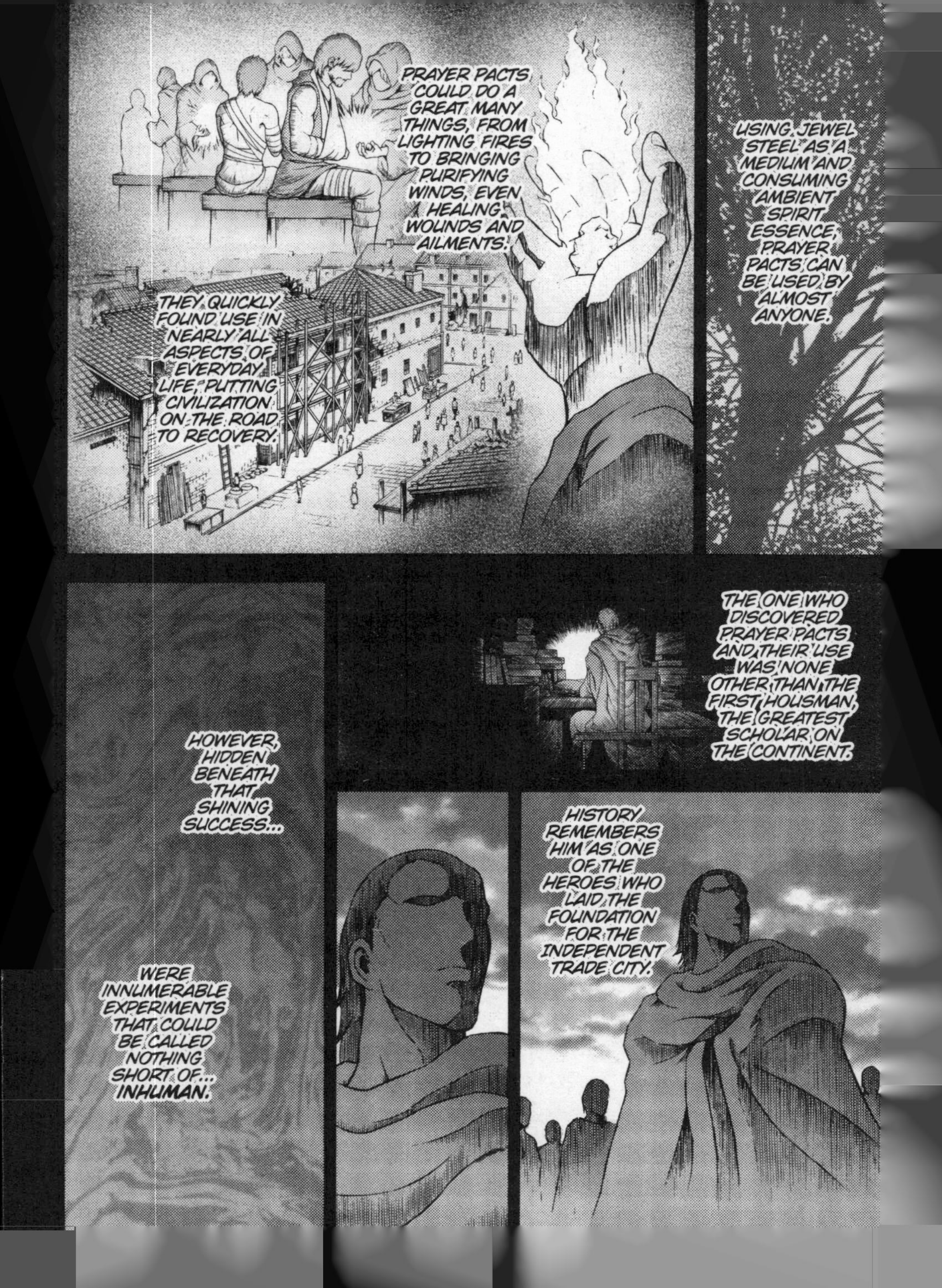
USING JEWEL STEEL AS A MEDIUM AND CONSUMING AMBIENT SPIRIT ESSENCE, PRAYER PACTS CAN BE USED BY ALMOST ANYONE.
PRAYER PACTS COULD DO A GREAT MANY THINGS, FROM LIGHTING FIRES TO BRINGING PURIFYING WINDS, EVEN HEALING WOUNDS AND AILMENTS.
THEY QUICKLY FOUND USE IN NEARLY ALL ASPECTS OF EVERYDAY LIFE, PUTTING CIVILIZATION ON THE ROAD TO RECOVERY.
THE ONE WHO DISCOVERED PRAYER PACTS AND THEIR USE WAS NONE OTHER THAN THE FIRST HOUSMAN, THE GREATEST SCHOLAR ON THE CONTINENT.
HISTORY REMEMBERS HIM AS ONE OF THE HEROES WHO LAID THE FOUNDATION FOR THE INDEPENDENT TRADE CITY.
HOWEVER, HIDDEN BENEATH THAT SHINING SUCCESS...
WERE INNUMERABLE EXPERIMENTS THAT COULD BE CALLED NOTHING SHORT OF... INHUMAN.

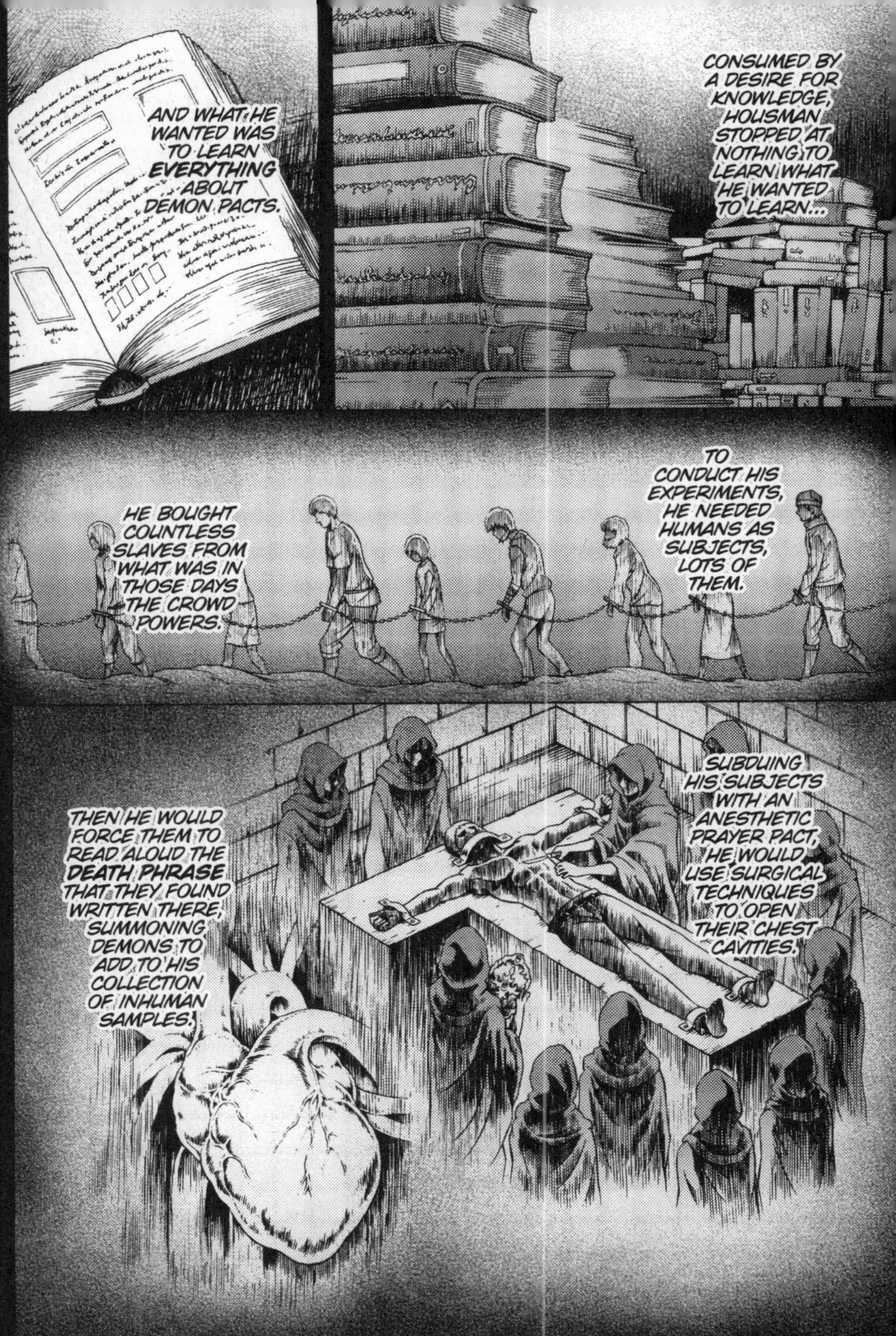
CONSUMED BY A DESIRE FOR KNOWLEDGE, HOUSMAN STOPPED AT NOTHING TO LEARN WHAT HE WANTED TO LEARN...
AND WHAT HE WANTED WAS TO LEARN EVERYTHING ABOUT DEMON PACTS.
TO CONDUCT HIS EXPERIMENTS, HE NEEDED HUMANS AS SUBJECTS, LOTS OF THEM.
HE BOUGHT COUNTLESS SLAVES FROM WHAT WAS IN THOSE DAYS THE CROWD POWERS.
SUBDUING HIS SUBJECTS WITH AN ANESTHETIC PRAYER PACT, HE WOULD USE SURGICAL TECHNIQUES TO OPEN THEIR CHEST CAVITIES.
THEN HE WOULD FORCE THEM TO READ ALOUD THE DEATH PHRASE THAT THEY FOUND WRITTEN THERE, SUMMONING DEMONS TO ADD TO HIS COLLECTION OF INHUMAN SAMPLES.

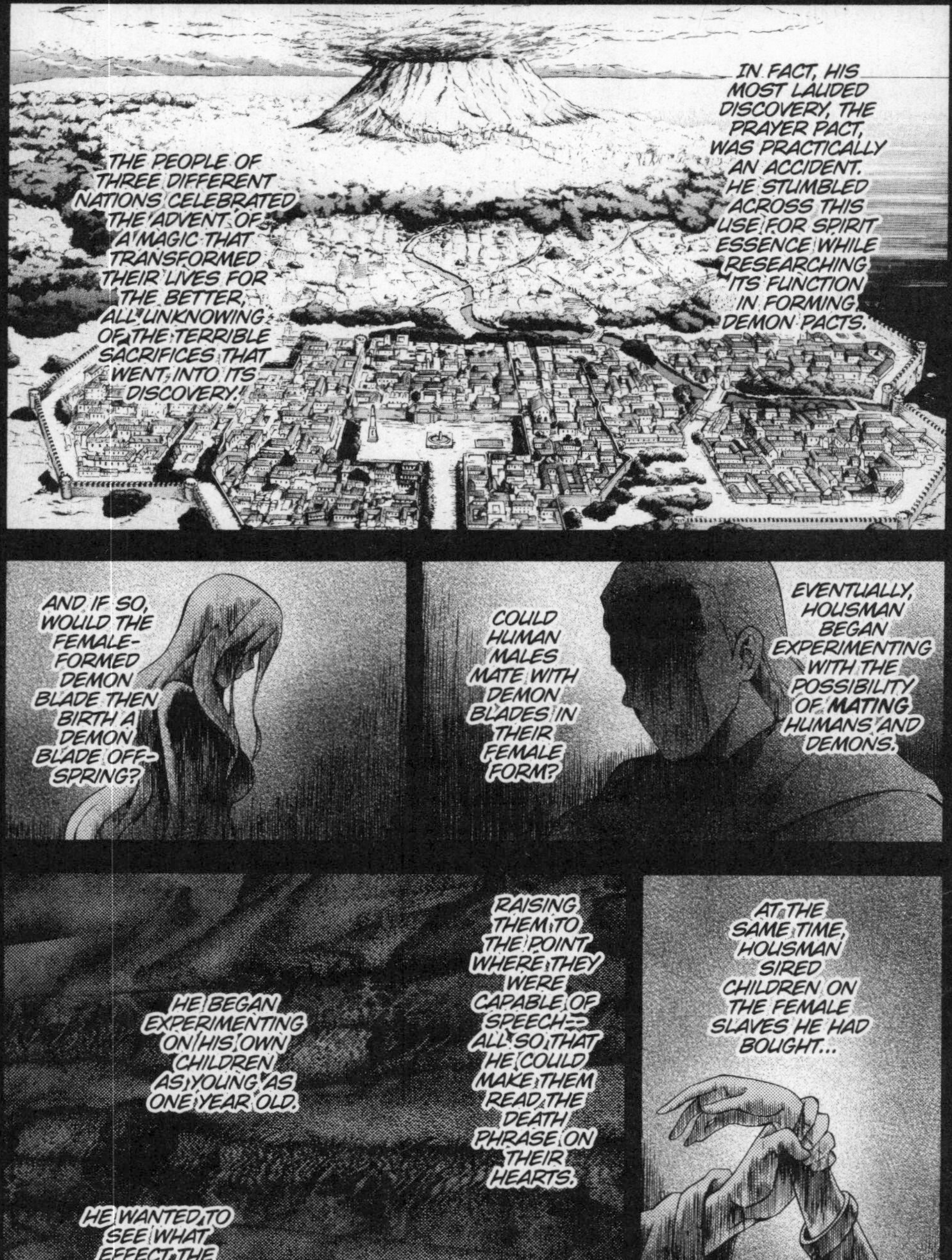
IN FACT, HIS MOST LAUDED DISCOVERY, THE PRAYER PACT, WAS PRACTICALLY AN ACCIDENT. HE STUMBLED ACROSS THIS USE FOR SPIRIT ESSENCE WHILE RESEARCHING ITS FUNCTION IN FORMING DEMON PACTS.
THE PEOPLE OF THREE DIFFERENT NATIONS CELEBRATED THE ADVENT OF A MAGIC THAT TRANSFORMED THEIR LIVES FOR THE BETTER, ALL UNKNOWING OF THE TERRIBLE SACRIFICES THAT WENT INTO ITS DISCOVERY.
EVENTUALLY, HOUSMAN BEGAN EXPERIMENTING WITH THE POSSIBILITY OF **MATING** HUMANS AND DEMONS.
COULD HUMAN MALES MATE WITH DEMON BLADES IN THEIR FEMALE FORM?
AND IF SO, WOULD THE FEMALE-FORMED DEMON BLADE THEN BIRTH A DEMON BLADE OFF-SPRING?
AT THE SAME TIME, HOUSMAN SIRED CHILDREN ON THE FEMALE SLAVES HE HAD BOUGHT...
RAISING THEM TO THE POINT WHERE THEY WERE CAPABLE OF SPEECH— ALL SO THAT HE COULD MAKE THEM READ THE DEATH PHRASE ON THEIR HEARTS.
HE BEGAN EXPERIMENTING ON HIS OWN CHILDREN AS YOUNG AS ONE YEAR OLD.
HE WANTED TO SEE WHAT EFFECT THE AGE OF THE CASTER WOULD HAVE ON A DEMON PACT.

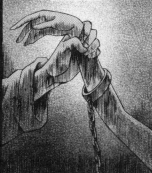

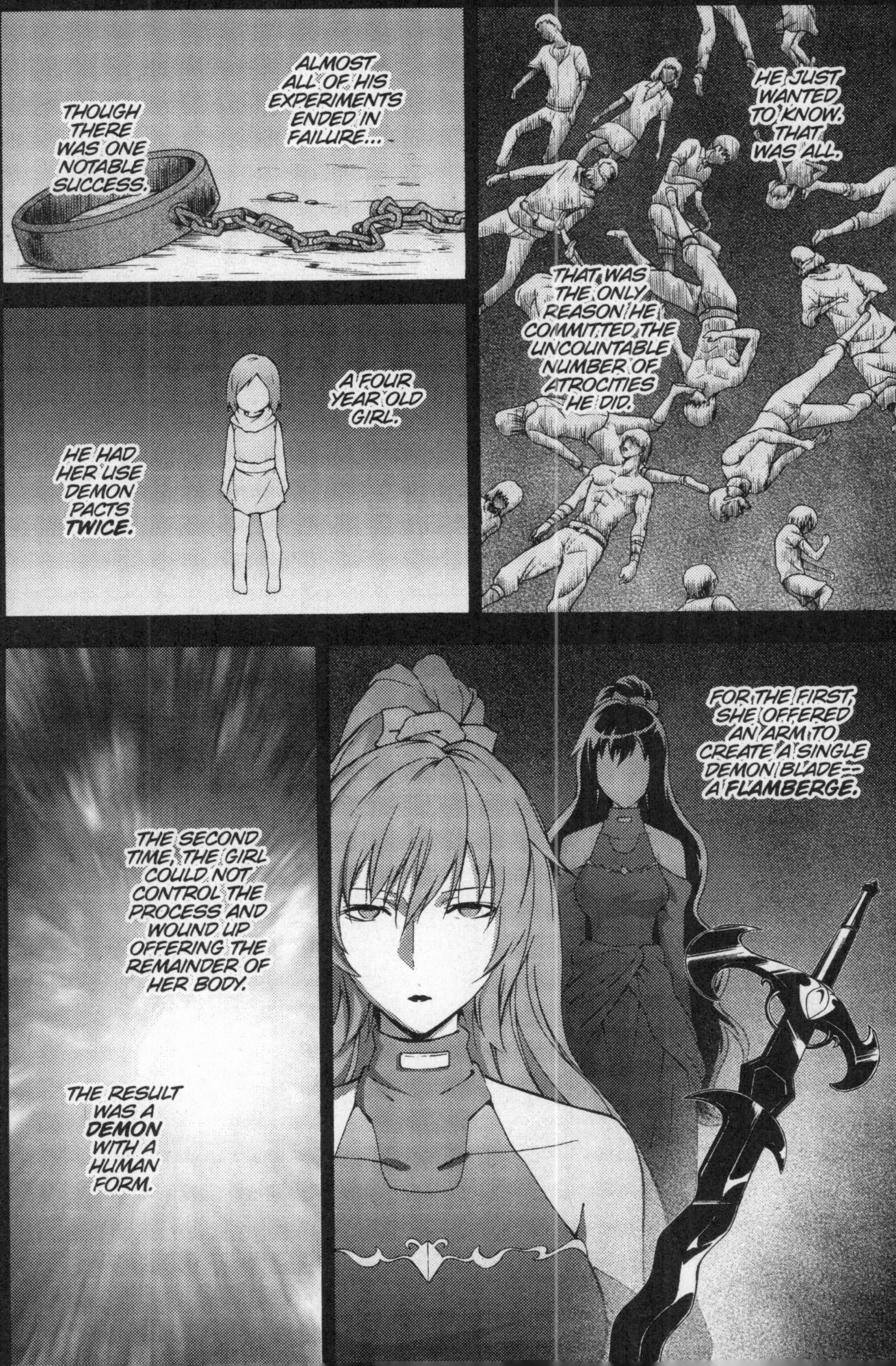
HE JUST WANTED TO KNOW. THAT WAS ALL.
THAT WAS THE ONLY REASON HE COMMITTED THE UNCOUNTABLE NUMBER OF ATROCITIES HE DID.
ALMOST ALL OF HIS EXPERIMENTS ENDED IN FAILURE...
THOUGH THERE WAS ONE NOTABLE SUCCESS.
A FOUR YEAR OLD GIRL.
HE HAD HER USE DEMON PACTS TWICE.
FOR THE FIRST, SHE OFFERED AN ARM TO CREATE A SINGLE DEMON BLADE-- A FLAMBERGE.
THE SECOND TIME, THE GIRL COULD NOT CONTROL THE PROCESS AND WOUND UP OFFERING THE REMAINDER OF HER BODY.
THE RESULT WAS A DEMON WITH A HUMAN FORM.

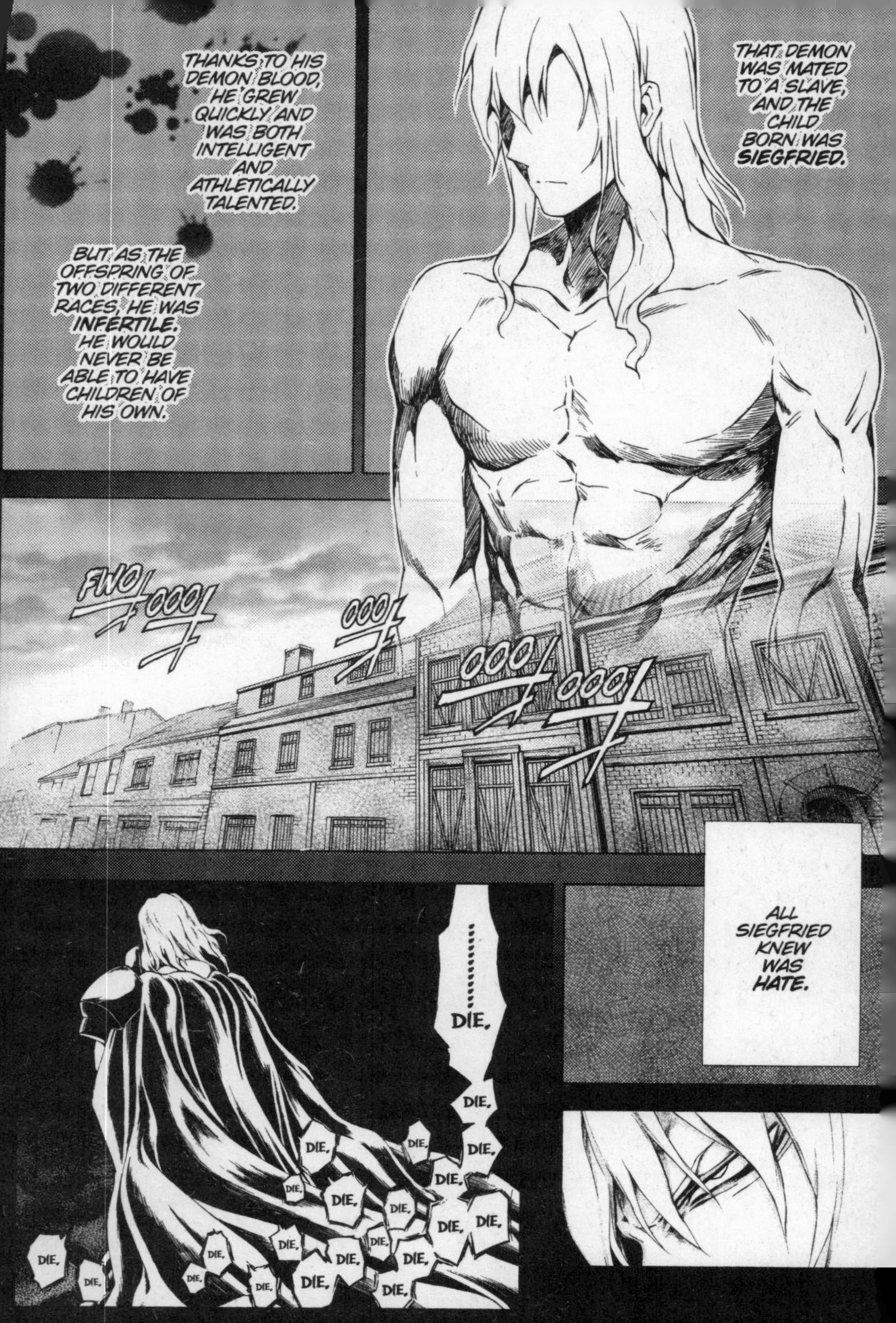
THAT DEMON WAS MATED TO A SLAVE, AND THE CHILD BORN WAS **SIEGFRIED.**
THANKS TO HIS DEMON BLOOD, HE GREW QUICKLY AND WAS BOTH INTELLIGENT AND ATHLETICALLY TALENTED.
BUT AS THE OFFSPRING OF TWO DIFFERENT RACES, HE WAS **INFERTILE.** HE WOULD NEVER BE ABLE TO HAVE CHILDREN OF HIS OWN.
FWOOOO
OOO
OOOOOO
ALL SIEGFRIED KNEW WAS **HATE.**
......
DIE.
DIE.
DIE.
DIE.
DIE.
DIE.
DIE.
DIE.
DIE.
DIE.
DIE.
DIE.
DIE.
DIE.
DIE.
DIE.
DIE.
DIE.
DIE.
DIE.
DIE.
DIE.
DIE.

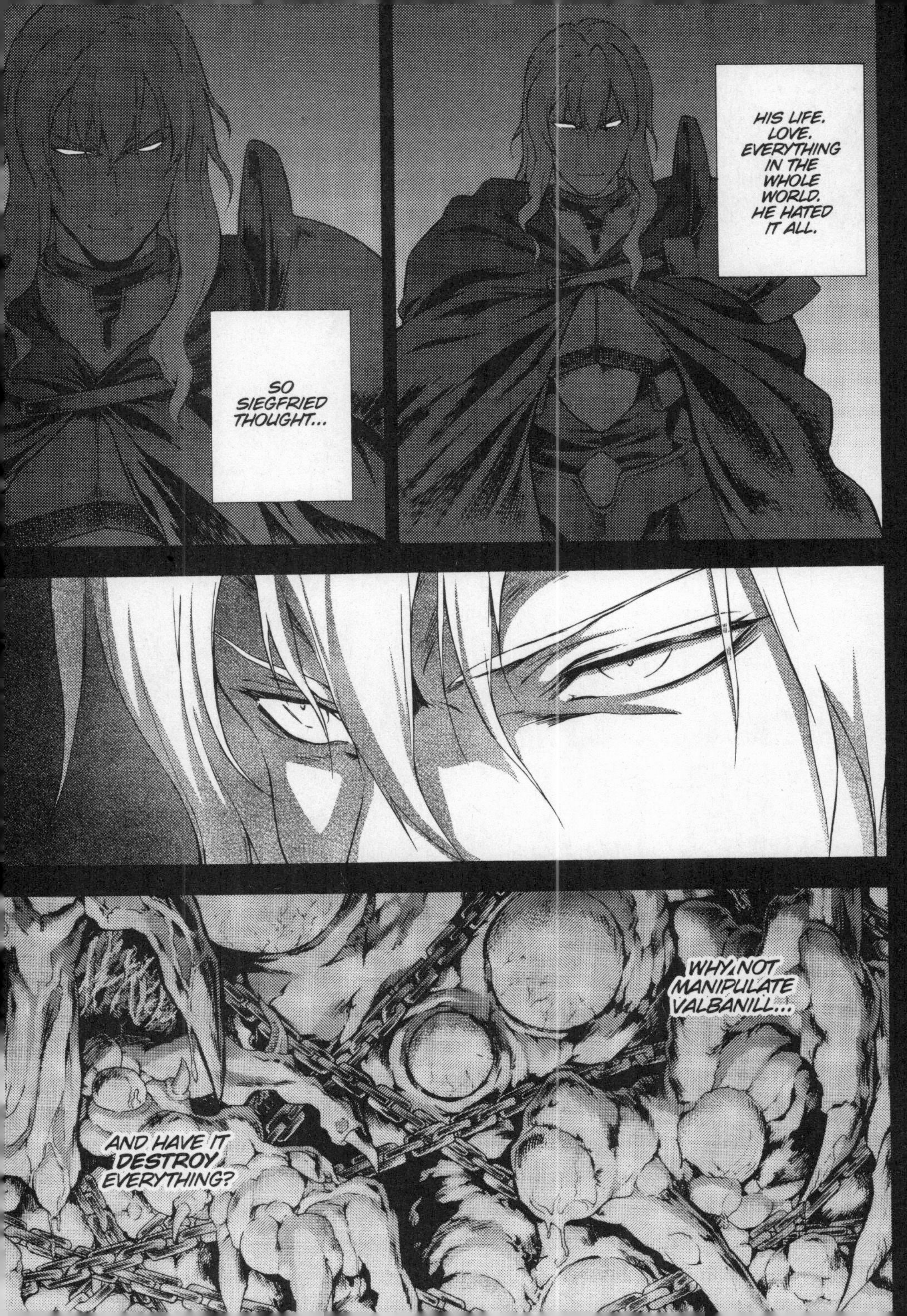
HIS LIFE. LOVE. EVERYTHING IN THE WHOLE WORLD. HE HATED IT ALL.
SO SIEGFRIED THOUGHT...
WHY NOT MANIPULATE VALBANILL...
AND HAVE IT DESTROY EVERYTHING?

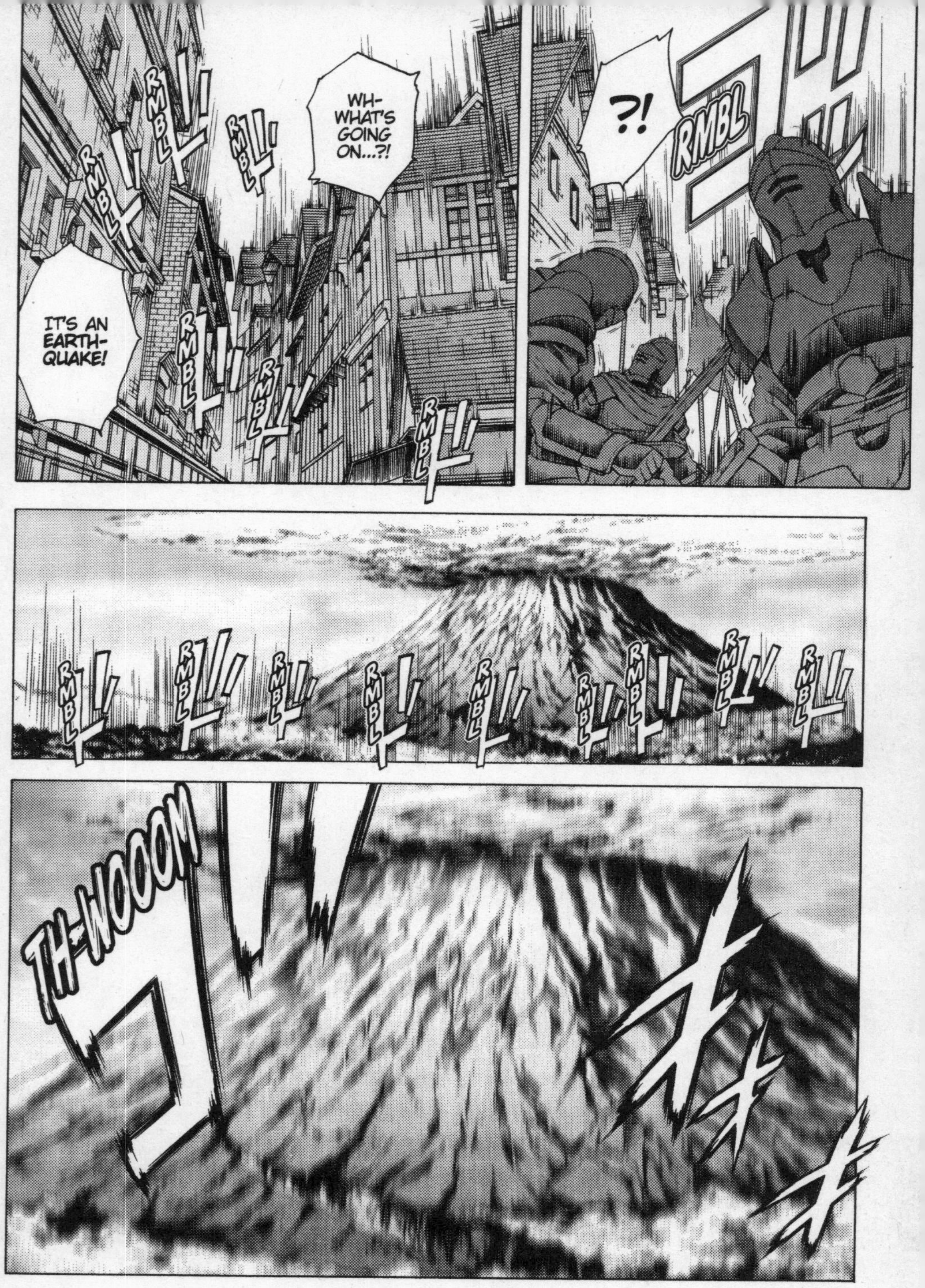
?!
RMBL
WH-WHAT'S GOING ON...?!
RMBL
RMBL
RMBL
IT'S AN EARTHQUAKE!
RMBL
RMBL
RMBL
RMBL
RMBL
RMBL
RMBL
RMBL
RMBL
RMBL
RMBL
RMBL
TH-WOOOM

The Sacred Blacksmith

聖剣の刀鍛治

The Sacred Blacksmith

聖剣の刀鍛冶

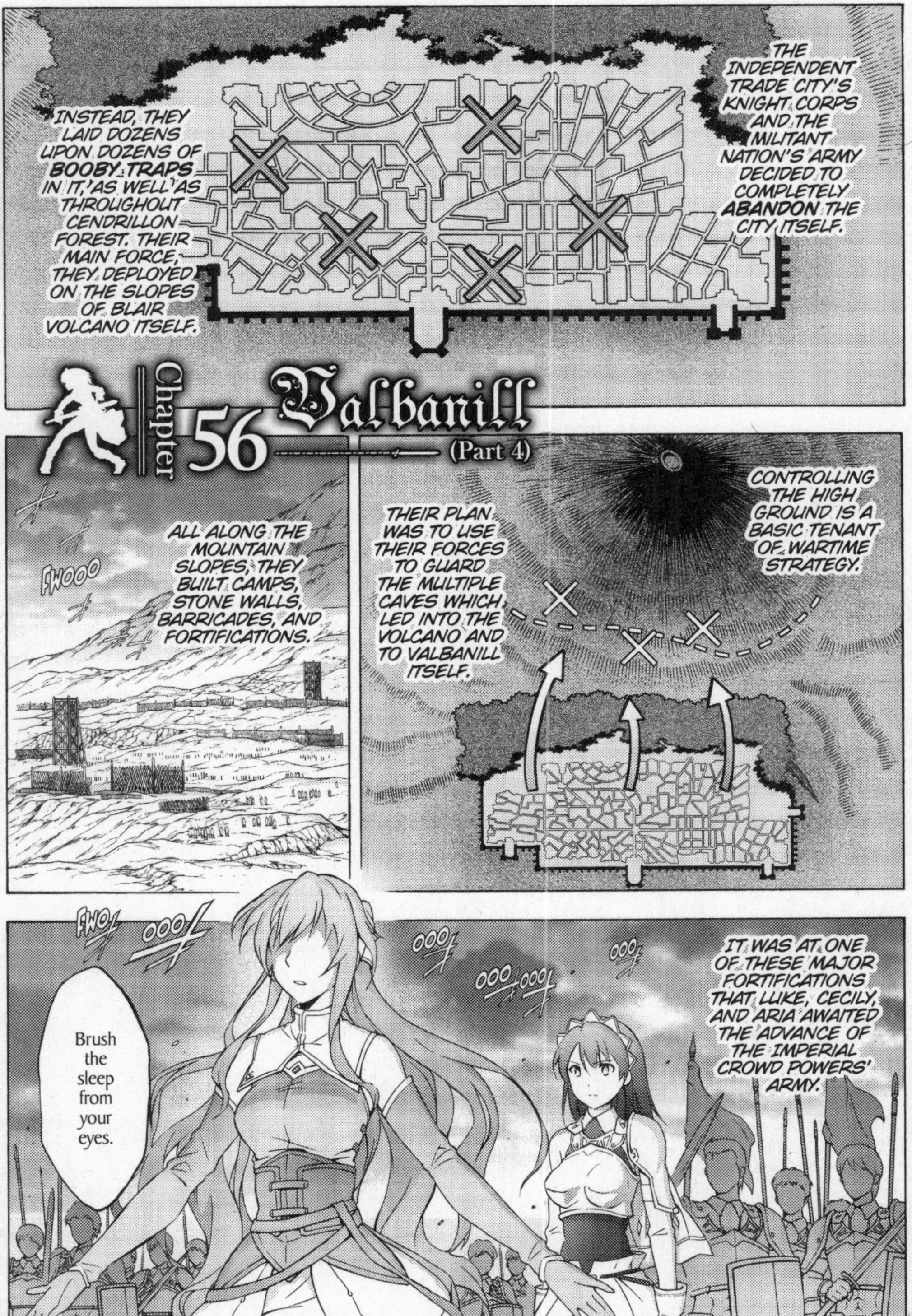
THE INDEPENDENT TRADE CITY'S KNIGHT CORPS AND THE MILITANT NATION'S ARMY DECIDED TO COMPLETELY ABANDON THE CITY ITSELF.
INSTEAD, THEY LAID DOZENS UPON DOZENS OF BOOBY TRAPS IN IT, AS WELL AS THROUGHOUT CENDRILLON FOREST. THEIR MAIN FORCE, THEY DEPLOYED ON THE SLOPES OF BLAIR VOLCANO ITSELF.
Chapter 56 Valbanill
(Part 4)
CONTROLLING THE HIGH GROUND IS A BASIC TENANT OF WARTIME STRATEGY.
THEIR PLAN WAS TO USE THEIR FORCES TO GUARD THE MULTIPLE CAVES WHICH LED INTO THE VOLCANO AND TO VALBANILL ITSELF.
ALL ALONG THE MOUNTAIN SLOPES, THEY BUILT CAMPS, STONE WALLS, BARRICADES, AND FORTIFICATIONS.
FWOOO
IT WAS AT ONE OF THESE MAJOR FORTIFICATIONS THAT LUKE, CECILY, AND ARIA AWAITED THE ADVANCE OF THE IMPERIAL CROWD POWERS' ARMY.
FWOOOOO
Brush the sleep from your eyes.

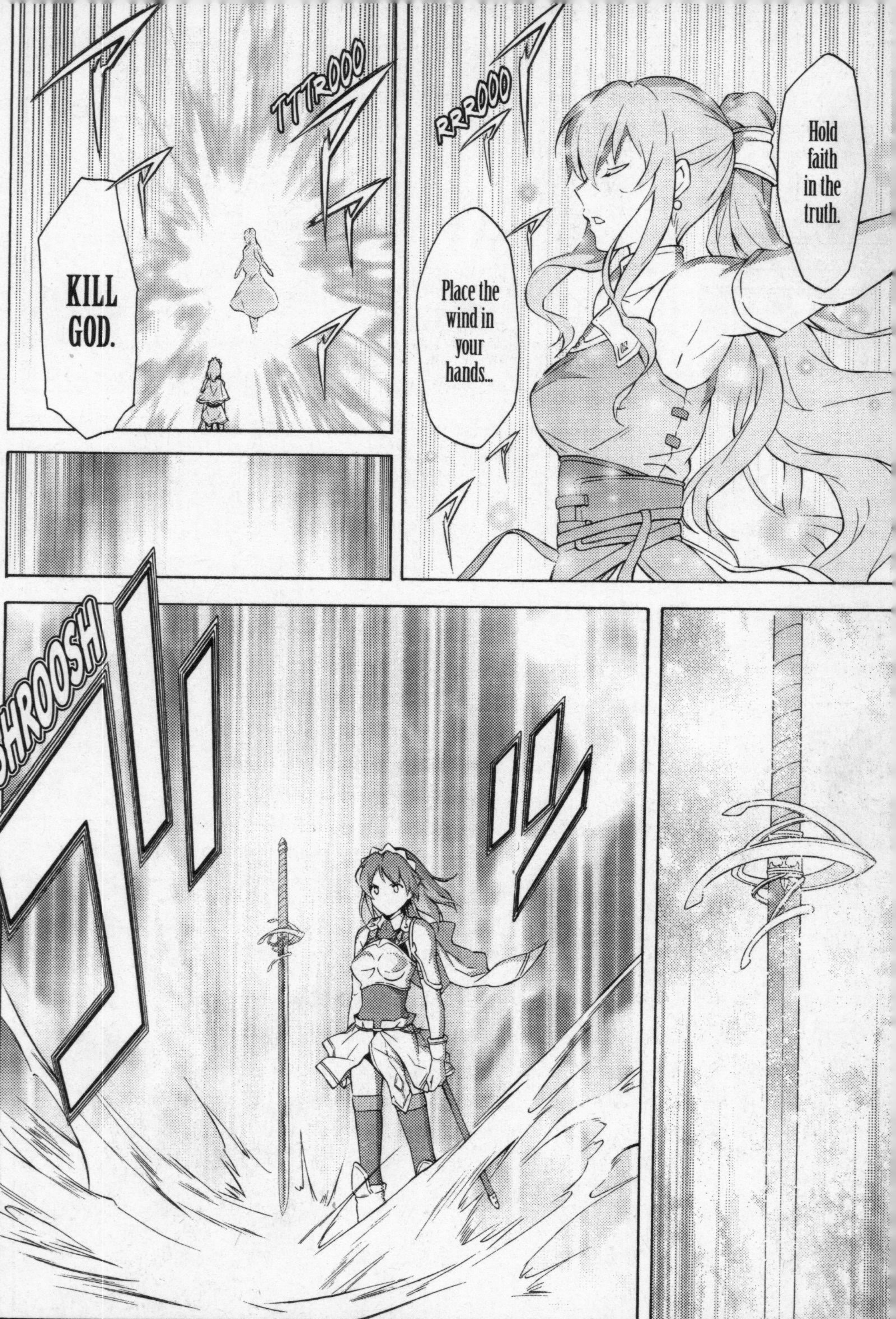
RRROOO
Hold faith in the truth.
Place the wind in your hands...
TTTROOO
KILL GOD.
SHROOSH

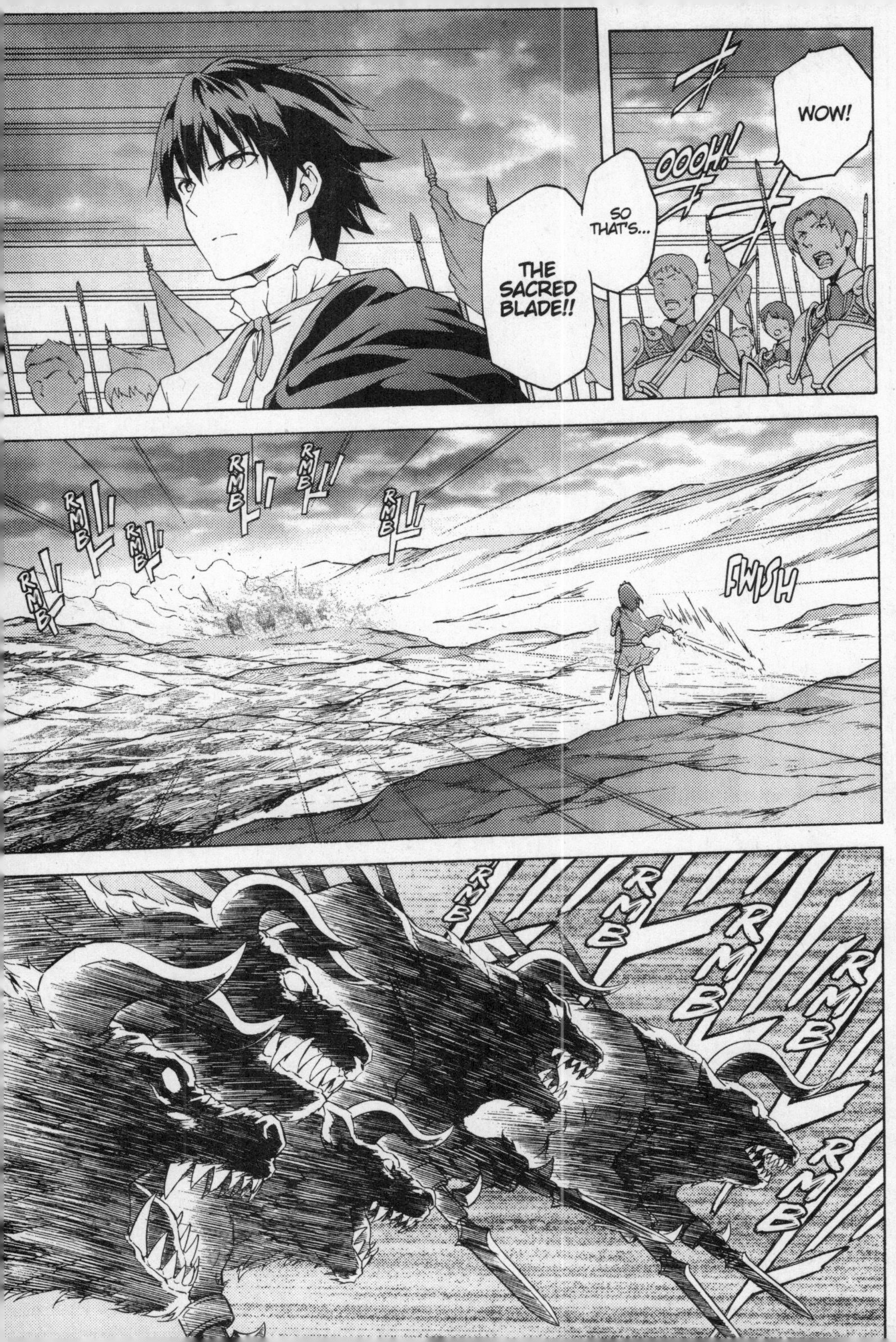
WOW!
OOOH!
SO THAT'S...
THE SACRED BLADE!!
FWISH
RMB
RMB
RMB
RMB
RMB
RMB
RMB
RMB
RMB
RMB
RMB

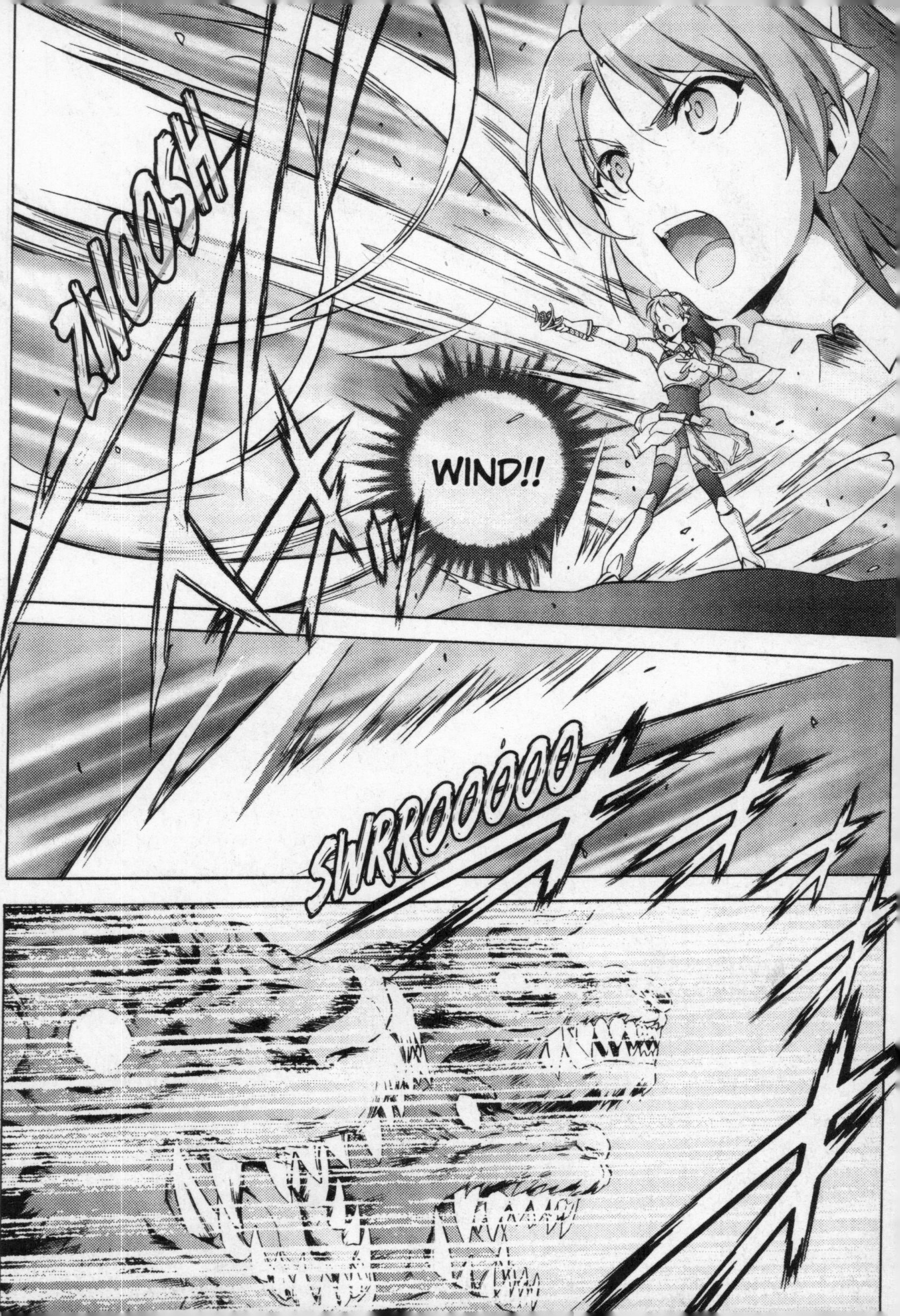
WIND!!
ZWOOSH
SWRROOOOOO

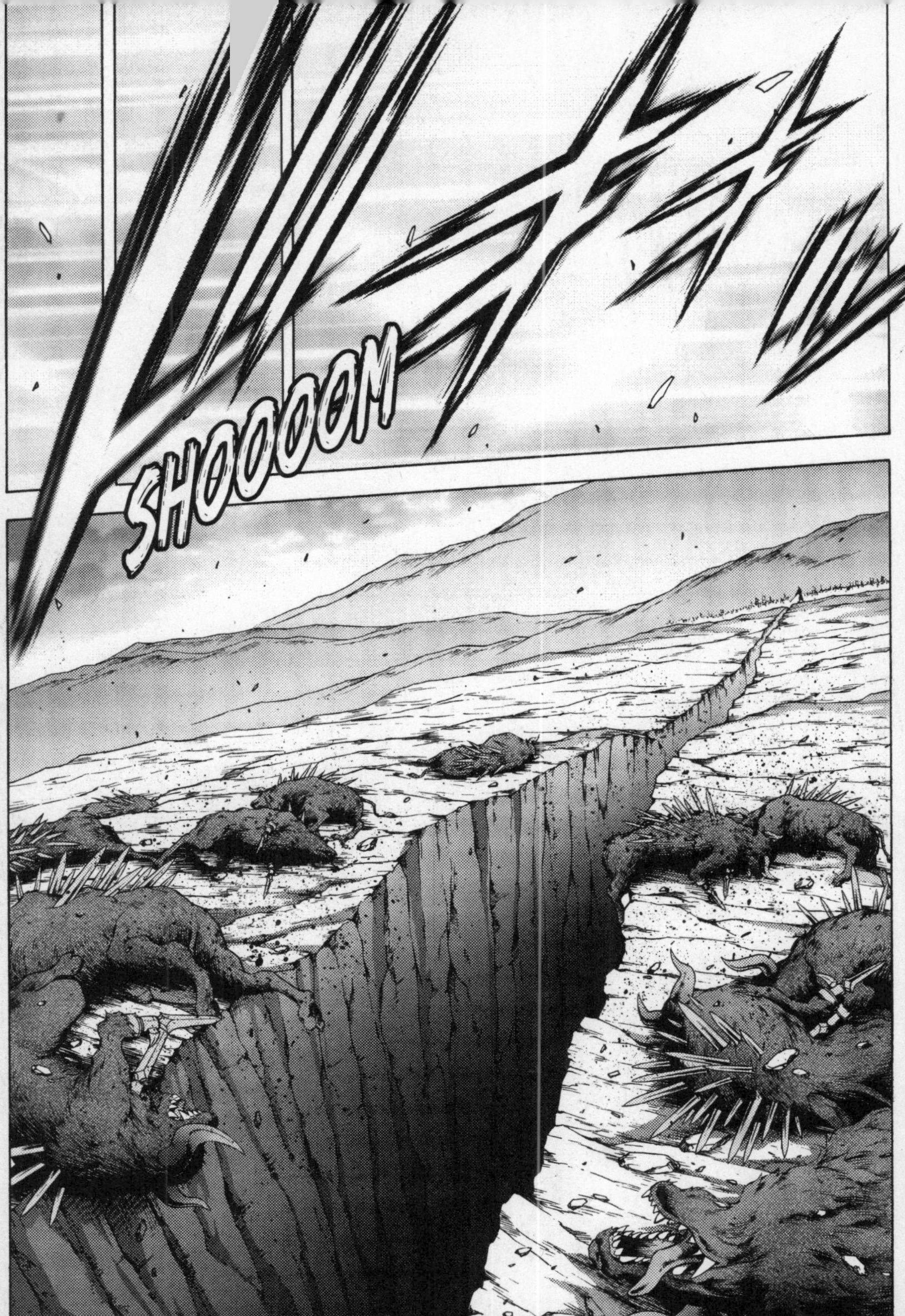
SHOOOOM

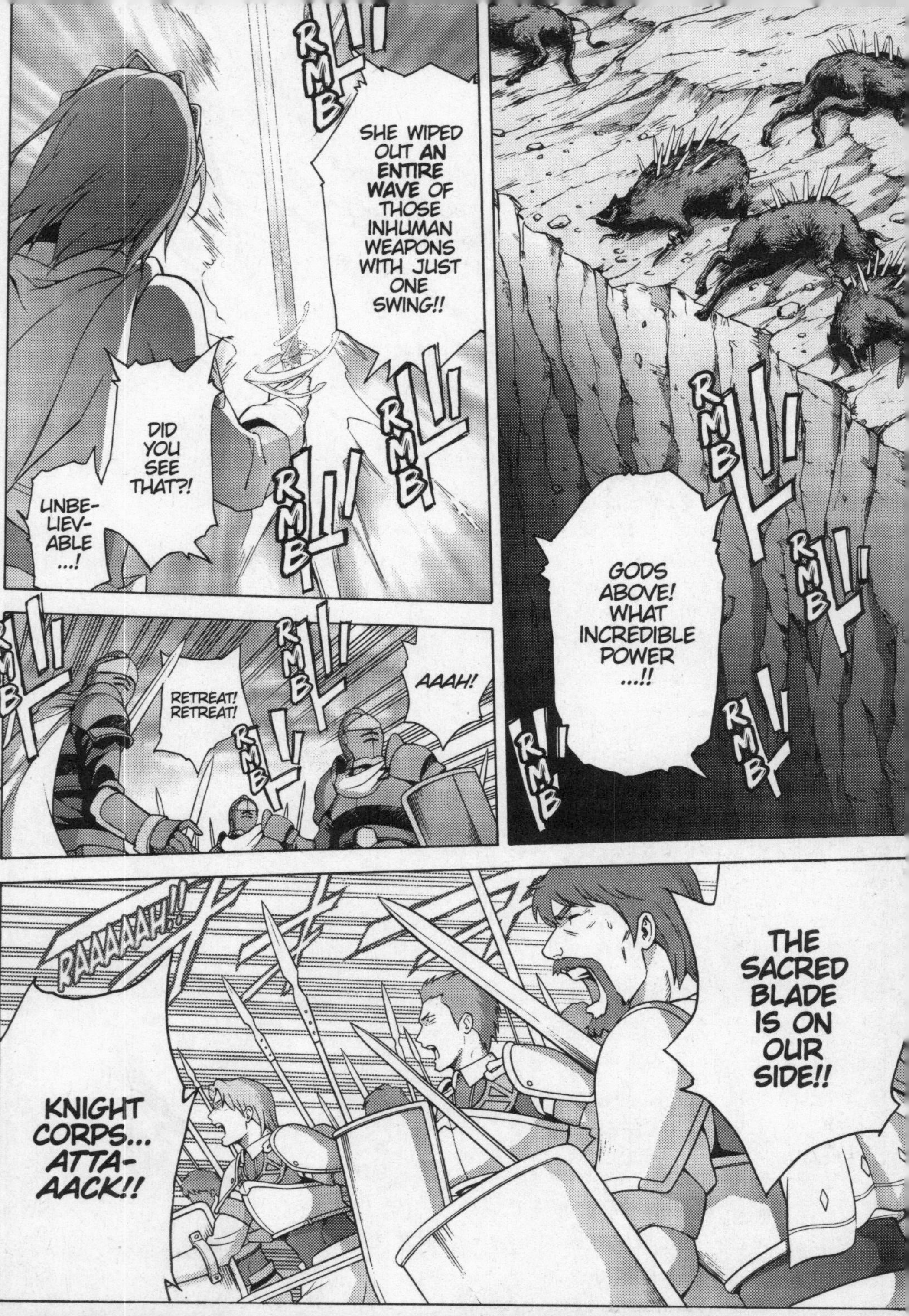

RMB
GODS ABOVE! WHAT INCREDIBLE POWER ...!!
RMB
RMB
RMB
RMB
SHE WIPED OUT AN ENTIRE WAVE OF THOSE INHUMAN WEAPONS WITH JUST ONE SWING!!
RMB
RMB
DID YOU SEE THAT?!
UNBE-LIEV-ABLE ...!
RMB
AAAH!
RMB
RETREAT! RETREAT!
RMB
THE SACRED BLADE IS ON OUR SIDE!!
RAAAAAAH!!
KNIGHT CORPS... ATTA-AACK!!

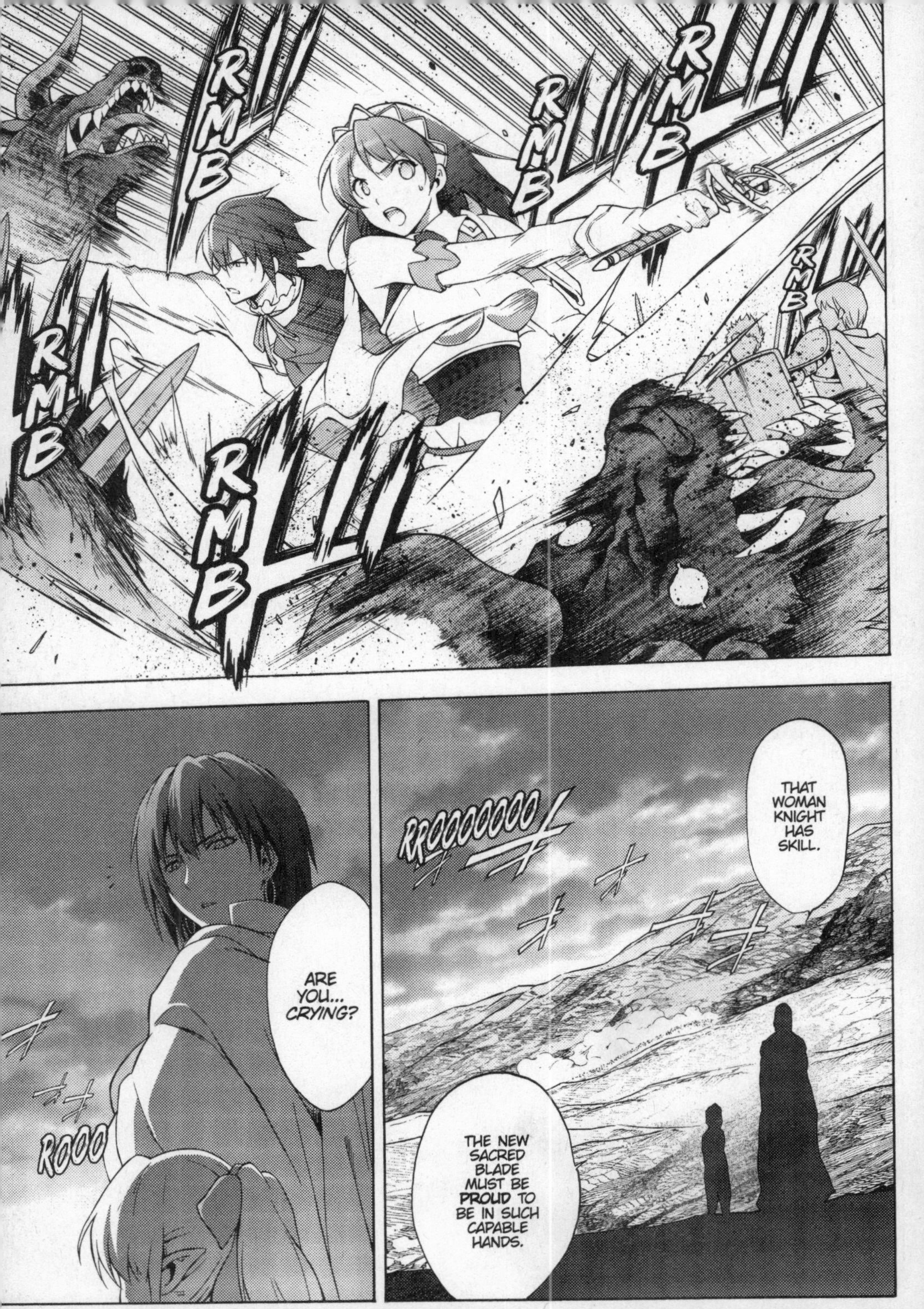
RMB
RMB
RMB
RMB
RMB
RMB
RMB
RROOOOOOO
THAT WOMAN KNIGHT HAS SKILL.
THE NEW SACRED BLADE MUST BE PROUD TO BE IN SUCH CAPABLE HANDS.
ARE YOU... CRYING?
ROOO

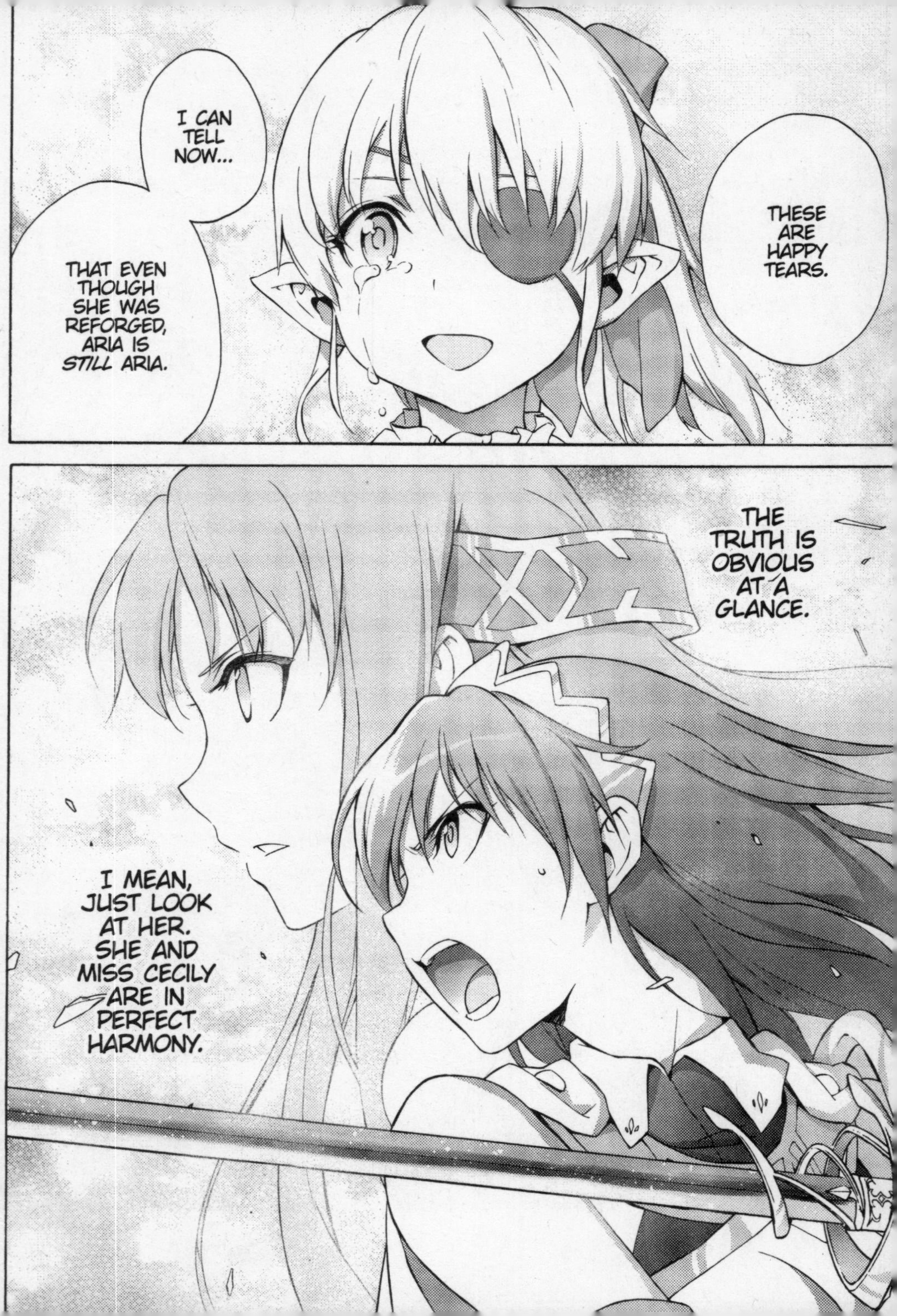
THESE ARE HAPPY TEARS.
I CAN TELL NOW...
THAT EVEN THOUGH SHE WAS REFORGED, ARIA IS *STILL* ARIA.
THE TRUTH IS OBVIOUS AT A GLANCE.
I MEAN, JUST LOOK AT HER. SHE AND MISS CECILY ARE IN PERFECT HARMONY.

The Sacred Blacksmith

聖剣の刀鍛冶

The Sacred Blacksmith

聖剣の刀鍛冶

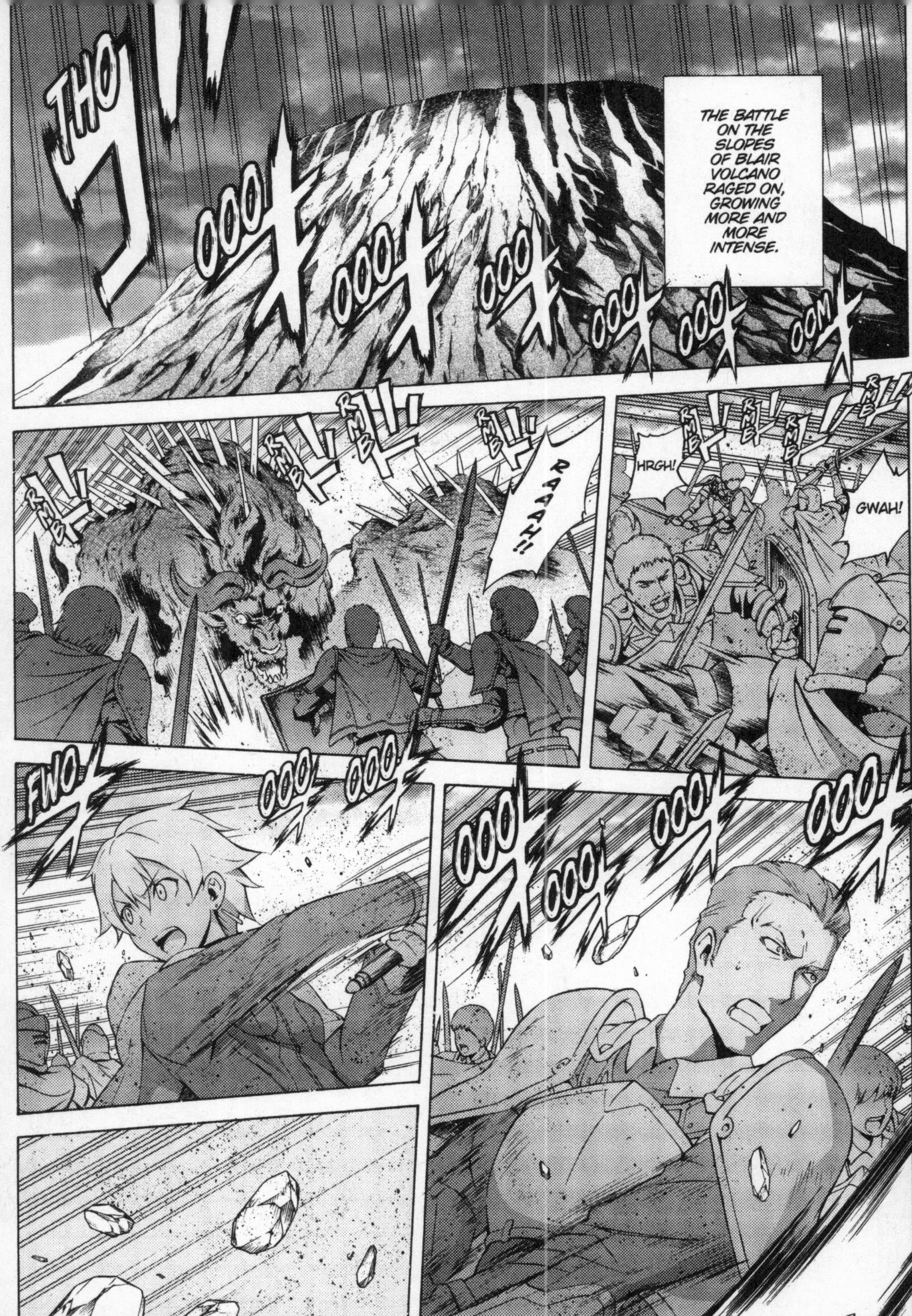
THE BATTLE ON THE SLOPES OF BLAIR VOLCANO RAGED ON, GROWING MORE AND MORE INTENSE.
THOOOOOOOOOOOOOOOOOOM
RMB!!
RMB!!
RMB!!
HRGH!
GWAH!
RMB!!
RMB!!
RMB!!
RMB!!
RAAAAH!!
FWOOOOOOOOOOOOOOOOO

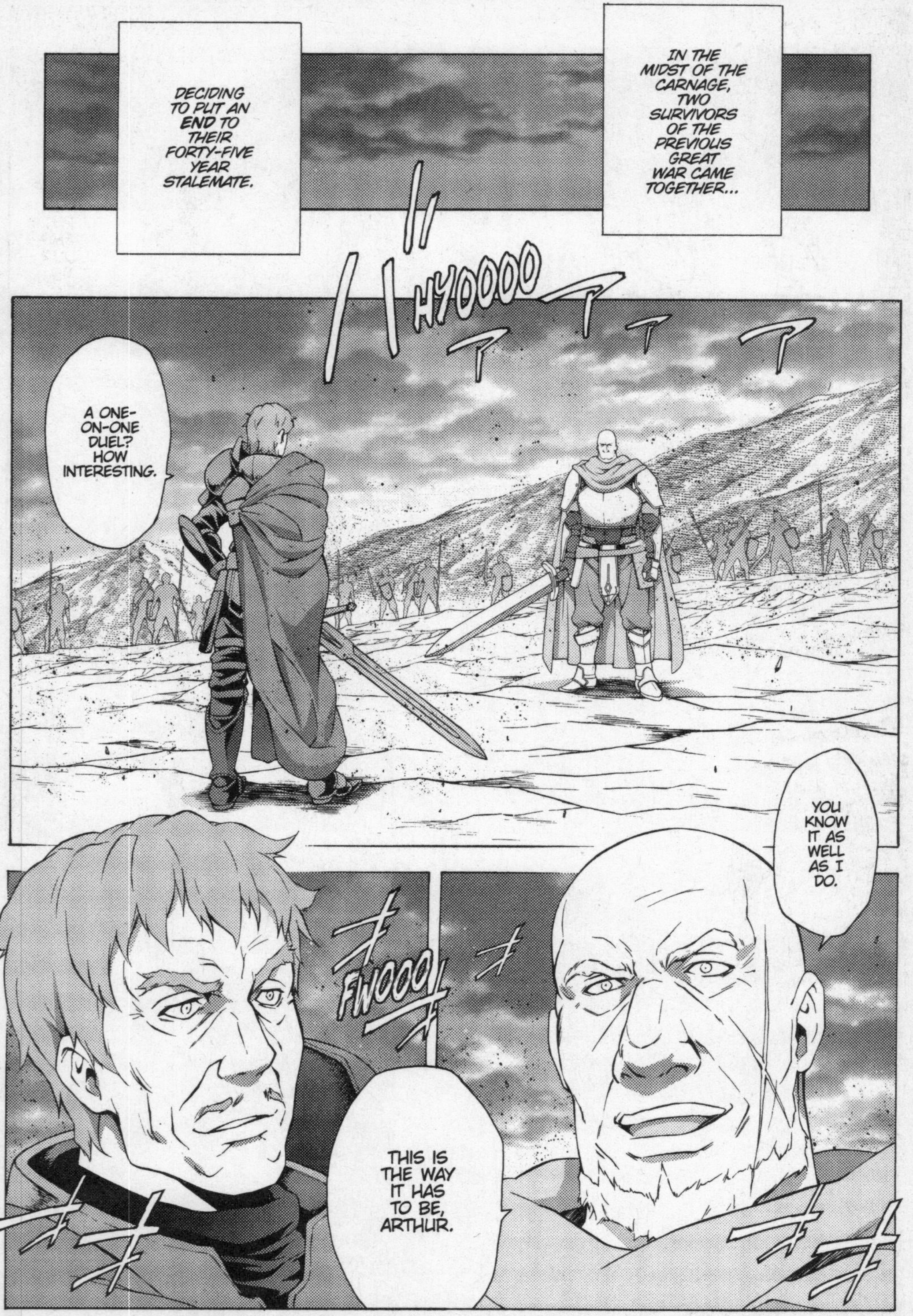
IN THE MIDST OF THE CARNAGE, TWO SURVIVORS OF THE PREVIOUS GREAT WAR CAME TOGETHER...
DECIDING TO PUT AN END TO THEIR FORTY-FIVE YEAR STALEMATE.
HYOOOO
A ONE-ON-ONE DUEL? HOW INTERESTING.
YOU KNOW IT AS WELL AS I DO.
FWOOO
THIS IS THE WAY IT HAS TO BE, ARTHUR.

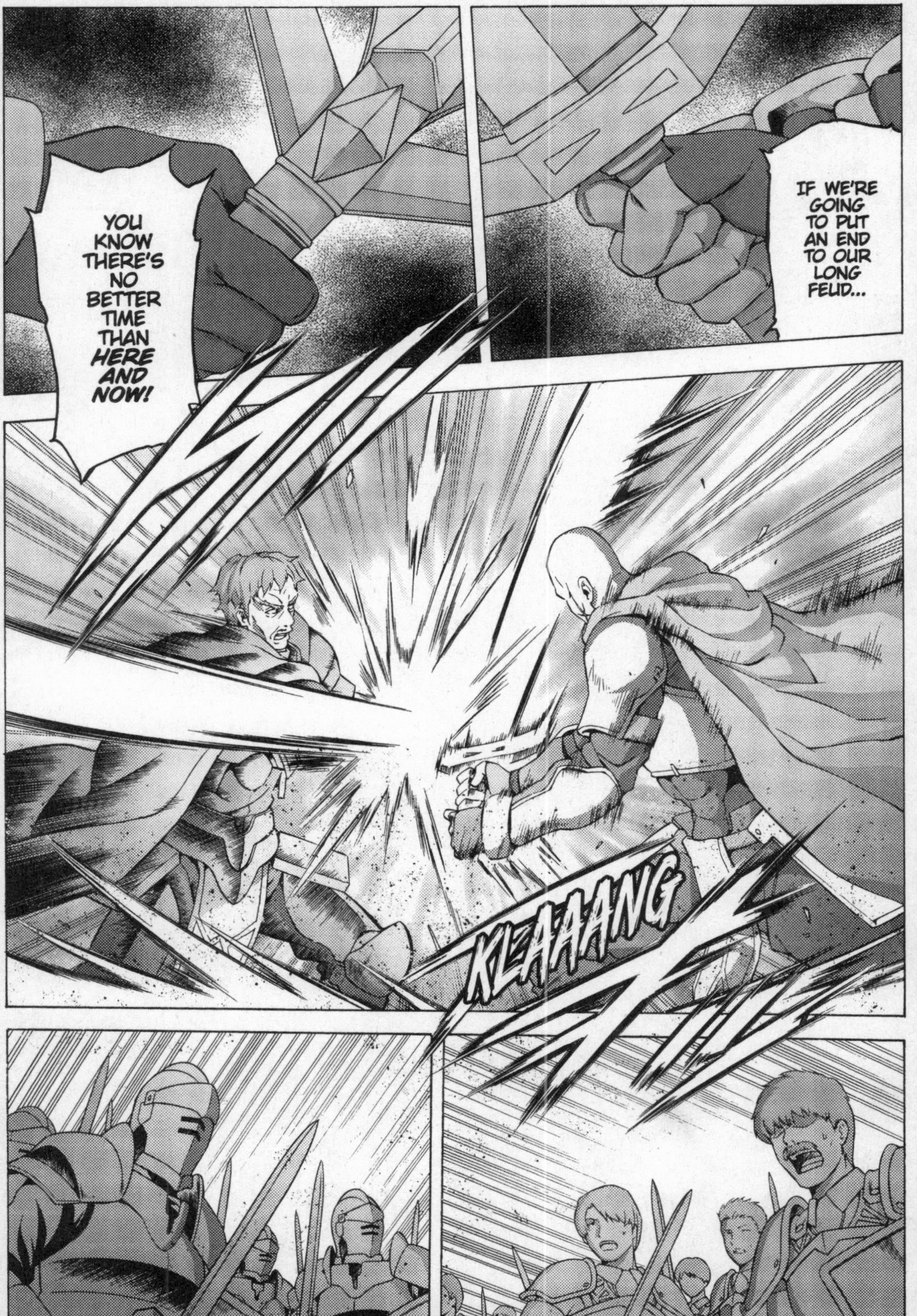
IF WE'RE GOING TO PUT AN END TO OUR LONG FEUD...
YOU KNOW THERE'S NO BETTER TIME THAN *HERE AND NOW!*
KLAAAANG

Chapt. 57 Valbanill
(Part 5)

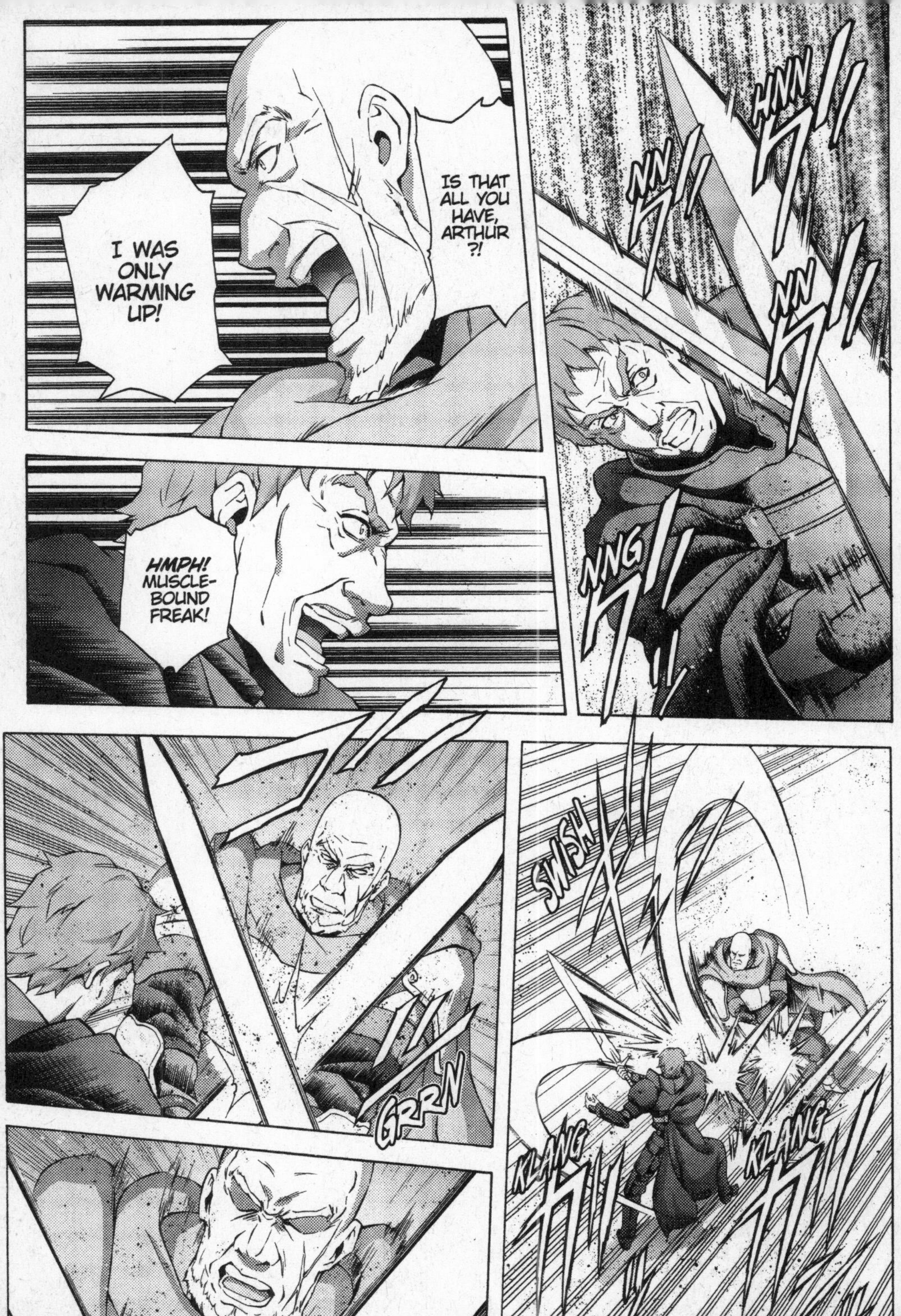
HNN
NN
NN
NNG
IS THAT ALL YOU HAVE, ARTHUR?!
I WAS ONLY WARMING UP!
HMPH! MUSCLE-BOUND FREAK!
SWISH
KLANG
KLANG
GRRN

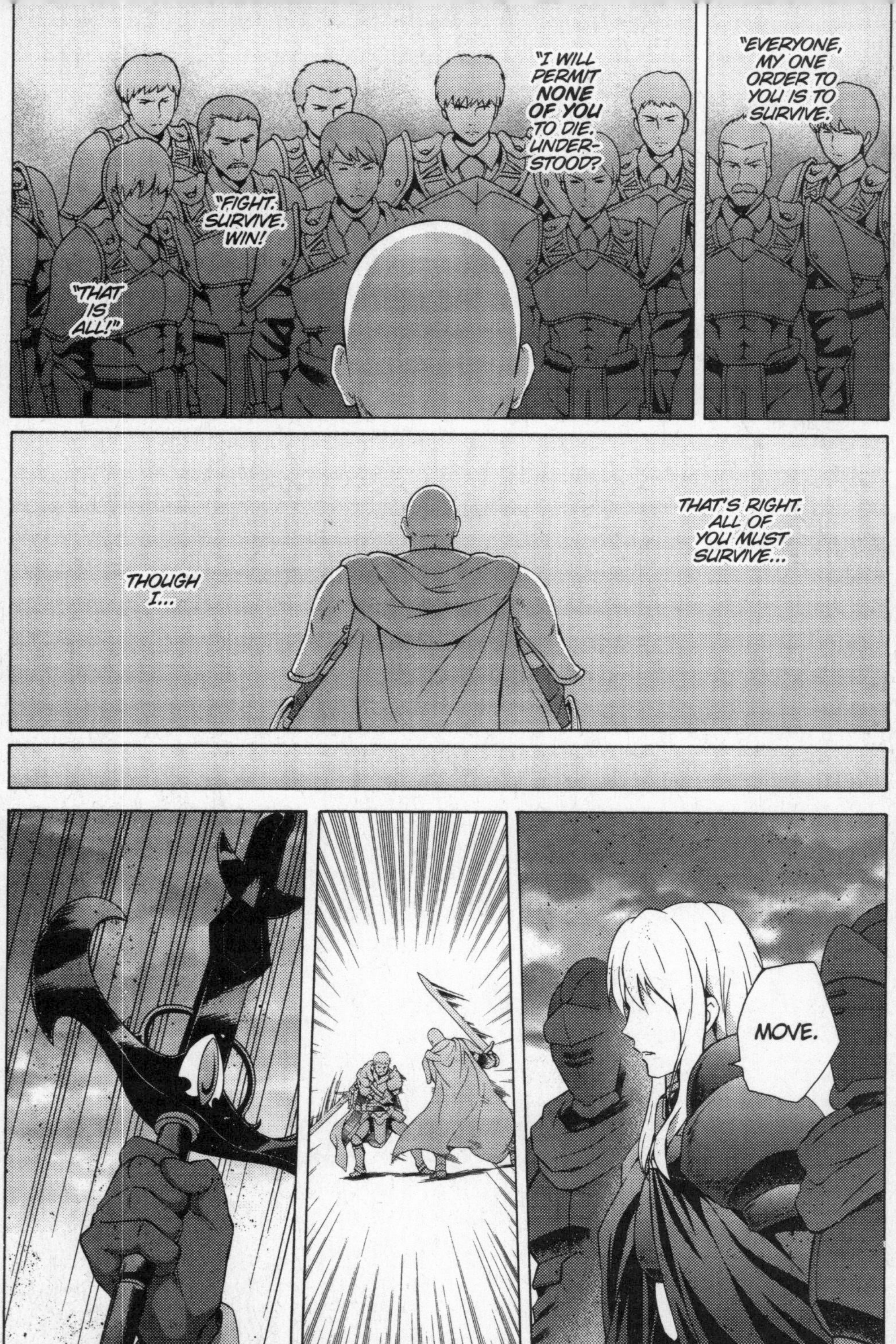
"EVERYONE, MY ONE ORDER TO YOU IS TO SURVIVE.
"I WILL PERMIT NONE OF YOU TO DIE. UNDER-STOOD?
"FIGHT. SURVIVE. WIN!
"THAT IS ALL!"
THAT'S RIGHT. ALL OF YOU MUST SURVIVE...
THOUGH I...
MOVE.

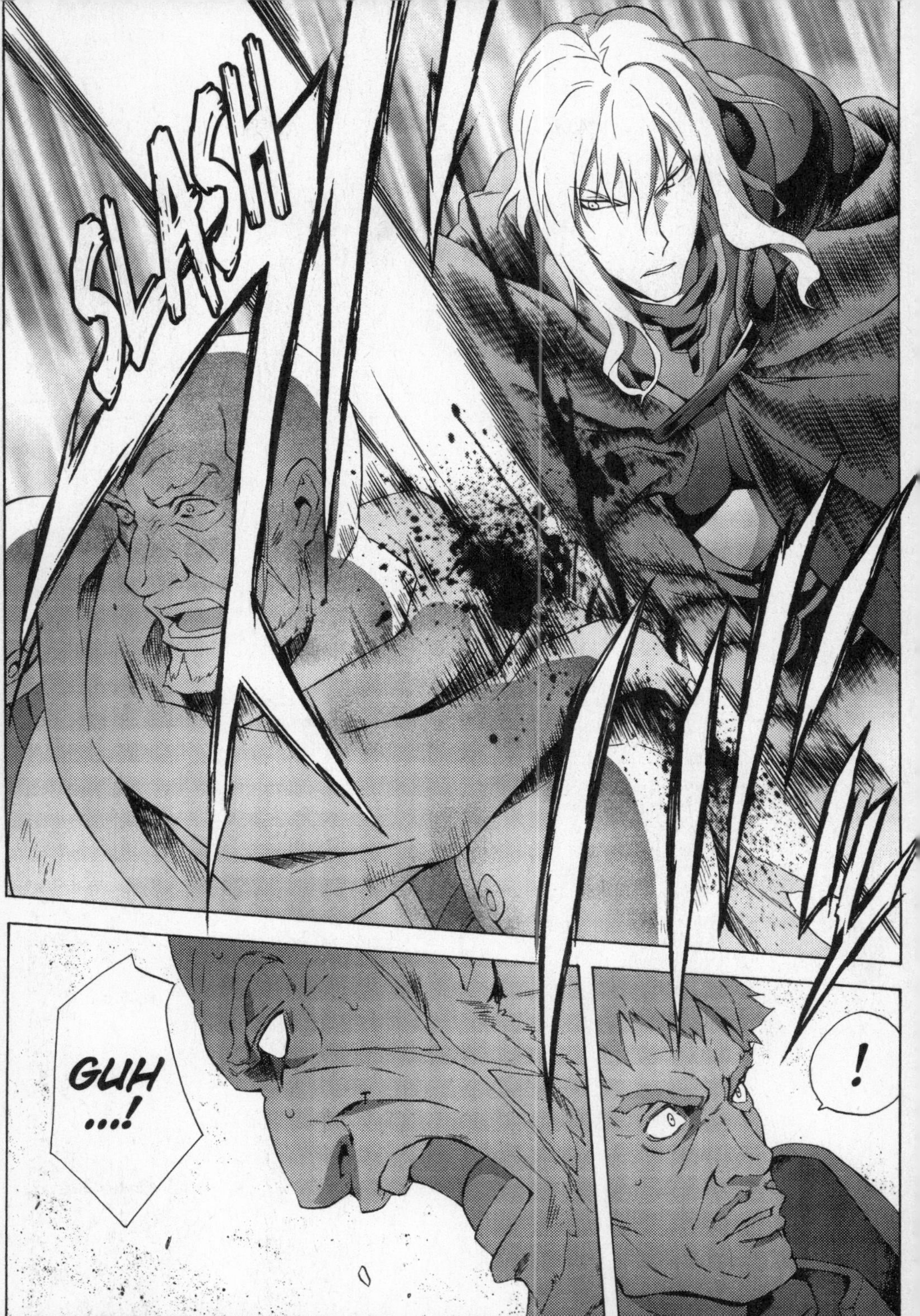
SLASH
!
GUH ...!

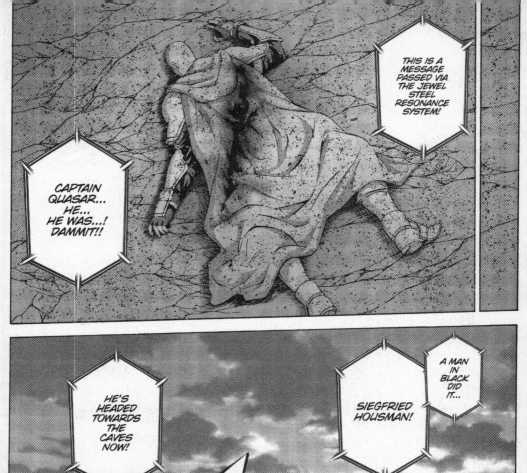

THIS IS A MESSAGE PASSED VIA THE JEWEL STEEL RESONANCE SYSTEM!

CAPTAIN QUASAR... HE... HE WAS...! DAMMIT!!

A MAN IN BLACK DID IT...

SIEGFRIED HOUSMAN!

HE'S HEADED TOWARDS THE CAVES NOW!

RAAAAAAH

PLEASE!!

SOME-BODY NEEDS TO STOP HIM!

!!

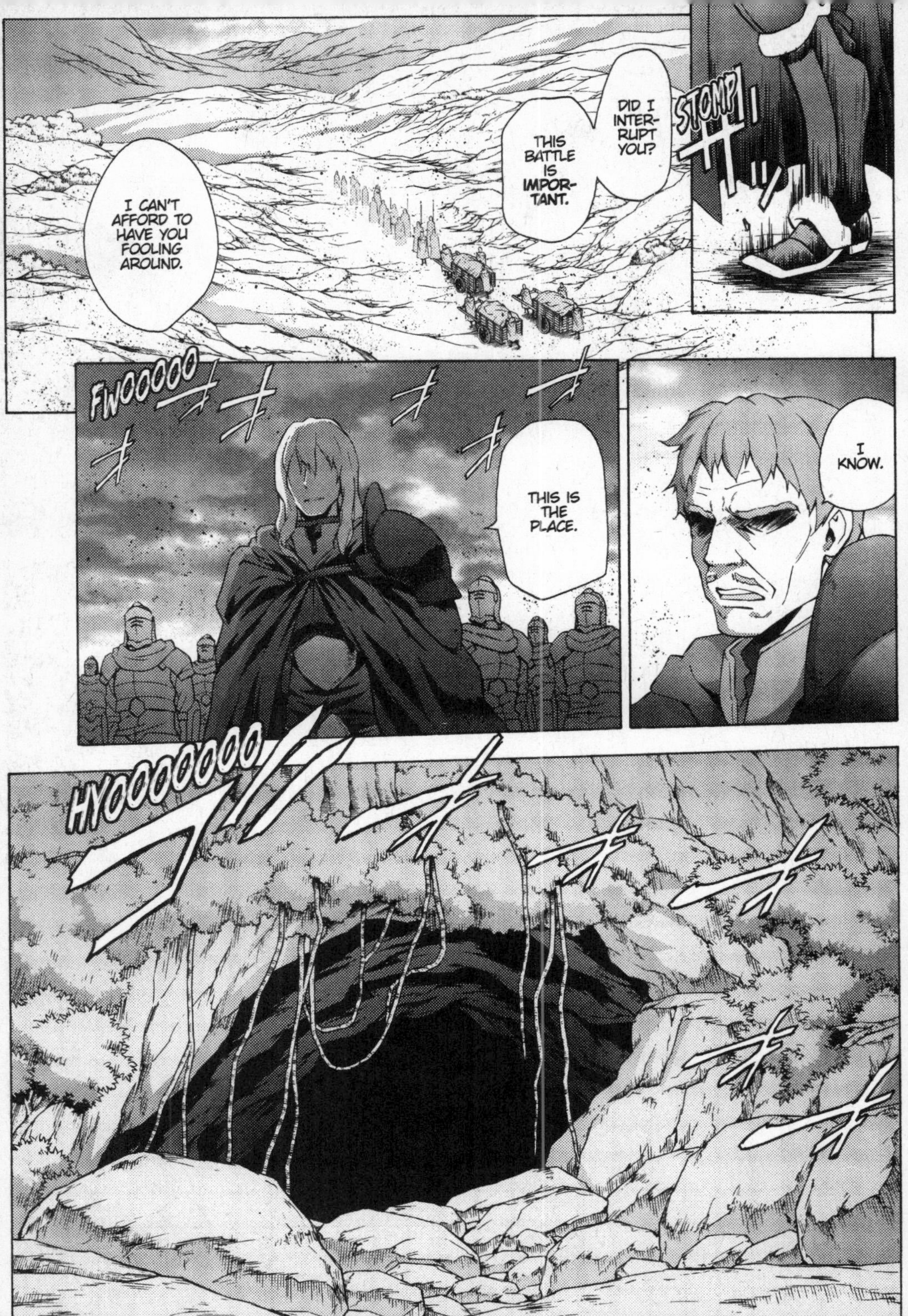
STOMP!
DID I INTERRUPT YOU?
THIS BATTLE IS IMPORTANT.
I CAN'T AFFORD TO HAVE YOU FOOLING AROUND.
I KNOW.
FWOOOOO
THIS IS THE PLACE.
HYOOOOOOO

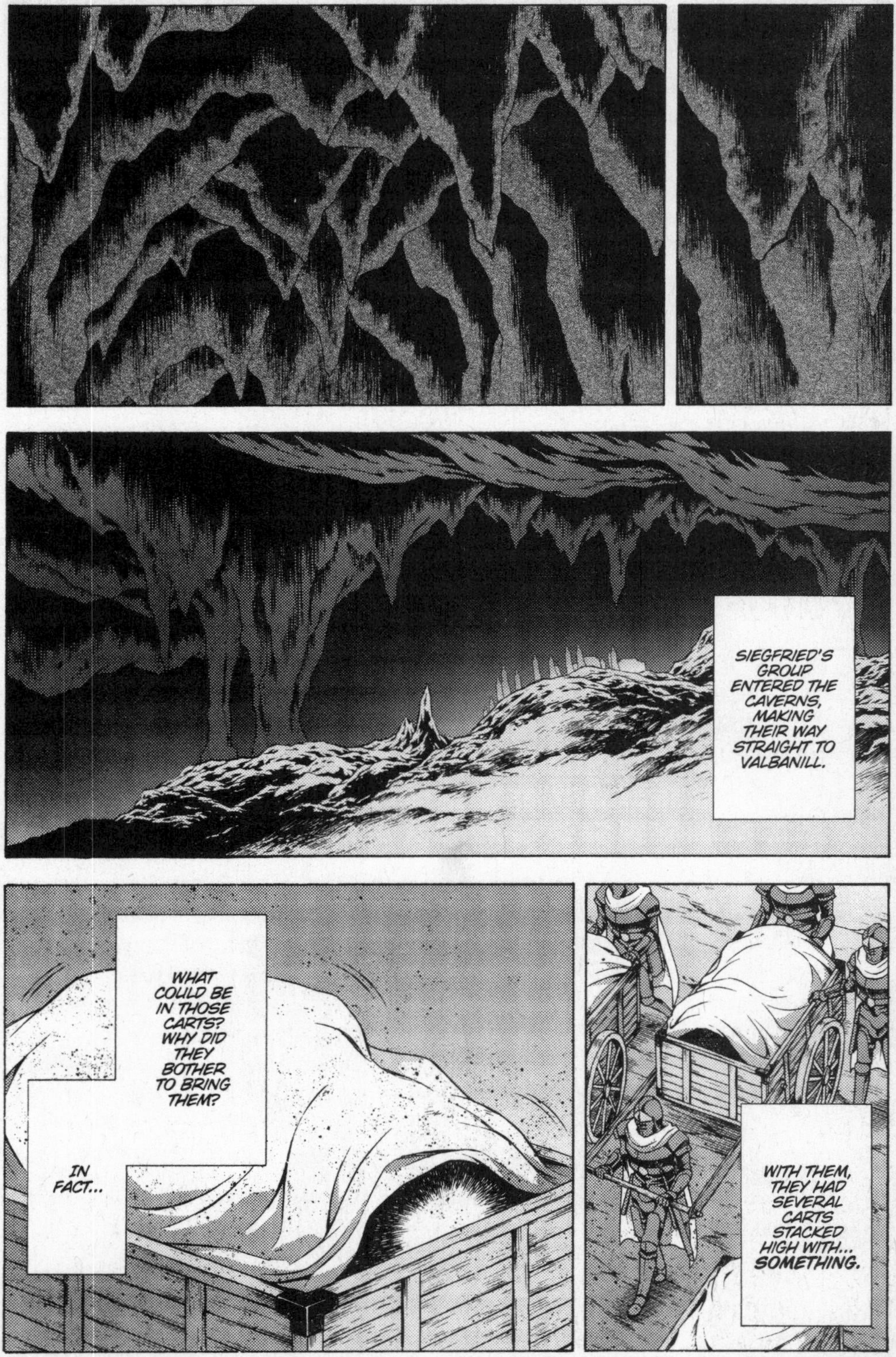
SIEGFRIED'S GROUP ENTERED THE CAVERNS, MAKING THEIR WAY STRAIGHT TO VALBANILL.
WITH THEM, THEY HAD SEVERAL CARTS STACKED HIGH WITH... **SOMETHING.**
WHAT COULD BE IN THOSE CARTS? WHY DID THEY BOTHER TO BRING THEM?
IN FACT...

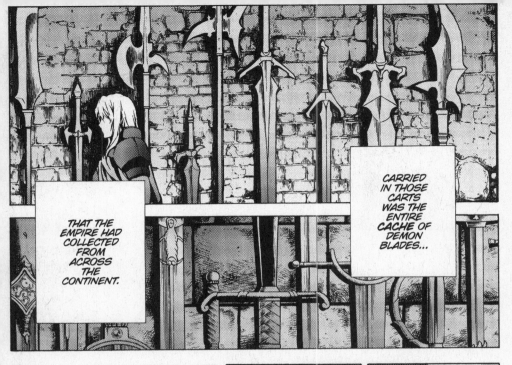

CARRIED IN THOSE CARTS WAS THE ENTIRE CACHE OF DEMON BLADES...

THAT THE EMPIRE HAD COLLECTED FROM ACROSS THE CONTINENT.

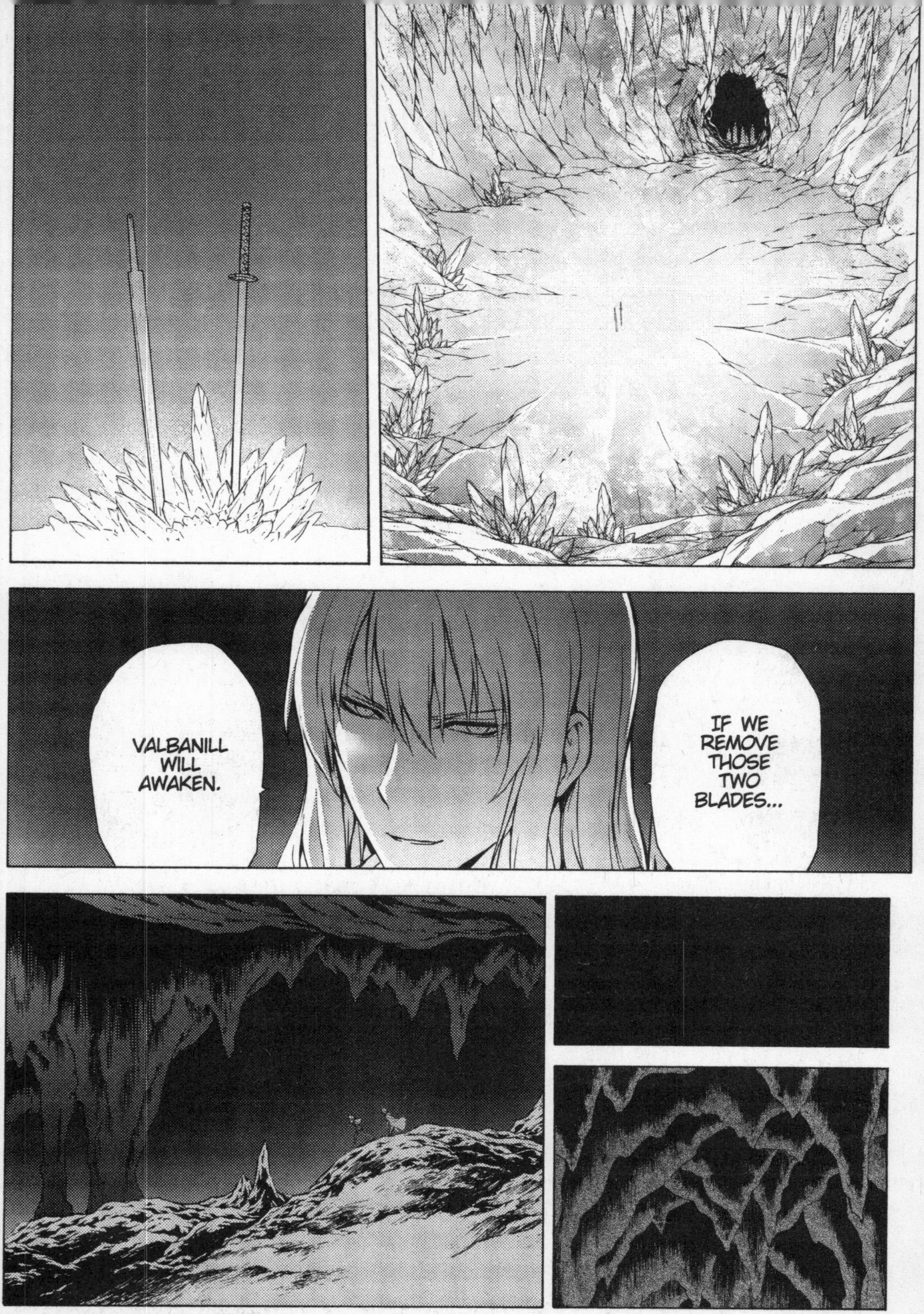
IF WE REMOVE THOSE TWO BLADES...
VALBANILL WILL AWAKEN.

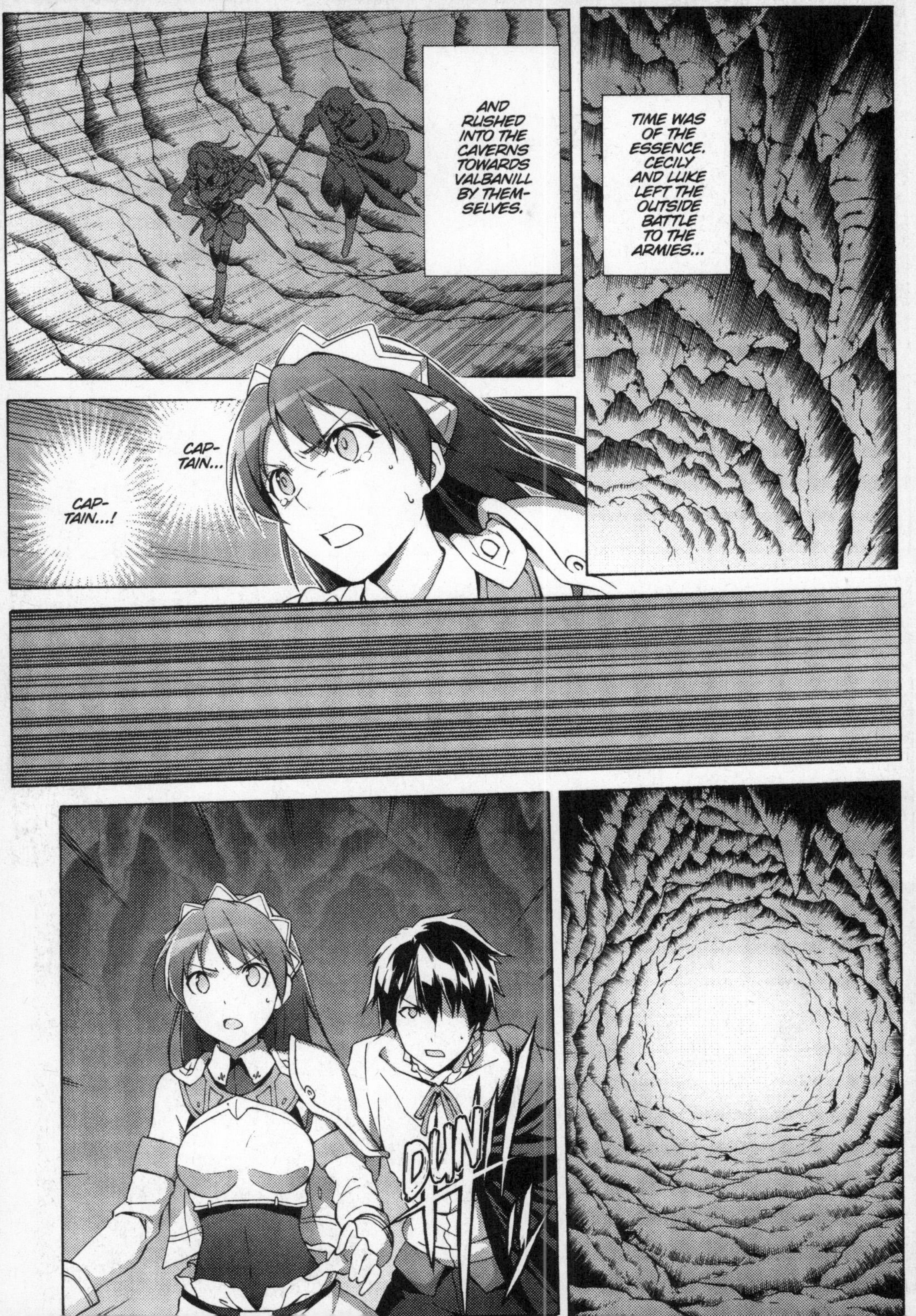
TIME WAS OF THE ESSENCE. CECILY AND LUKE LEFT THE OUTSIDE BATTLE TO THE ARMIES...
AND RUSHED INTO THE CAVERNS TOWARDS VALBANILL BY THEM-SELVES.
CAP-TAIN...
CAP-TAIN...!
DUN!!

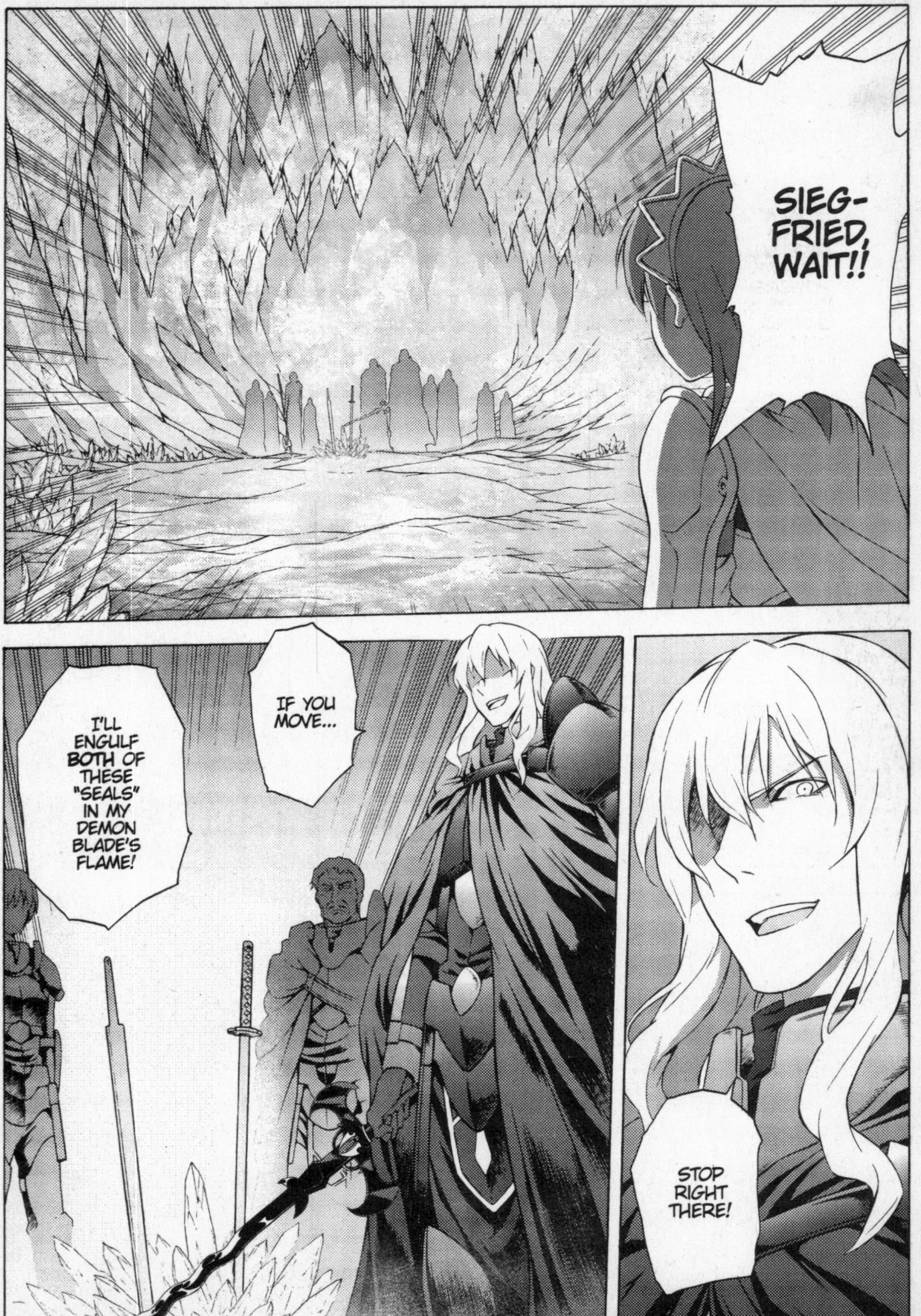
SIEG-FRIED, WAIT!!
STOP RIGHT THERE!
IF YOU MOVE...
I'LL ENGULF BOTH OF THESE "SEALS" IN MY DEMON BLADE'S FLAME!

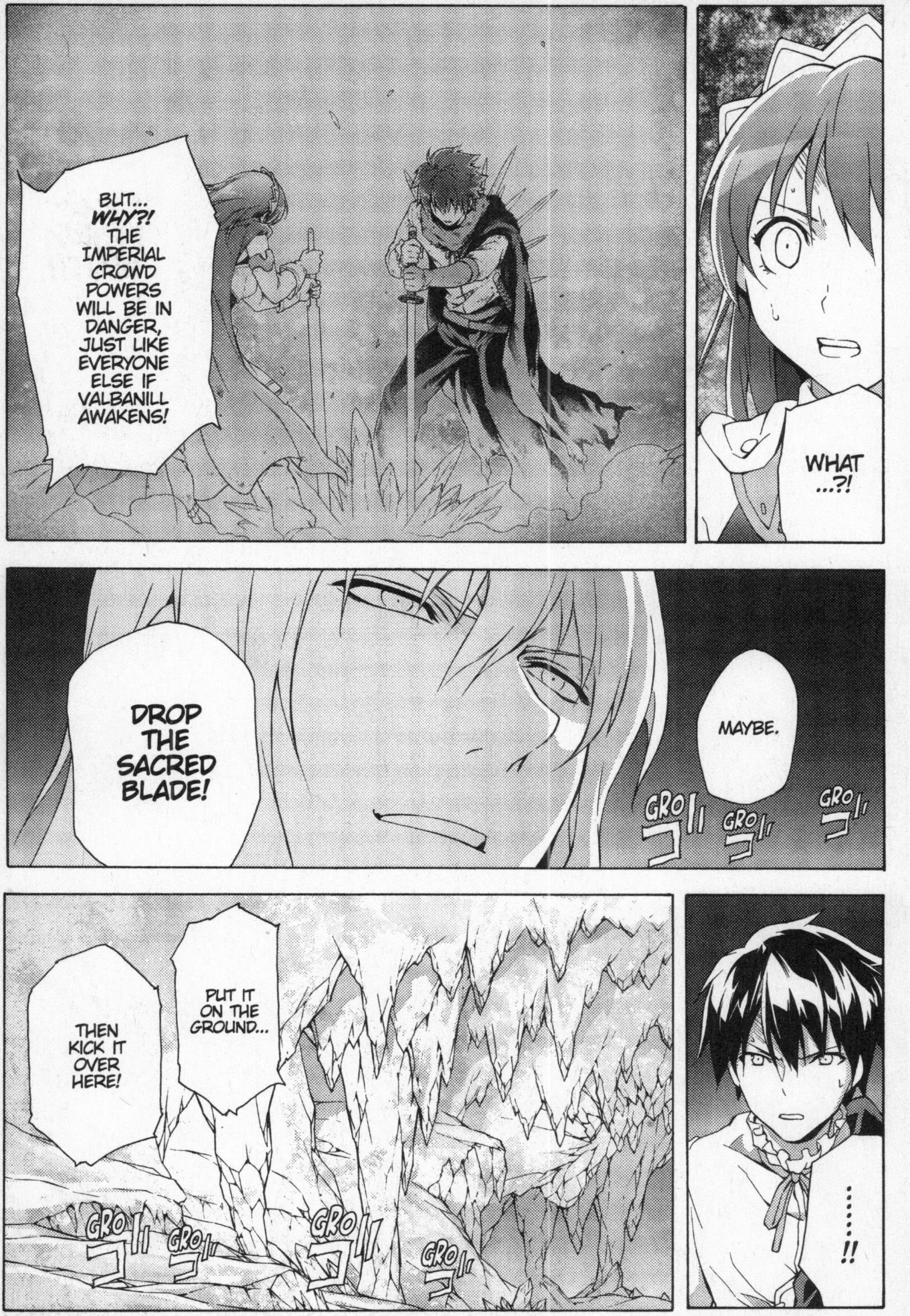
WHAT ...?!
BUT... *WHY?!* THE IMPERIAL CROWD POWERS WILL BE IN DANGER, JUST LIKE EVERYONE ELSE IF VALBANILL AWAKENS!
MAYBE.
GRO
GRO
GRO
DROP THE SACRED BLADE!
......!!
PUT IT ON THE GROUND...
THEN KICK IT OVER HERE!
GRO
GRO
GRO
GRO

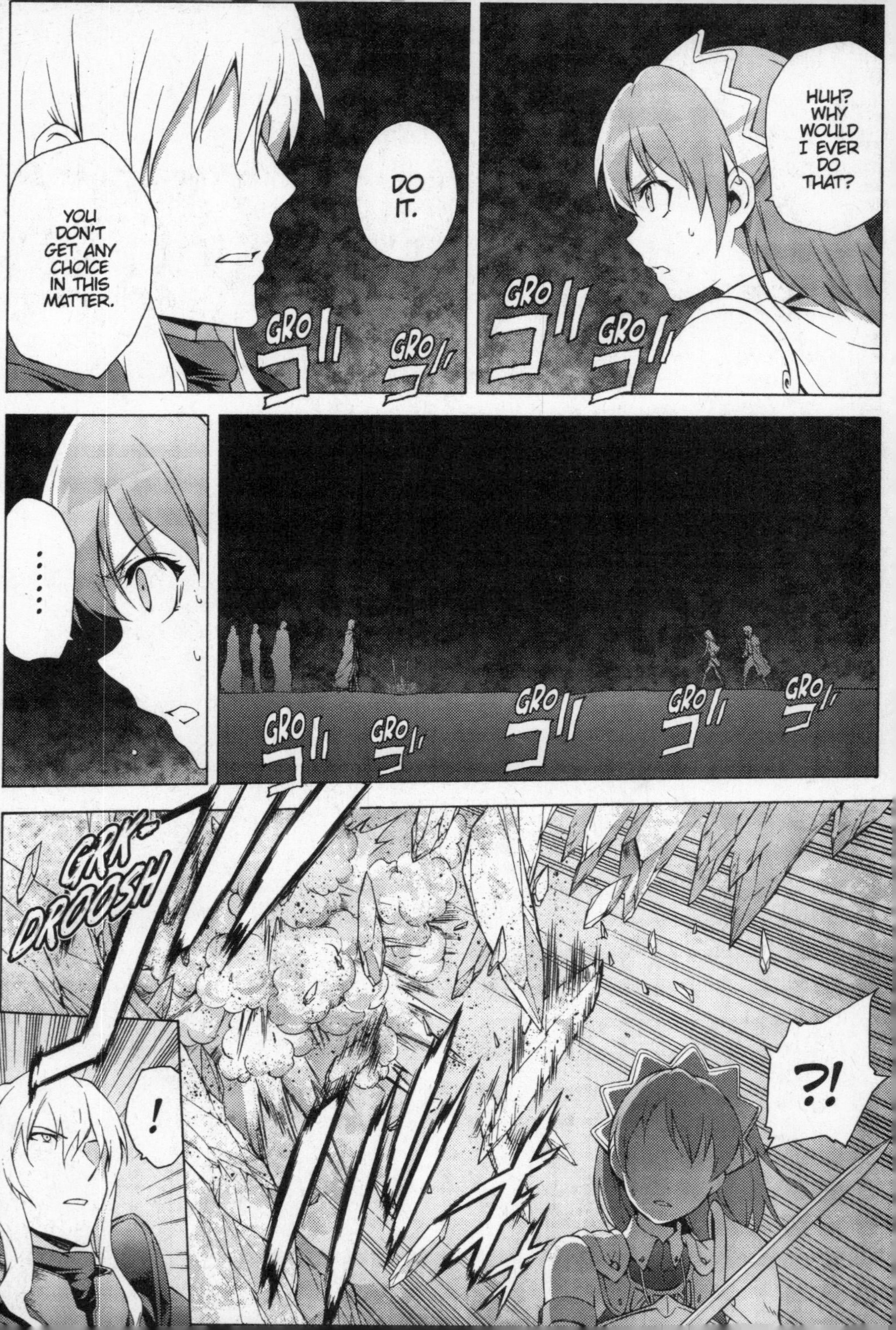
HUH? WHY WOULD I EVER DO THAT?
GRO
GRO
DO IT.
YOU DON'T GET ANY CHOICE IN THIS MATTER.
GRO
GRO
GRO
GRO
GRO
GRO
GRO
......
GRK-DROOSH
?!
!

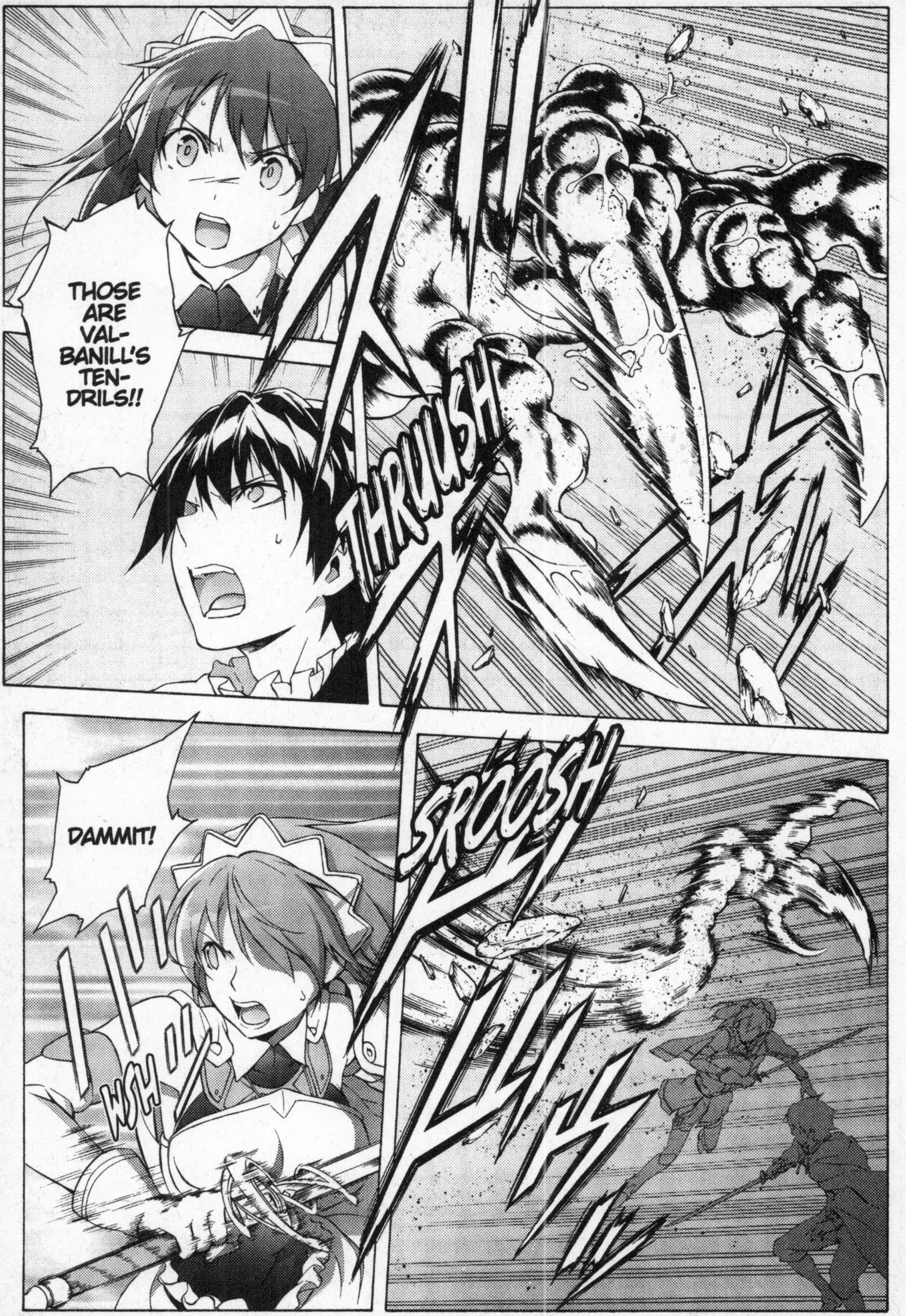
THRUUSH
THOSE ARE VAL-BANILL'S TEN-DRILS!!
SPOOSH
DAMMIT!
WSH

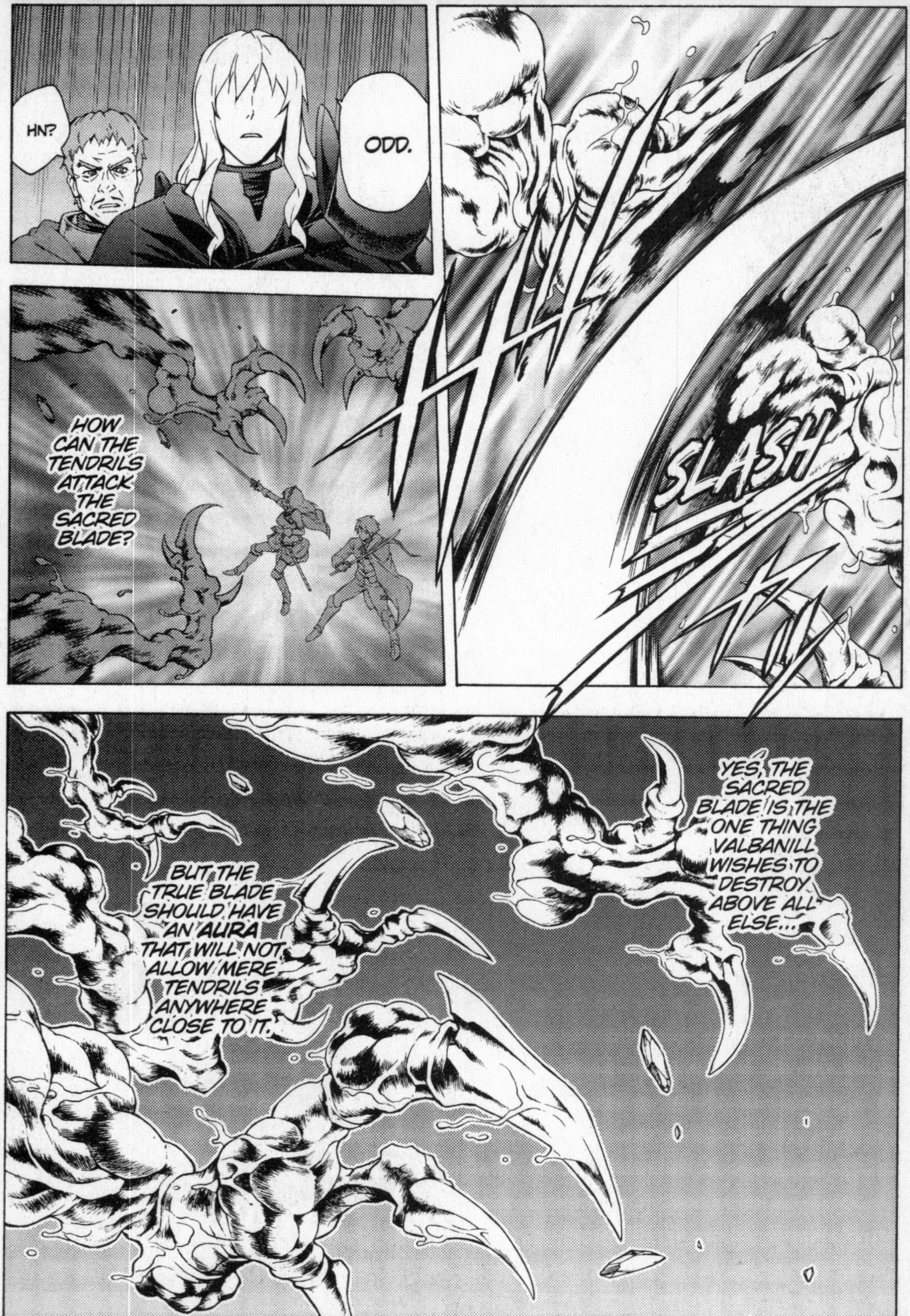

HN?
ODD.
SLASH
HOW CAN THE TENDRILS ATTACK THE SACRED BLADE?
YES, THE SACRED BLADE IS THE ONE THING VALBANILL WISHES TO DESTROY ABOVE ALL ELSE...
BUT THE TRUE BLADE SHOULD HAVE AN AURA THAT WILL NOT ALLOW MERE TENDRILS ANYWHERE CLOSE TO IT.

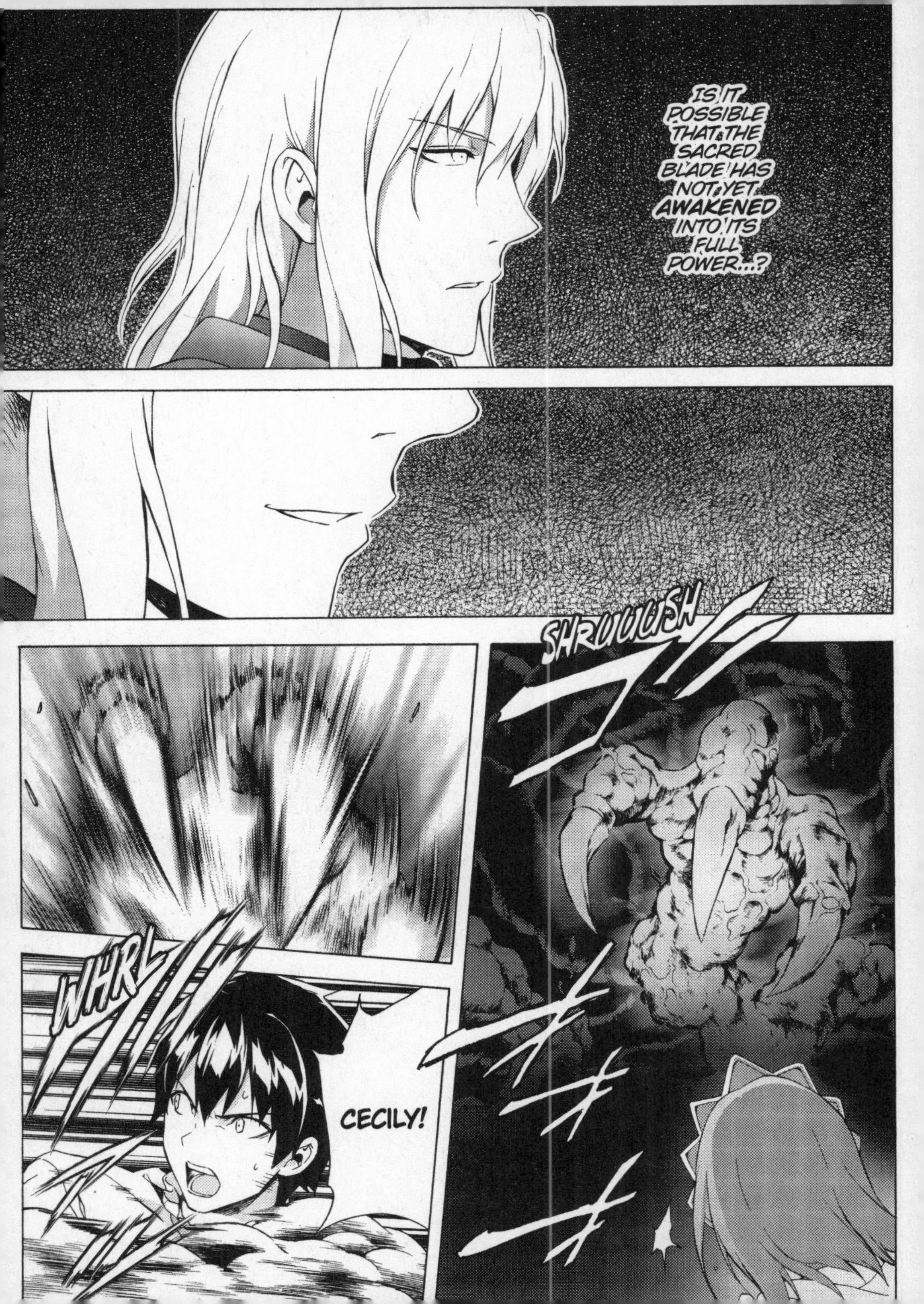
IS IT POSSIBLE THAT THE SACRED BLADE HAS NOT YET AWAKENED INTO ITS FULL POWER...?
SHRUUUSH
WHRL
CECILY!

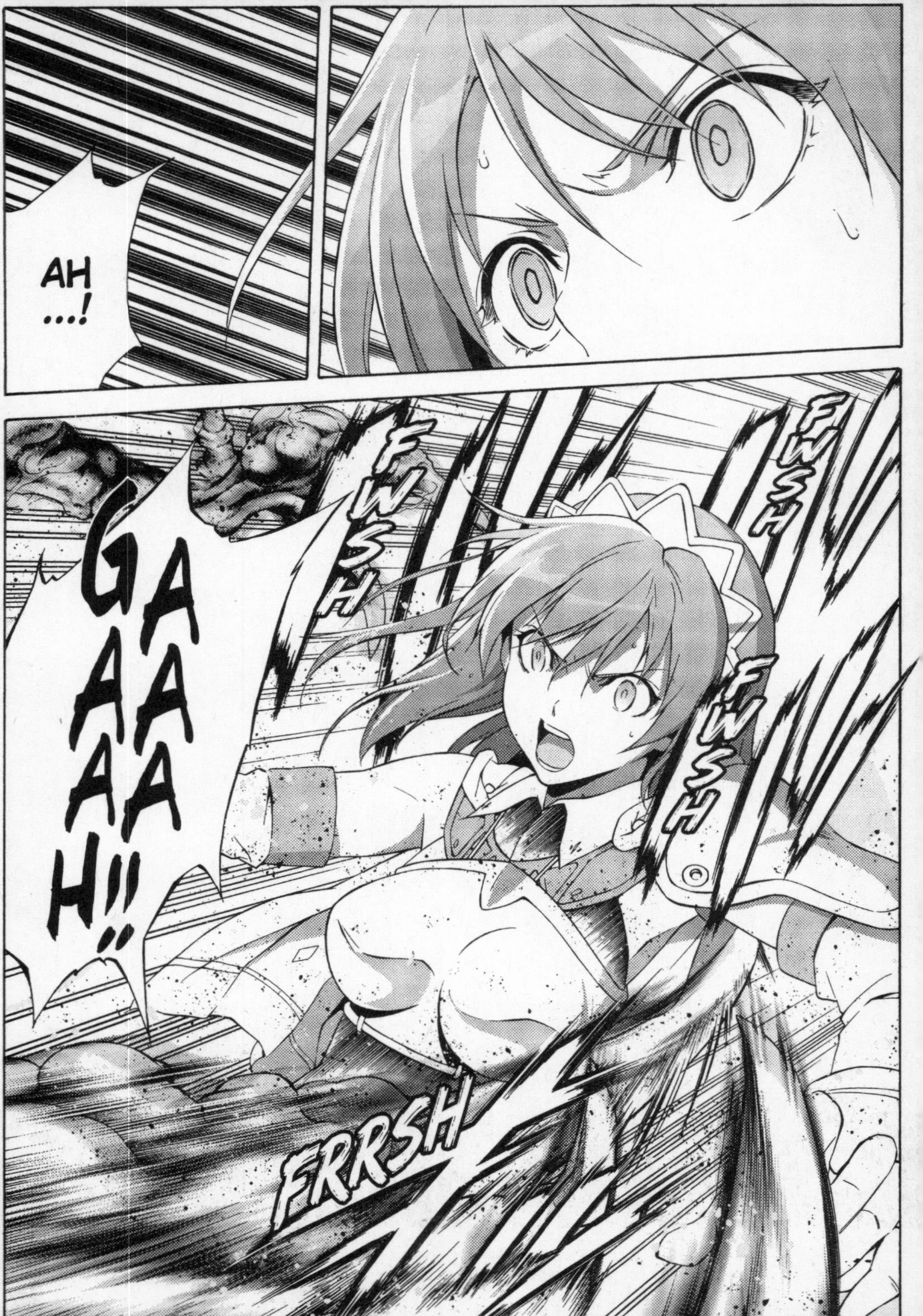
AH ...!
FWSH
FWSH
GAAAAAH!!
FWSH
FRRSH

The Sacred Blacksmith

聖剣の刀鍛冶

The Sacred Blacksmith

聖剣の刀鍛治

MRR-
RGH
....!

SKWEEZ

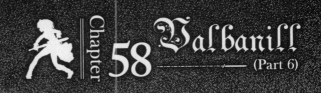

Chapter 58 Valbanill
(Part 6)

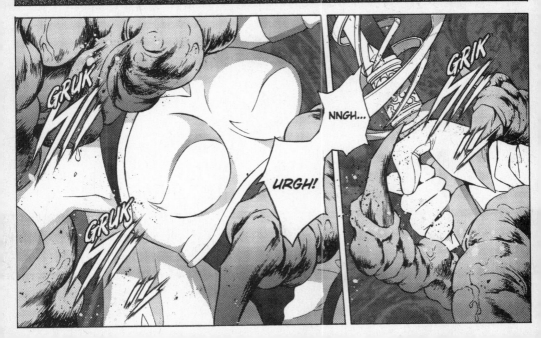

GRUK

GRUK

NNGH...

URGH!

GRIK

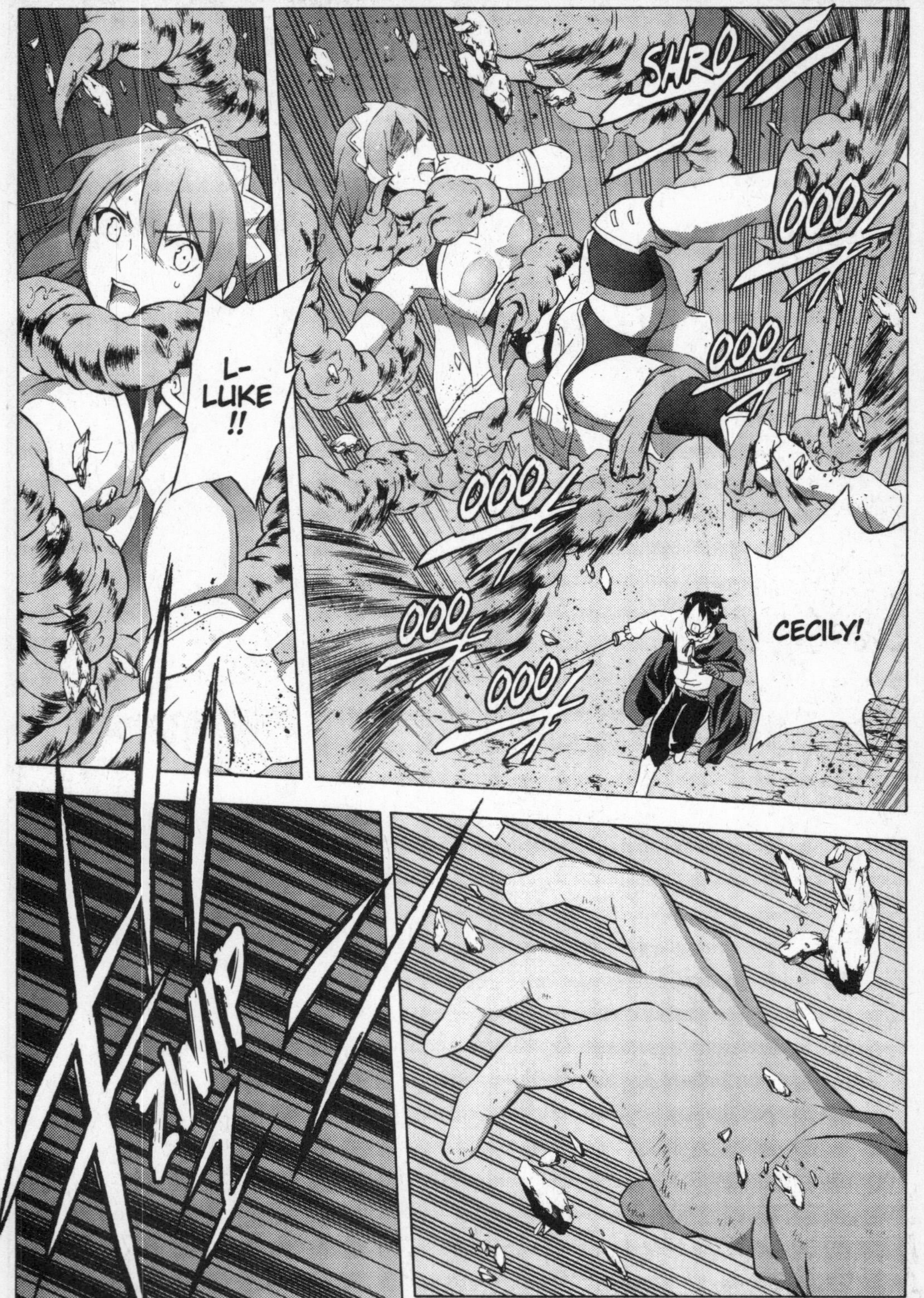
SHRO
OOO
OOO
OOO
CECILY!
OOO
OOO
L-LUKE!!
ZWIP

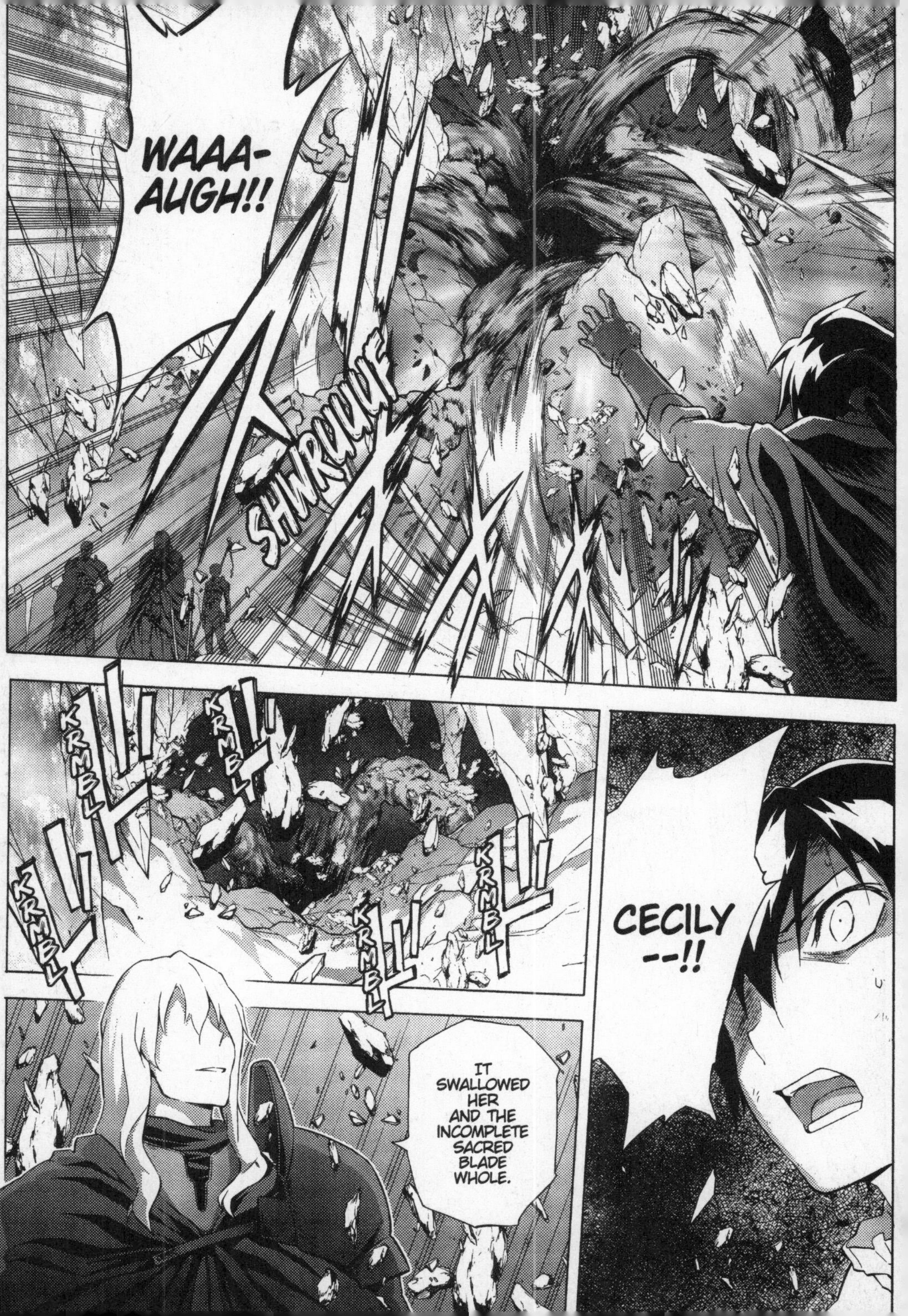
WAAAA-
AUGH!!
SHWRUUUF
CECILY
--!!
KRMBL
KRMBL
KRMBL
KRMBL
KRMBL
IT SWALLOWED HER AND THE INCOMPLETE SACRED BLADE WHOLE.

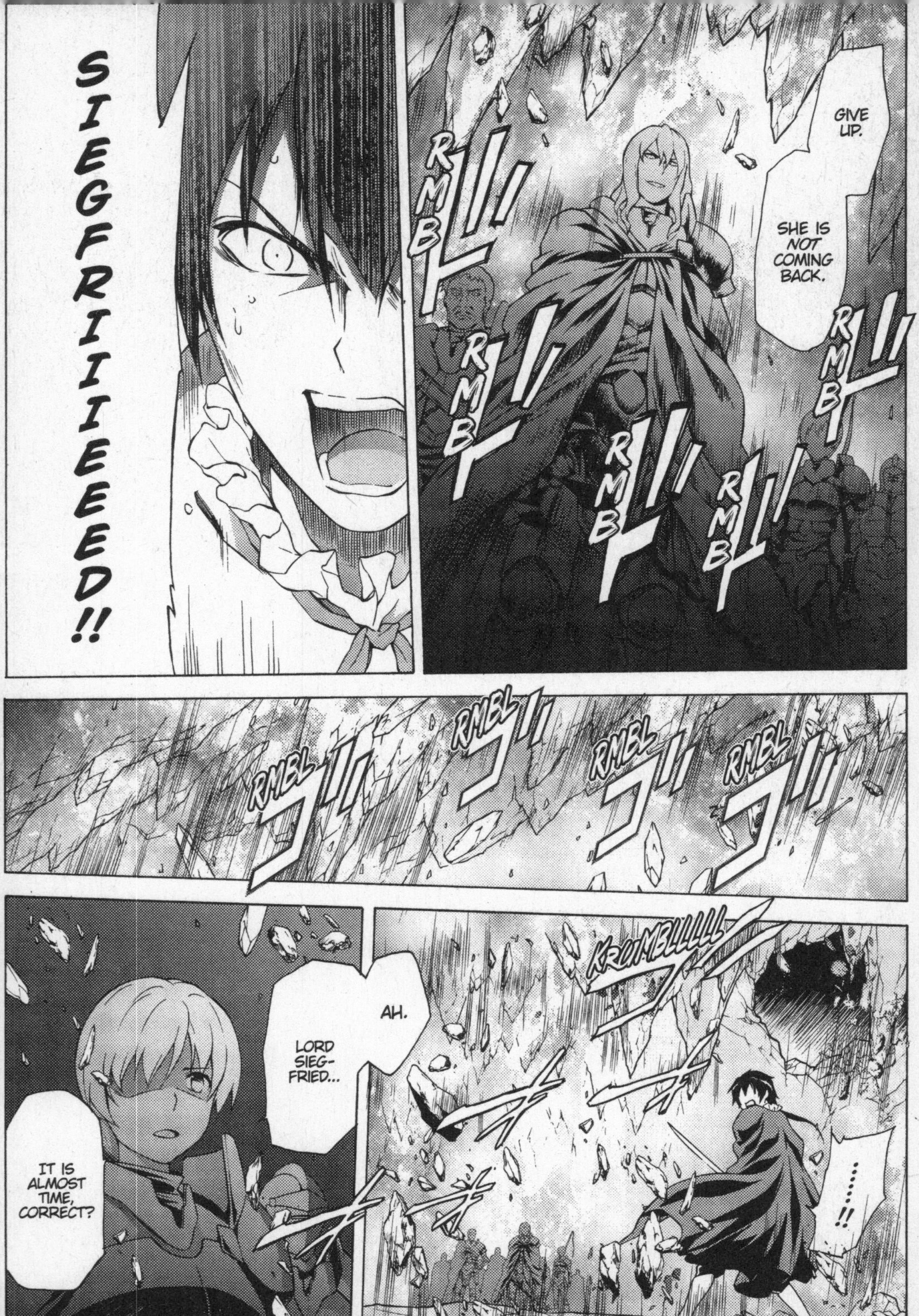
GIVE UP.
SHE IS NOT COMING BACK.
RMB RMB RMB RMB RMB
SIEGFRIIIEEEED!!
RMBL RMBL RMBL RMBL
KRUMBLLLLL
......!!
AH.
LORD SIEG-FRIED...
IT IS ALMOST TIME, CORRECT?

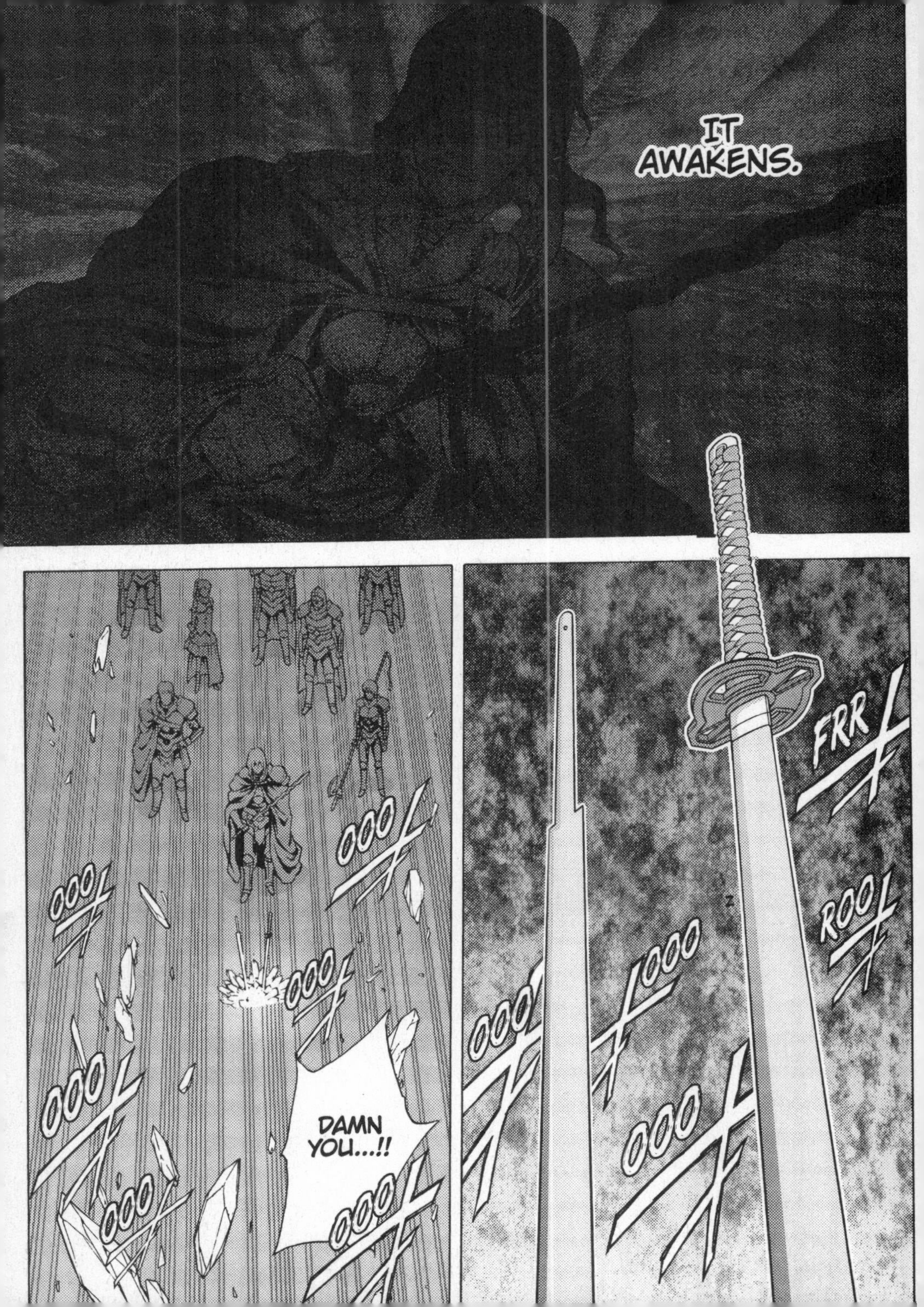
IT AWAKENS.
FRR
ROO
OOO
OOO
OOO
OOO
OOO
OOO
OOO
DAMN YOU...!!
OOO
OOO

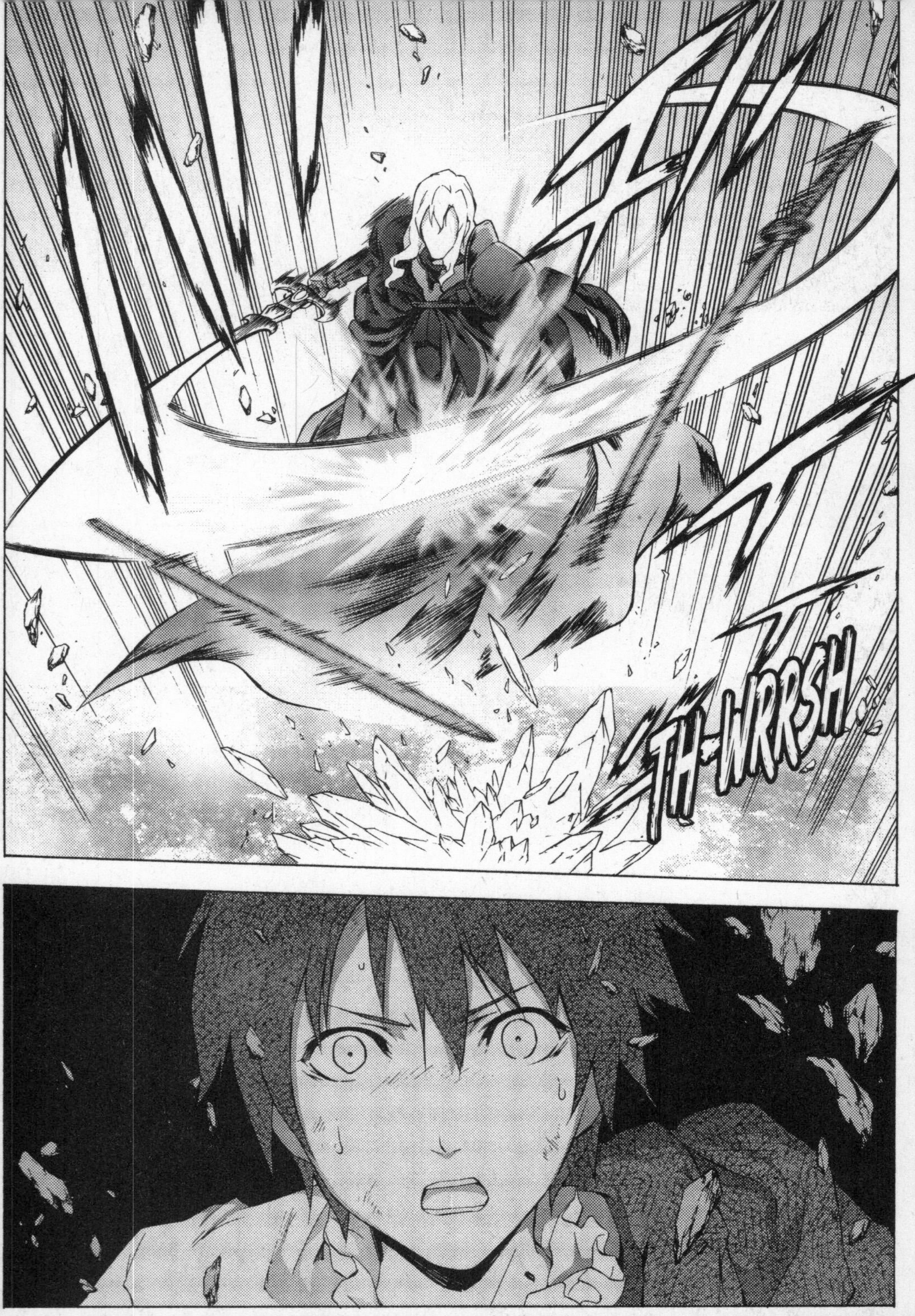
TH-WRRSH

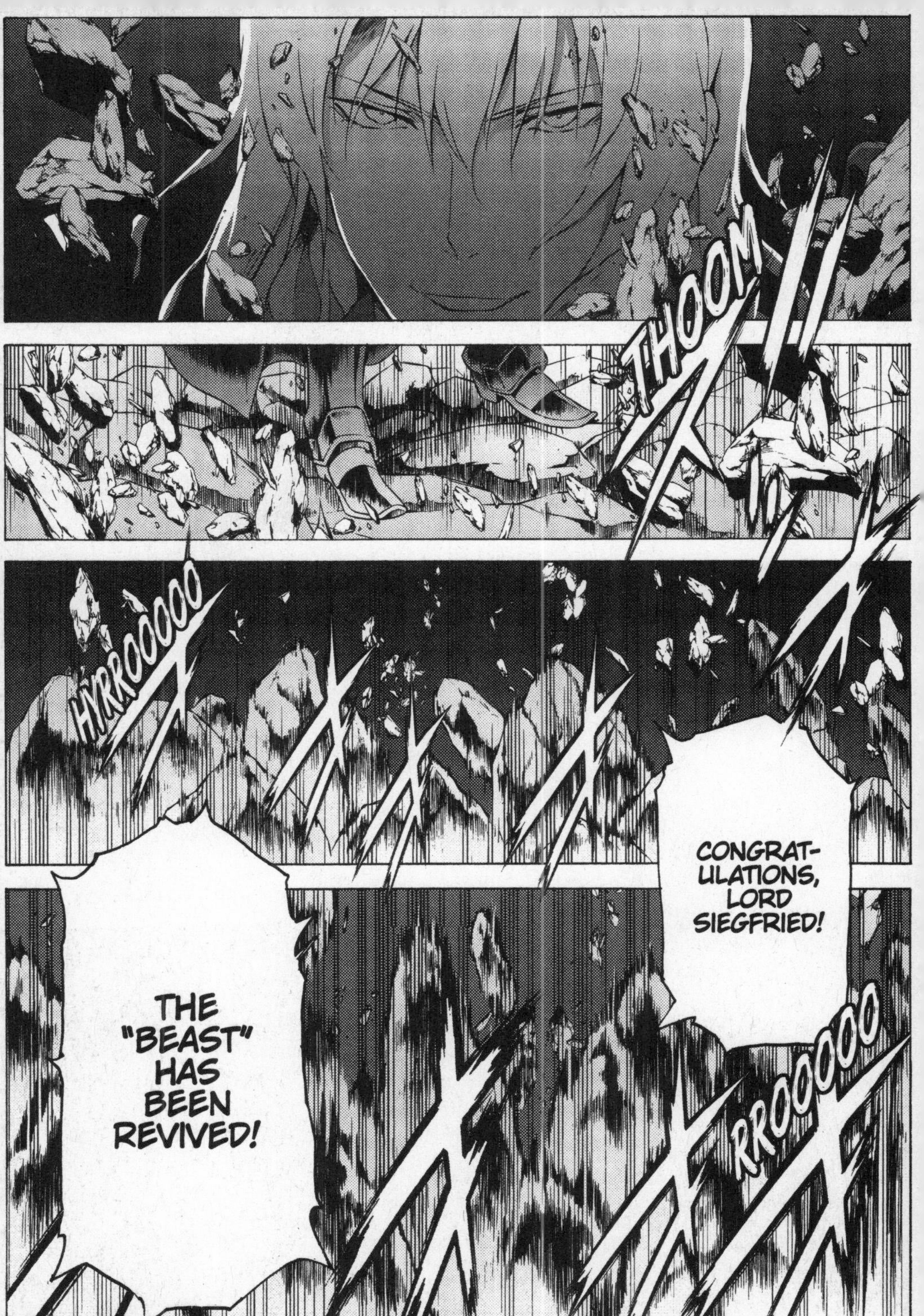
THOOM
HYRROOOOO
CONGRAT-
ULATIONS,
LORD
SIEGFRIED!
THE
"BEAST"
HAS
BEEN
REVIVED!
RROOOOO

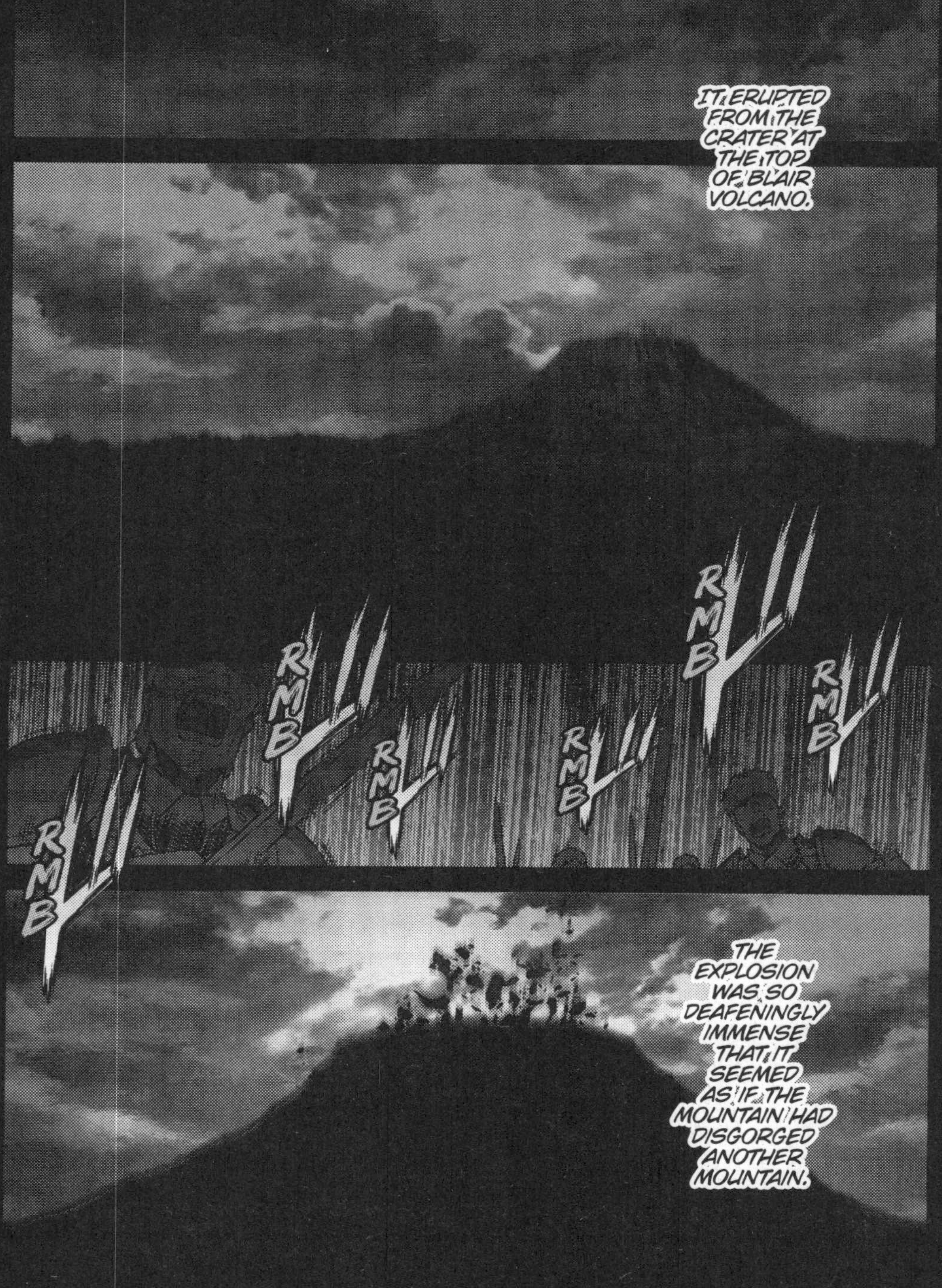
IT ERUPTED FROM THE CRATER AT THE TOP OF BLAIR VOLCANO.
RMB
RMB
RMB
RMB
RMB
RMB
THE EXPLOSION WAS SO DEAFENINGLY IMMENSE THAT IT SEEMED AS IF THE MOUNTAIN HAD DISGORGED ANOTHER MOUNTAIN.

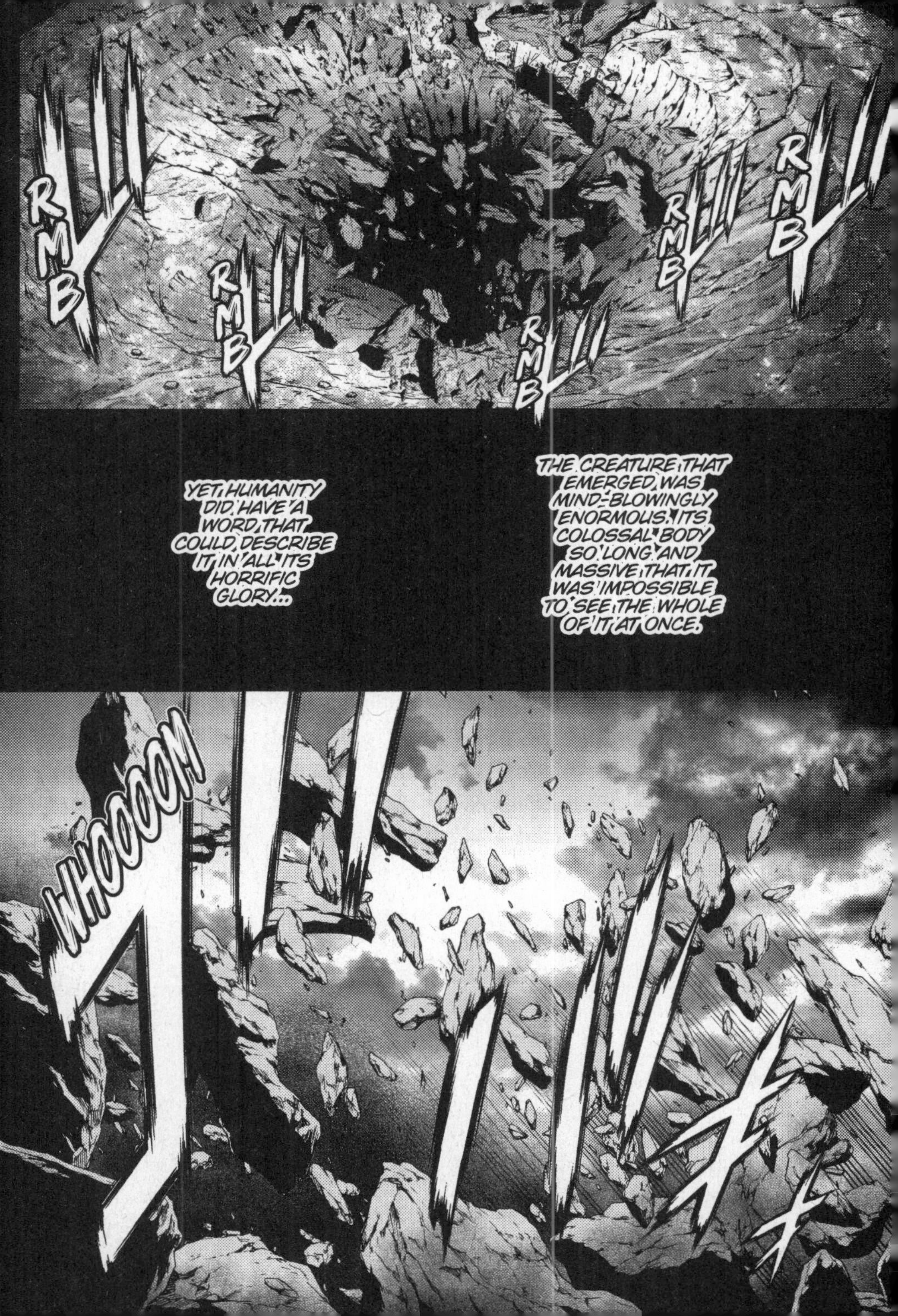
RMB
RMB
RMB
RMB
RMB
THE CREATURE THAT EMERGED WAS MIND-BLOWINGLY ENORMOUS. ITS COLOSSAL BODY SO LONG AND MASSIVE THAT IT WAS IMPOSSIBLE TO SEE THE WHOLE OF IT AT ONCE.
YET HUMANITY DID HAVE A WORD THAT COULD DESCRIBE IT IN ALL ITS HORRIFIC GLORY...
WHOOOOM

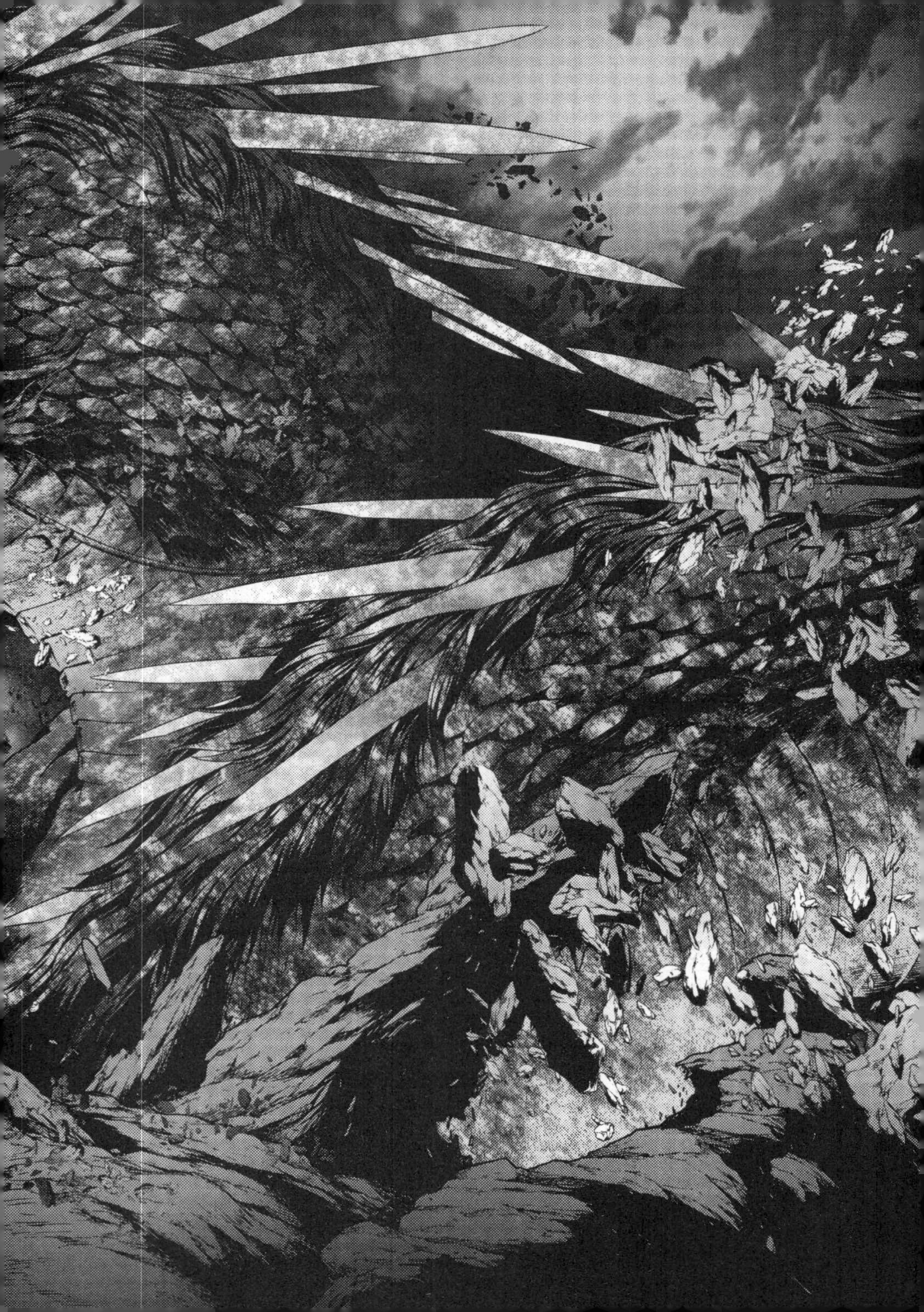

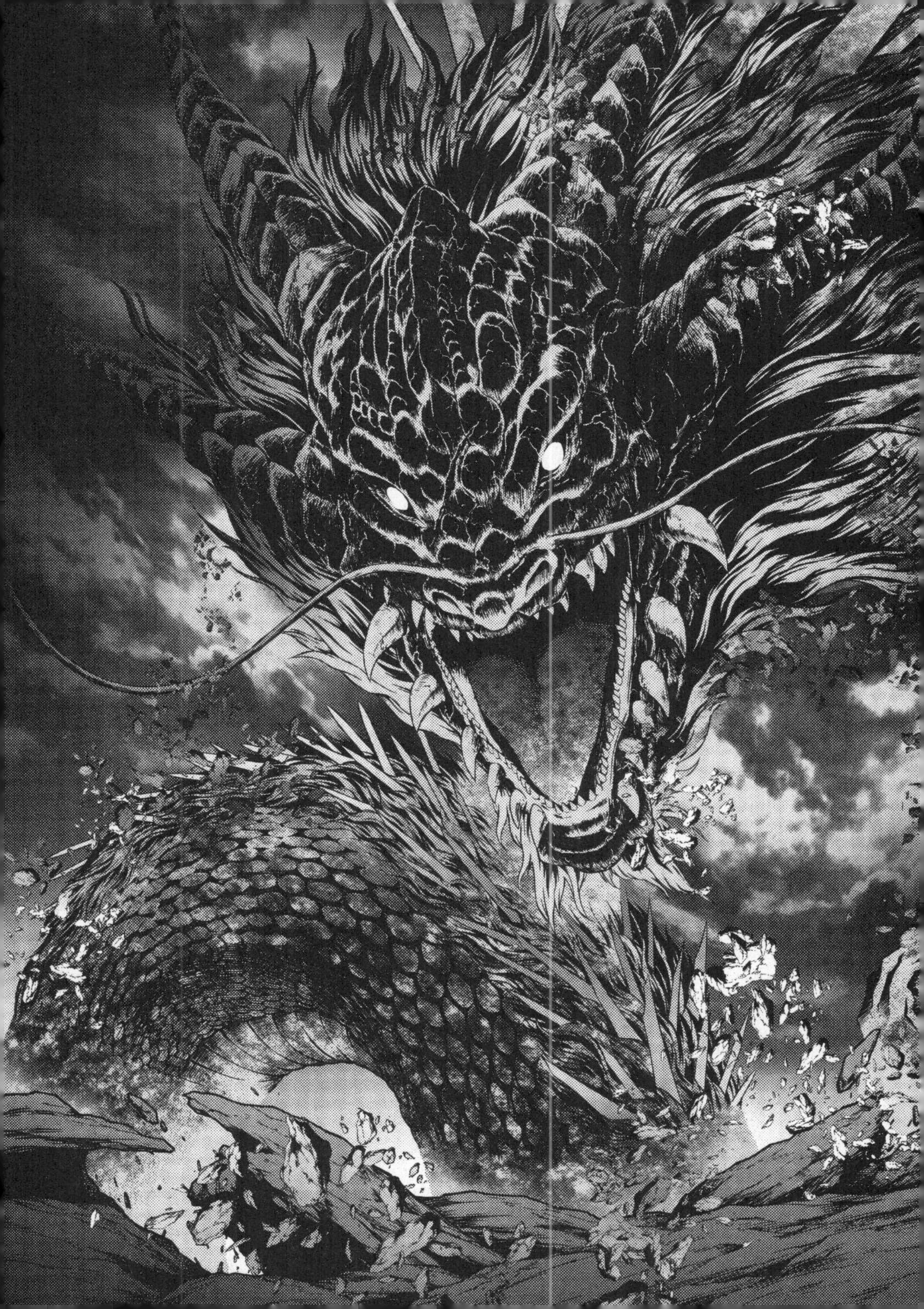

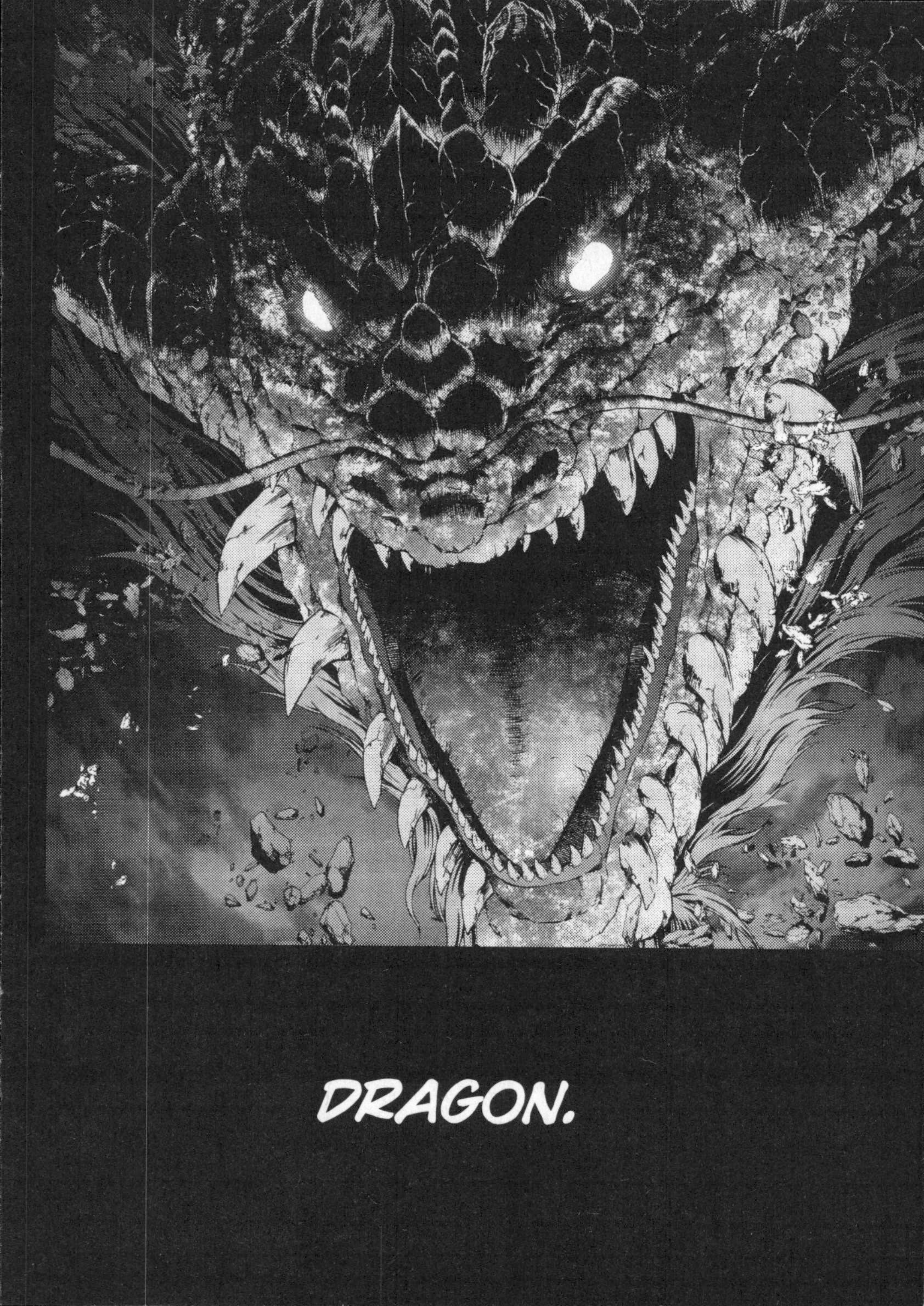
DRAGON.

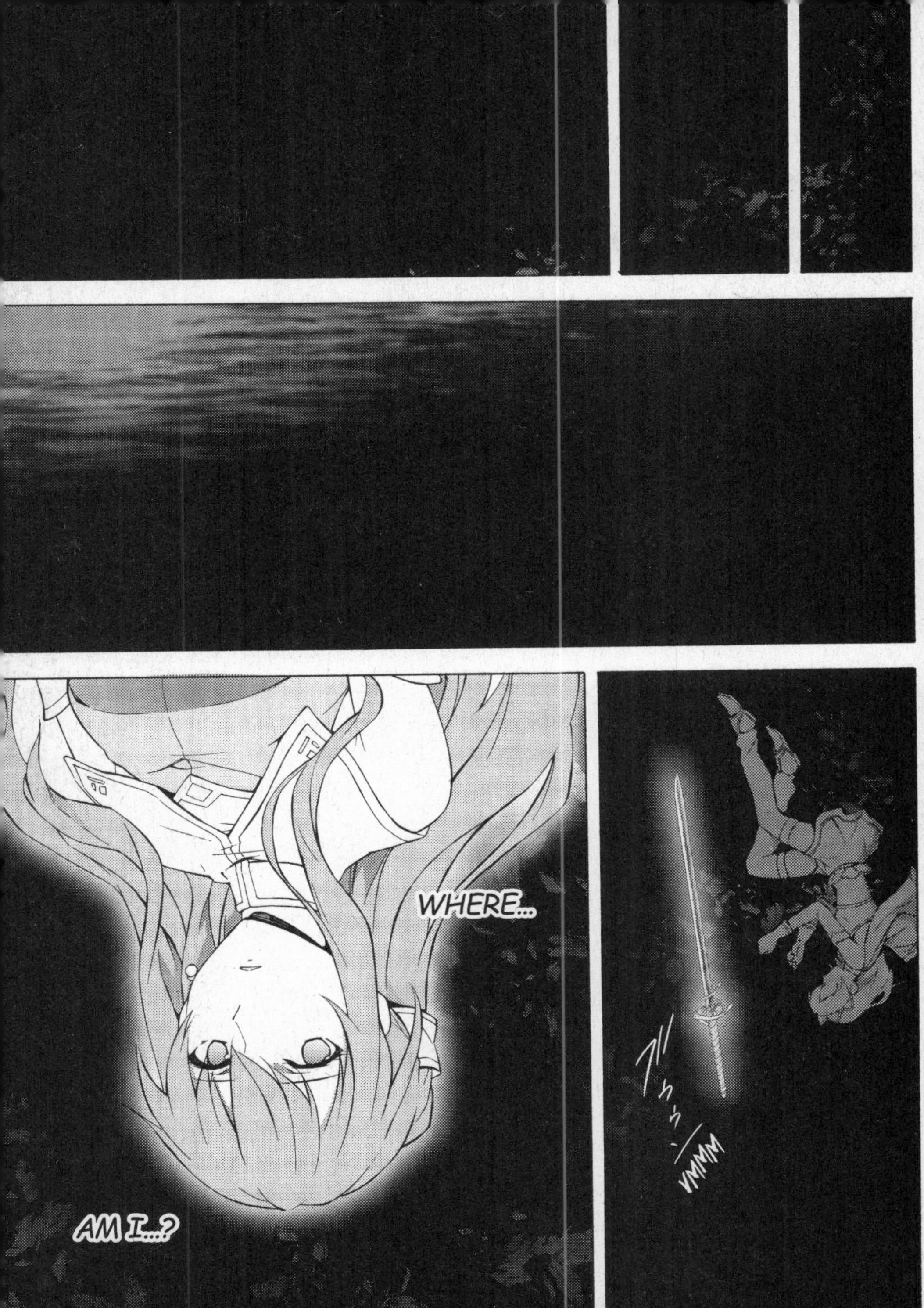
ブゥゥン
VMMM
WHERE...
AM I...?

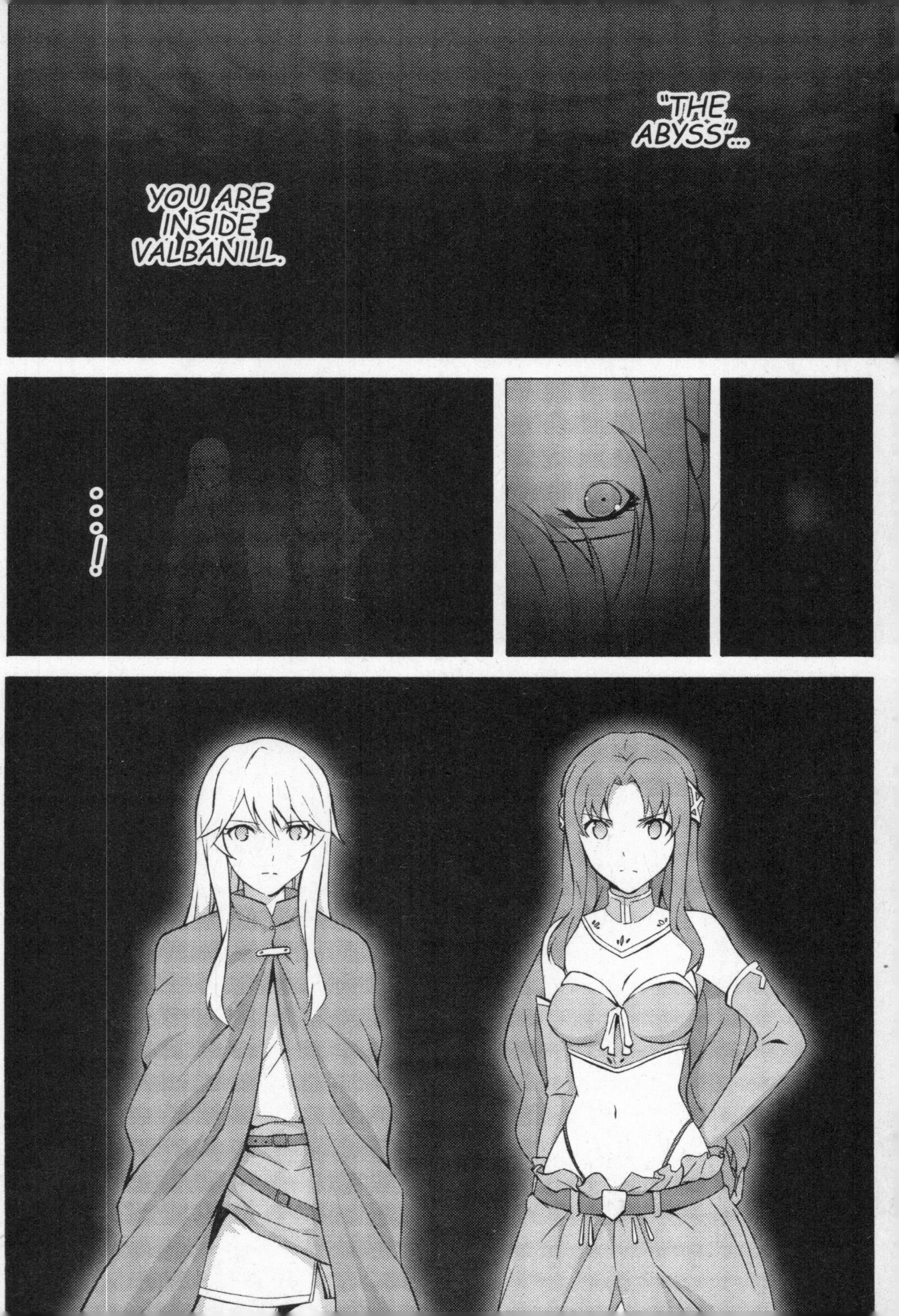
"THE ABYSS"...
YOU ARE INSIDE VALBANILL.
...!

The Sacred Blacksmith

聖剣の刀鍛治

The Sacred Blacksmith

聖剣の刀鍛冶

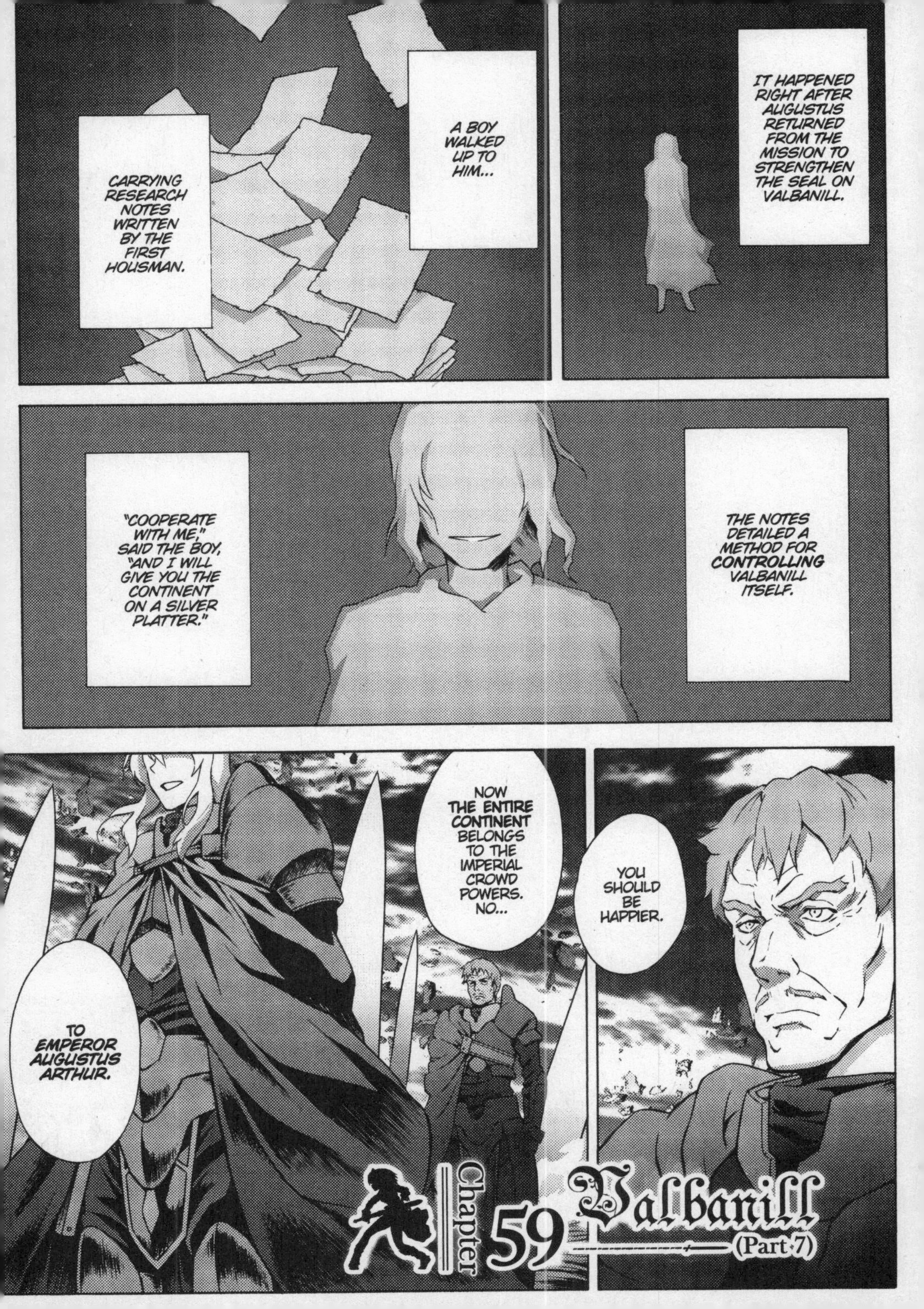
IT HAPPENED RIGHT AFTER AUGUSTUS RETURNED FROM THE MISSION TO STRENGTHEN THE SEAL ON VALBANILL.
A BOY WALKED UP TO HIM...
CARRYING RESEARCH NOTES WRITTEN BY THE FIRST HOUSMAN.
THE NOTES DETAILED A METHOD FOR **CONTROLLING** VALBANILL ITSELF.
"COOPERATE WITH ME," SAID THE BOY, "AND I WILL GIVE YOU THE CONTINENT ON A SILVER PLATTER."
YOU SHOULD BE HAPPIER.
NOW THE ENTIRE CONTINENT BELONGS TO THE IMPERIAL CROWD POWERS. NO...
TO EMPEROR AUGUSTUS ARTHUR.
Chapter 59 Valbanill (Part 7)

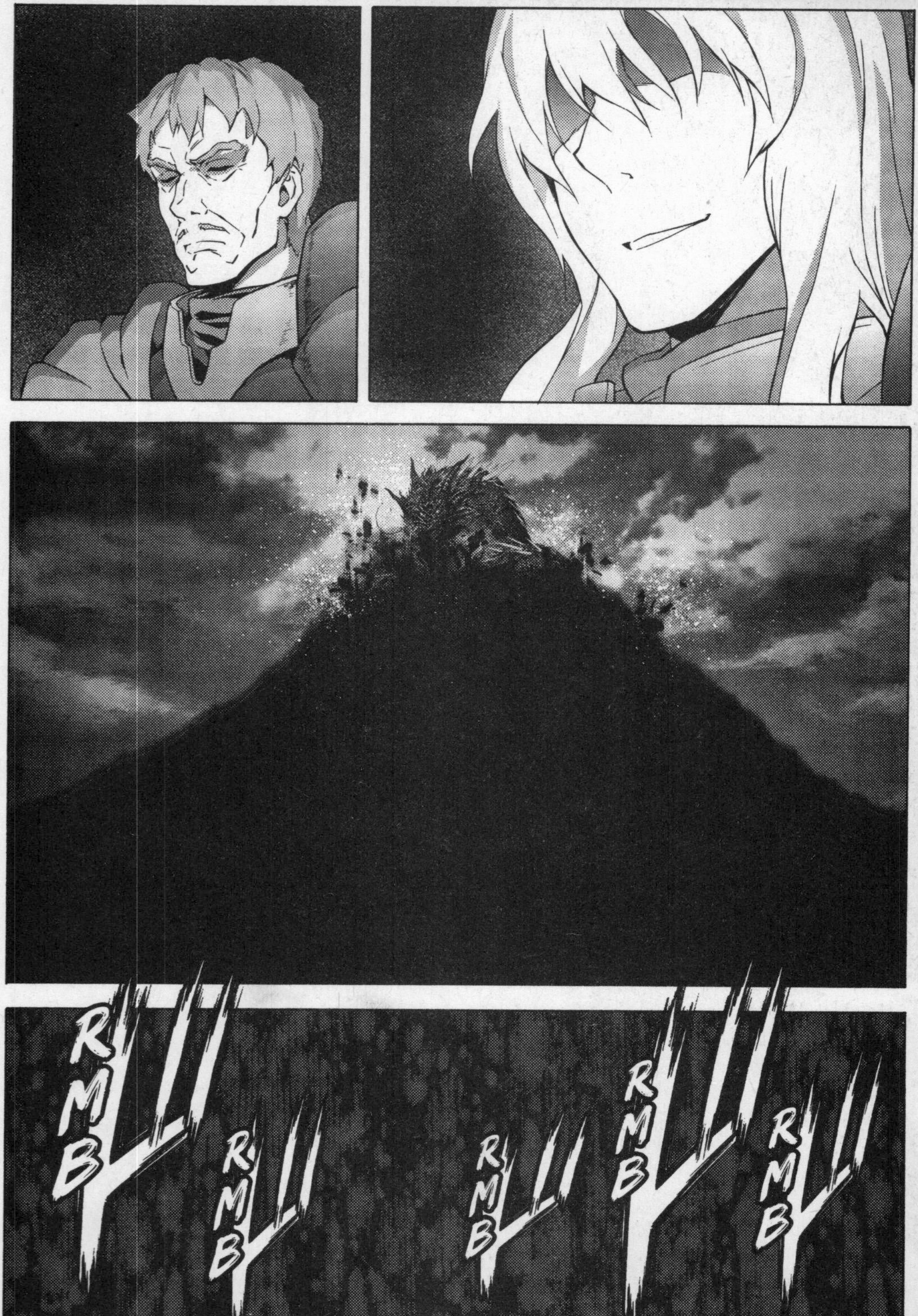
RMB
RMB
RMB
RMB
RMB

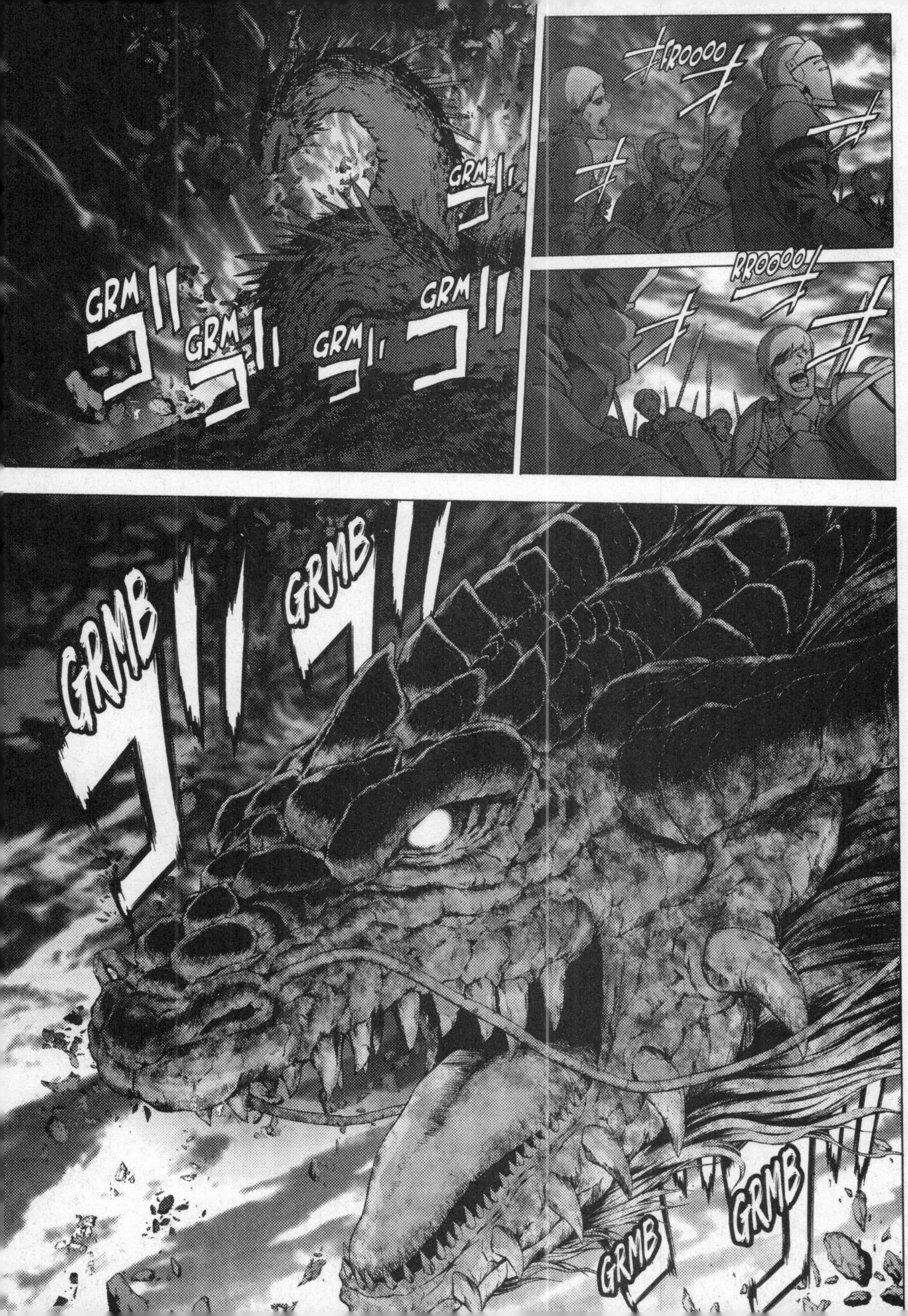
RROOOO
RROOOO
GRM
GRM
GRM
GRM
GRM
GRMB
GRMB
GRMB
GRMB

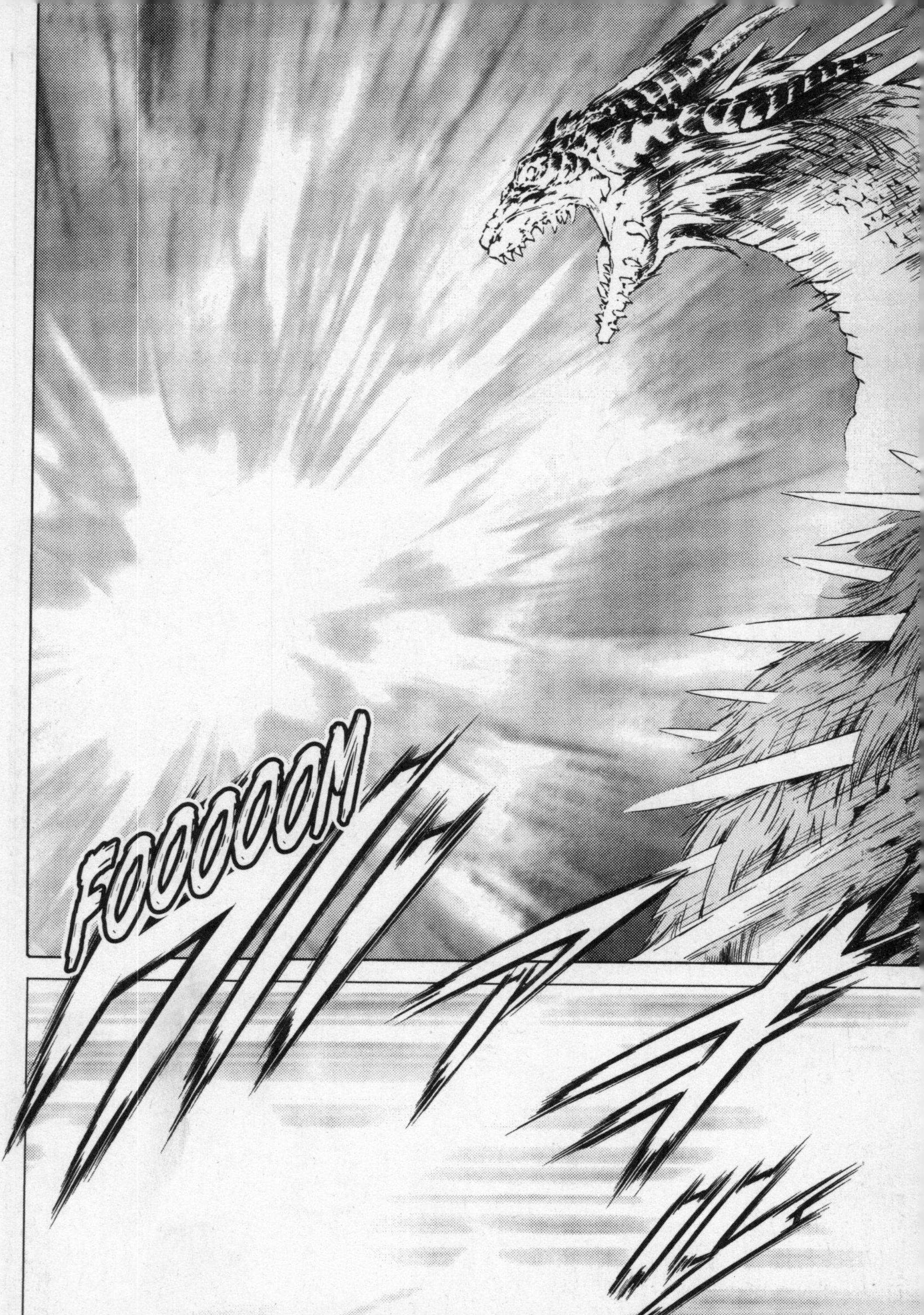
FOOOOOM

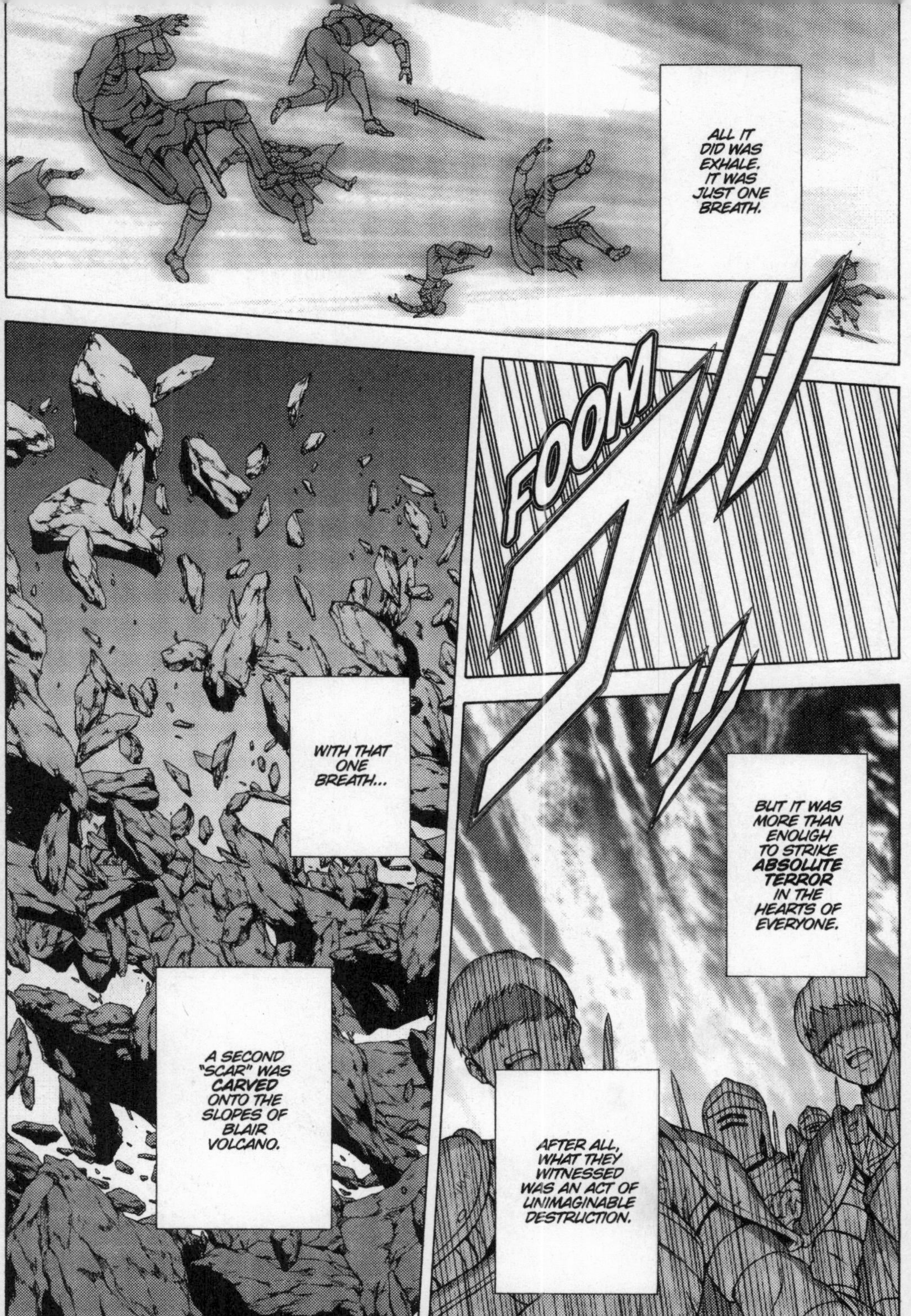
ALL IT DID WAS EXHALE. IT WAS JUST ONE BREATH.
FOOM
BUT IT WAS MORE THAN ENOUGH TO STRIKE **ABSOLUTE TERROR** IN THE HEARTS OF EVERYONE.
AFTER ALL, WHAT THEY WITNESSED WAS AN ACT OF UNIMAGINABLE DESTRUCTION.
WITH THAT ONE BREATH...
A SECOND "SCAR" WAS **CARVED** ONTO THE SLOPES OF BLAIR VOLCANO.

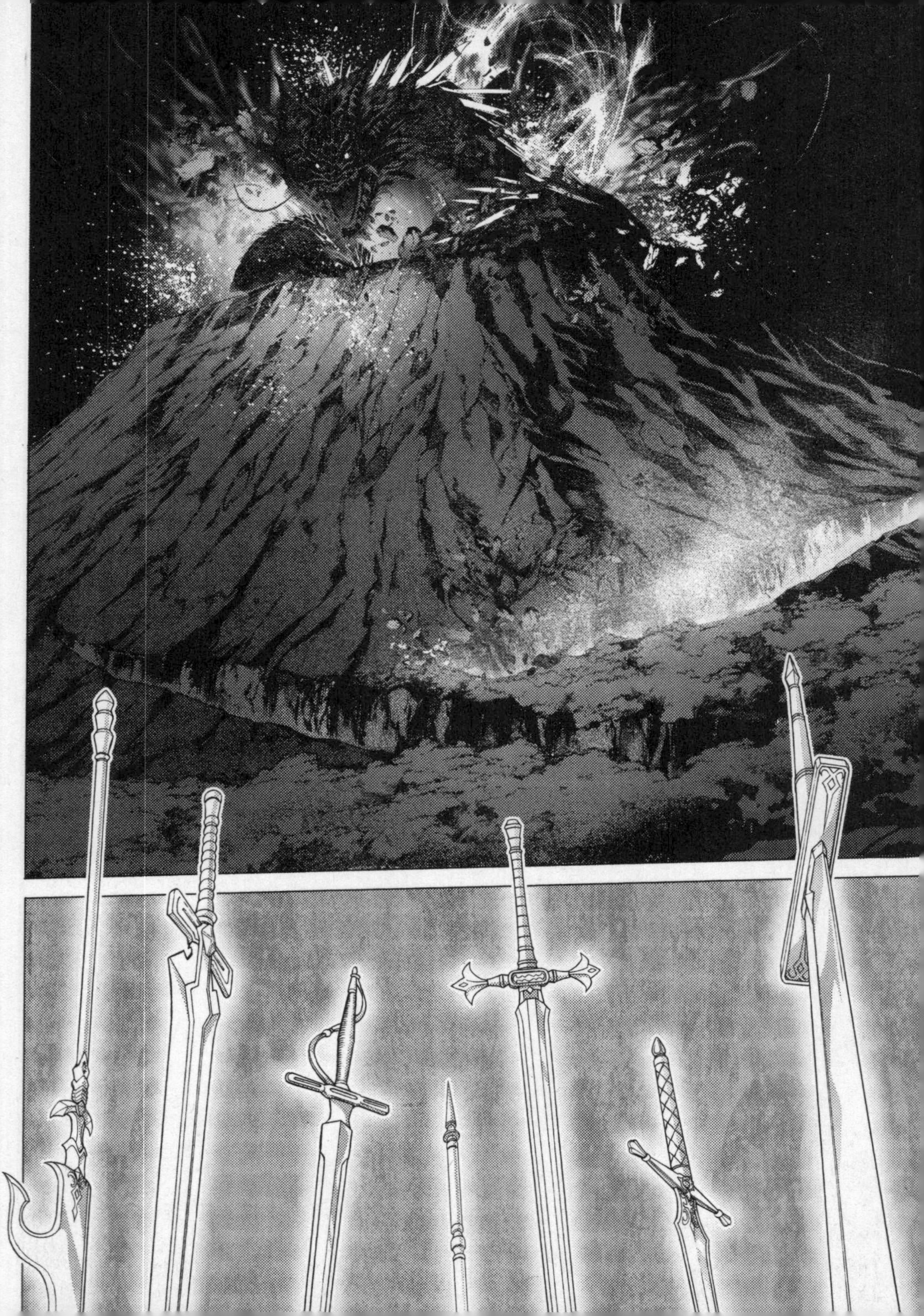

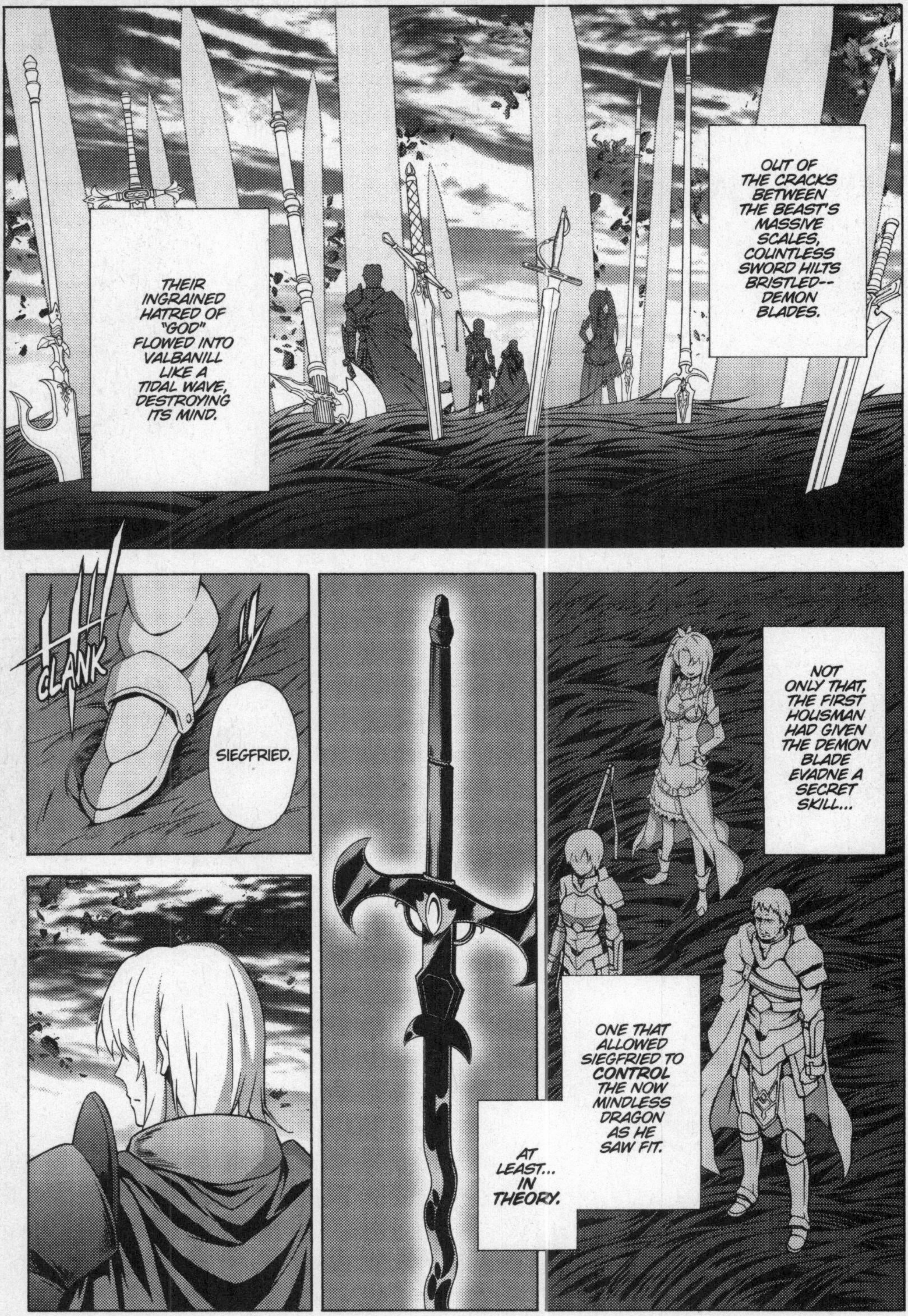
OUT OF THE CRACKS BETWEEN THE BEAST'S MASSIVE SCALES, COUNTLESS SWORD HILTS BRISTLED-- DEMON BLADES.
THEIR INGRAINED HATRED OF "GOD" FLOWED INTO VALBANILL LIKE A TIDAL WAVE, DESTROYING ITS MIND.
NOT ONLY THAT, THE FIRST HOUSMAN HAD GIVEN THE DEMON BLADE EVADNE A SECRET SKILL...
ONE THAT ALLOWED SIEGFRIED TO CONTROL THE NOW MINDLESS DRAGON AS HE SAW FIT.
AT LEAST... IN THEORY.
CLANK
SIEGFRIED.

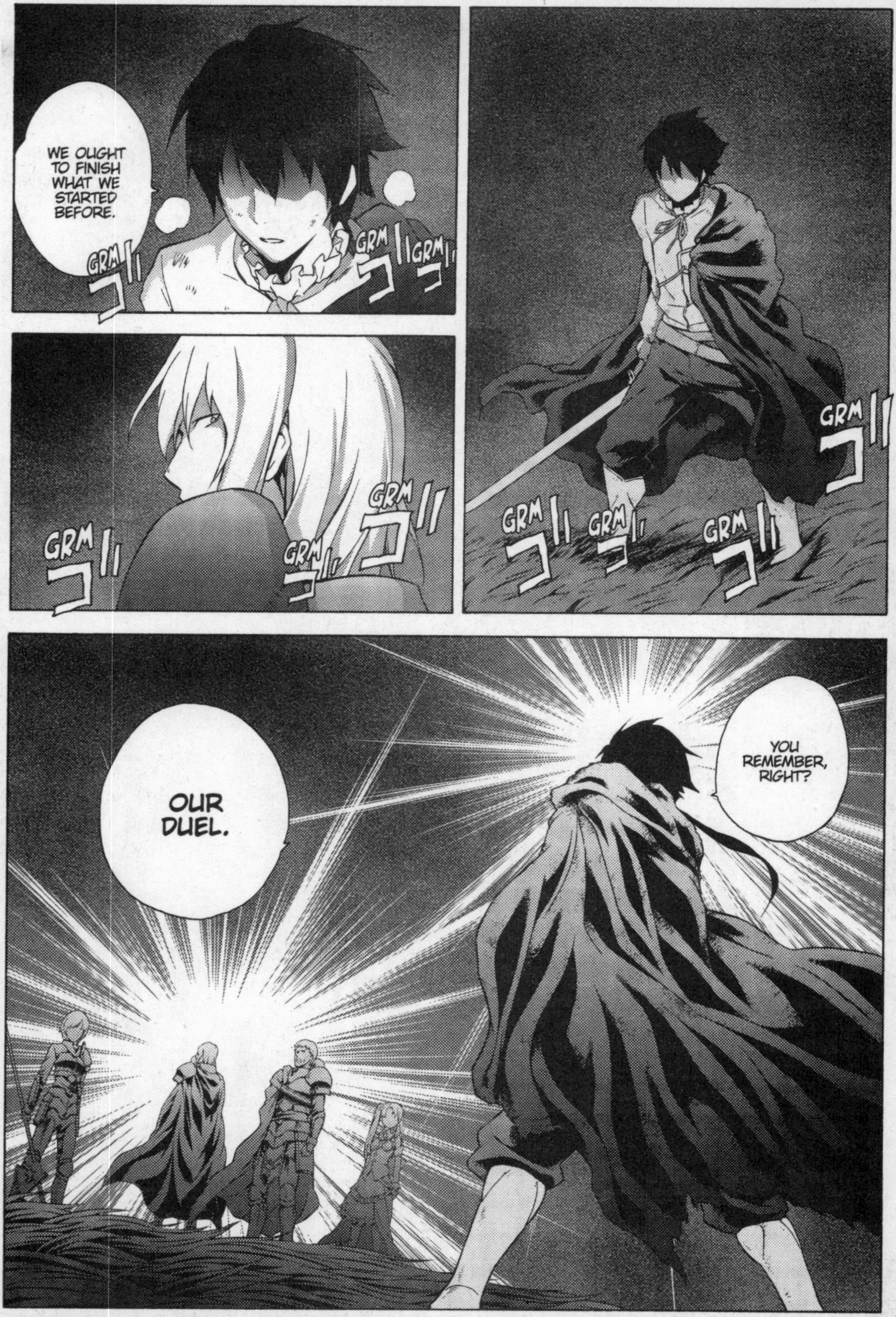
GRM
GRM
GRM
GRM
WE OUGHT TO FINISH WHAT WE STARTED BEFORE.
GRM
GRM
GRM
GRM
GRM
GRM
YOU REMEMBER, RIGHT?
OUR DUEL.

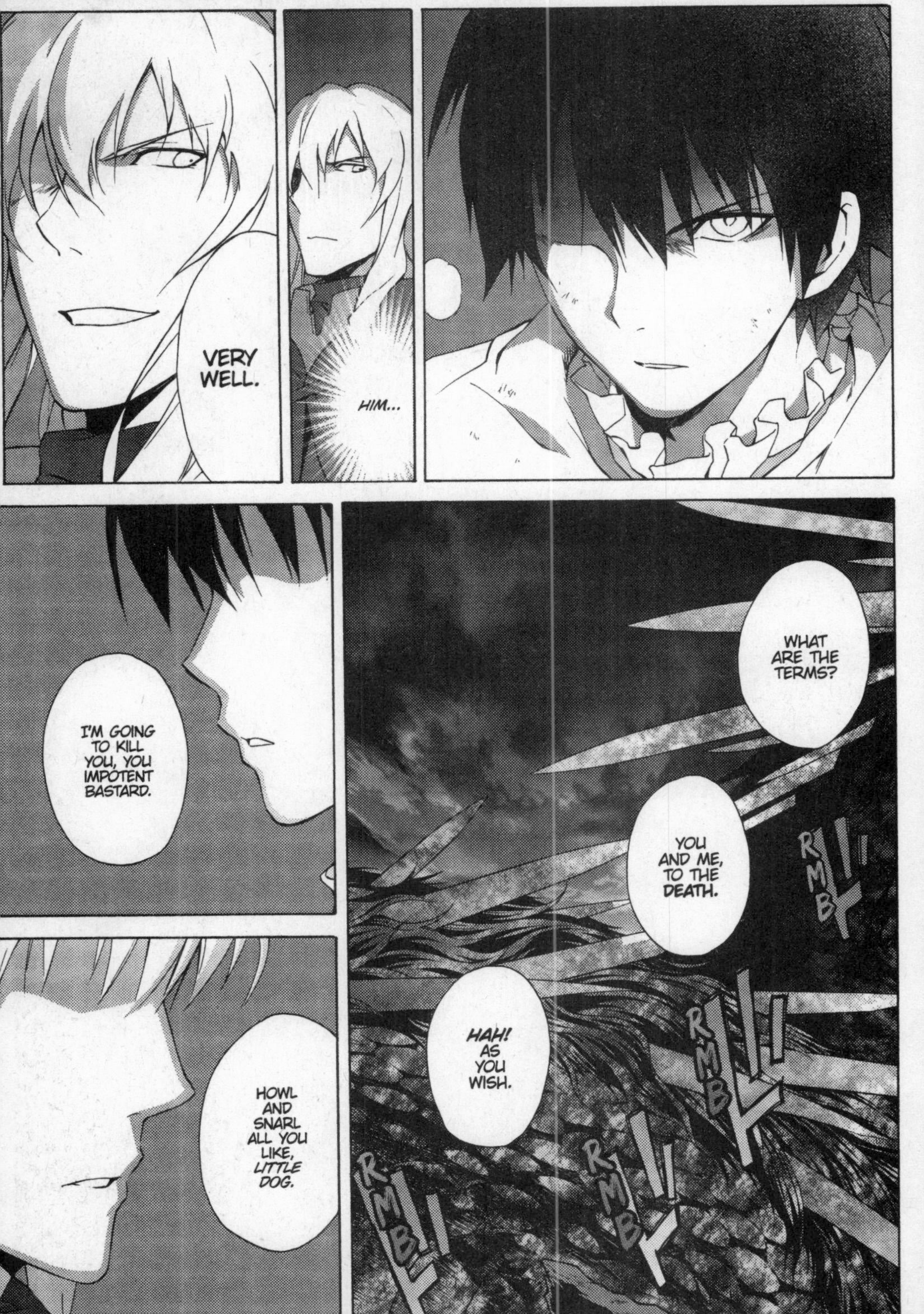
HIM...
VERY WELL.
WHAT ARE THE TERMS?
YOU AND ME, TO THE DEATH.
RMB
HAH! AS YOU WISH.
RMB
RMB
RMB
I'M GOING TO KILL YOU, YOU IMPOTENT BASTARD.
HOWL AND SNARL ALL YOU LIKE, LITTLE DOG.

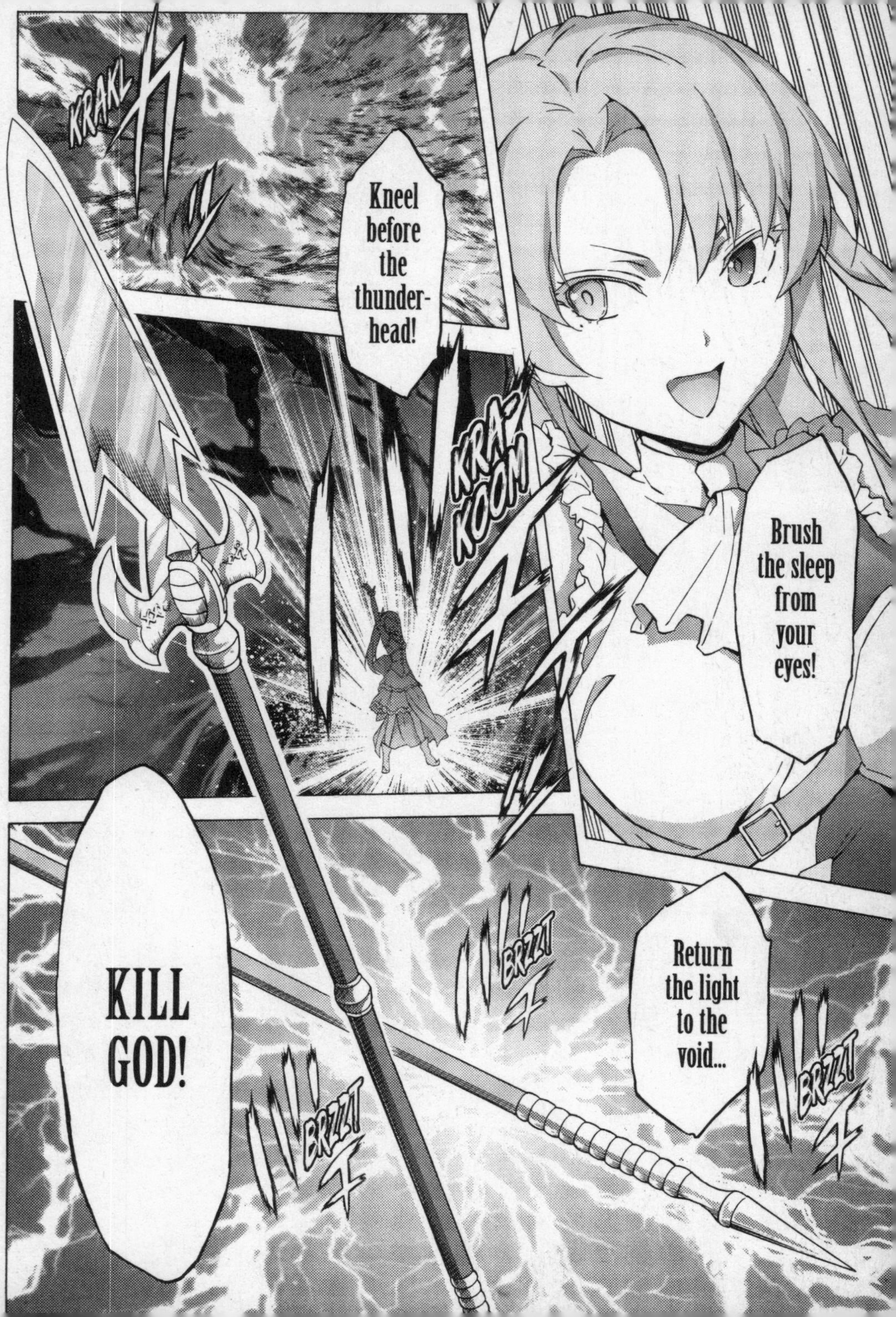
Kneel before the thunderhead!
Brush the sleep from your eyes!
KRAKL
KRA-KOOM
Return the light to the void...
BRZZT
BRZZT
KILL GOD!
BRZZT

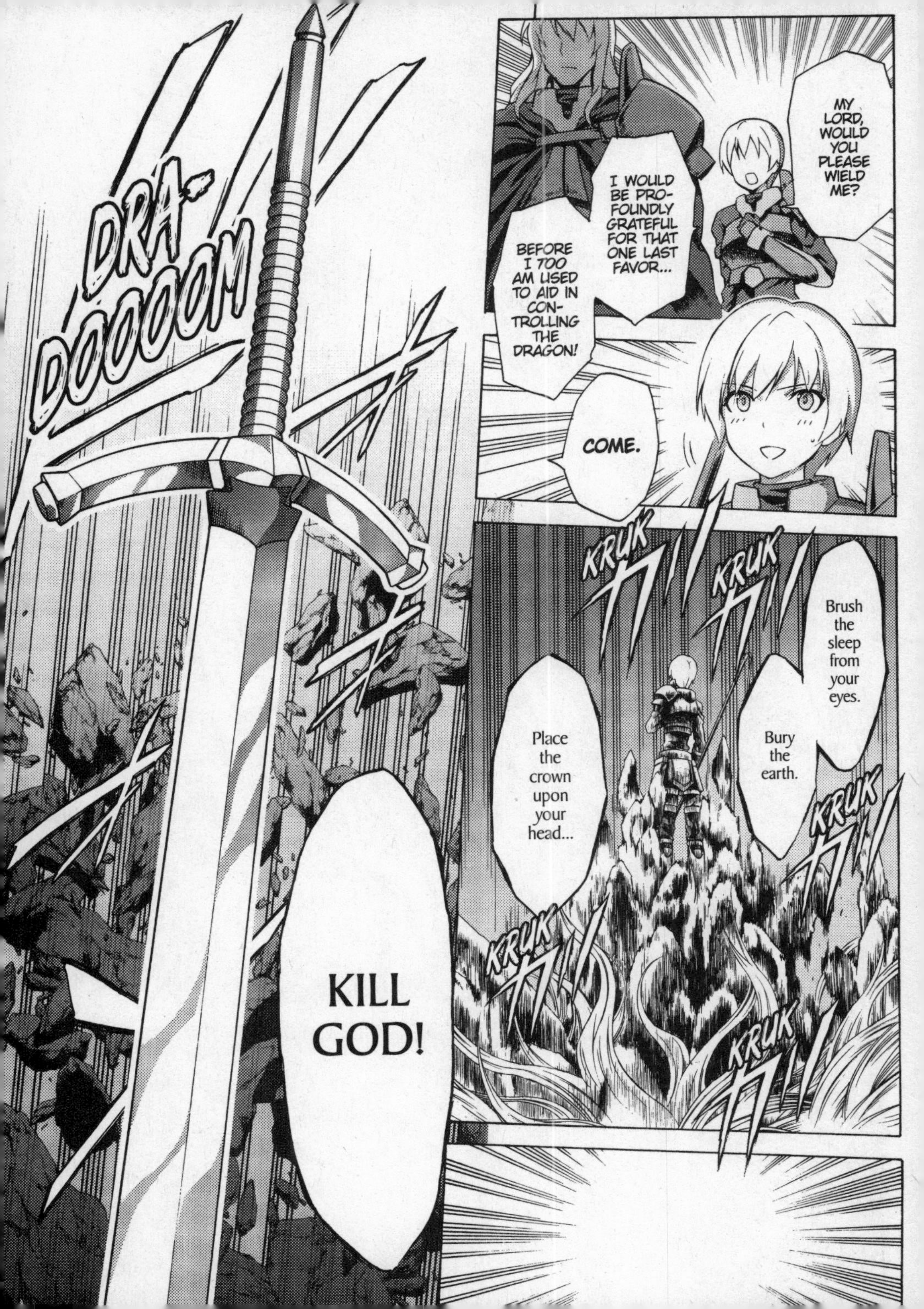
MY LORD, WOULD YOU PLEASE WIELD ME?
I WOULD BE PRO-FOUNDLY GRATEFUL FOR THAT ONE LAST FAVOR...
BEFORE I TOO AM USED TO AID IN CON-TROLLING THE DRAGON!
COME.
KRUK
KRUK
Brush the sleep from your eyes.
Bury the earth.
Place the crown upon your head...
KRUK
KRUK
KRUK
DRA-DOOOOM
KILL GOD!

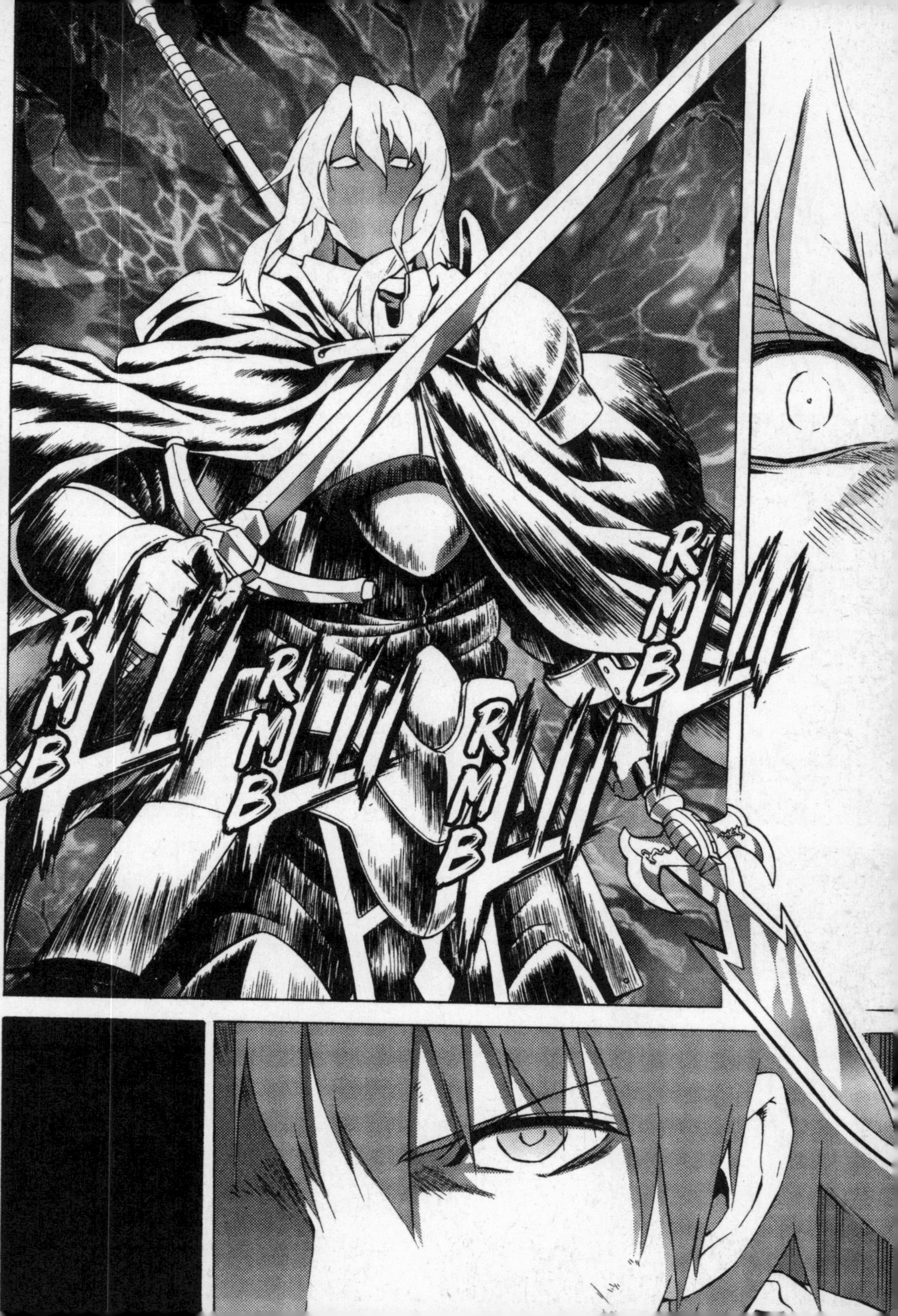
RMB
RMB
RMB
RMB

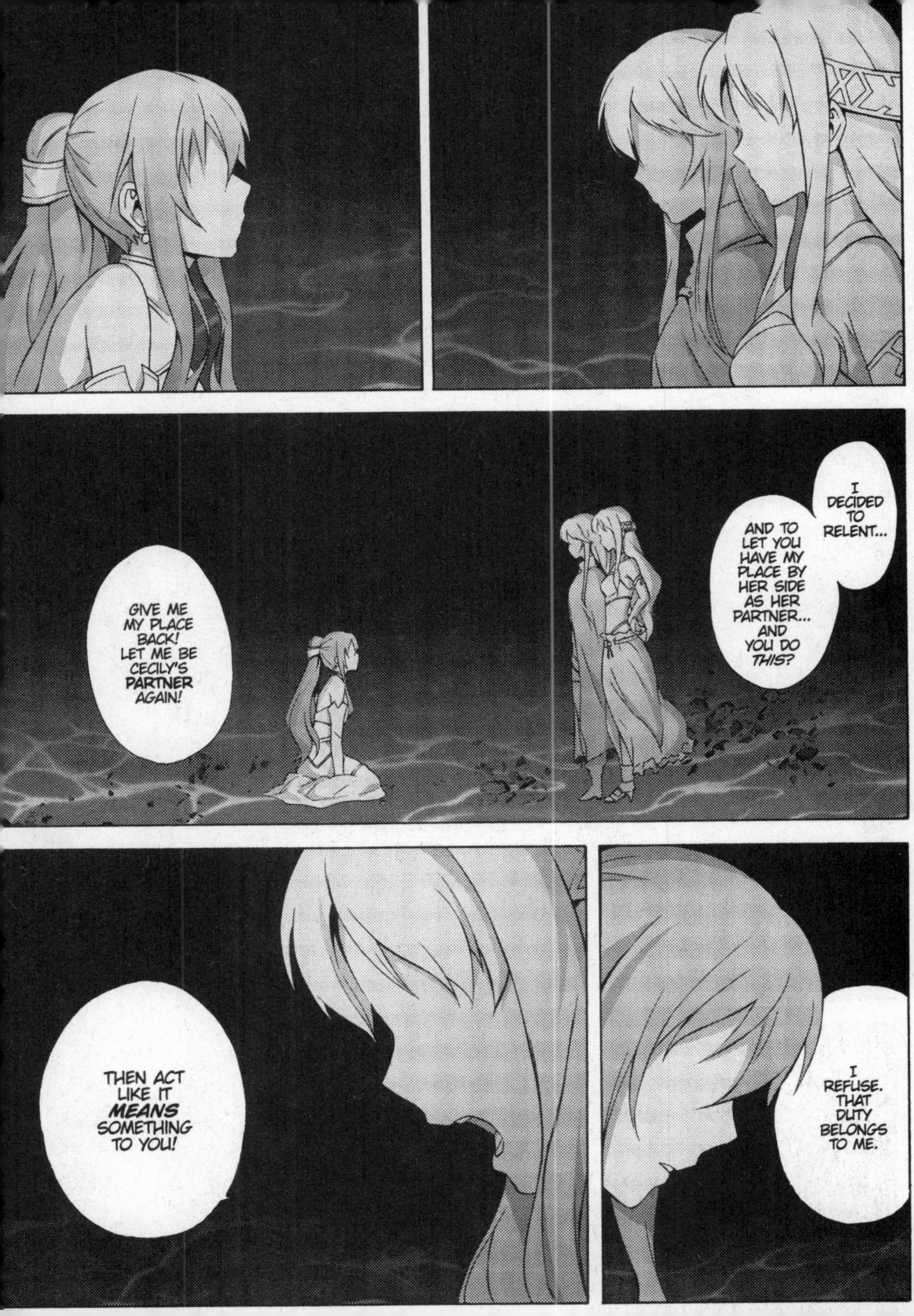
I DECIDED TO RELENT...
AND TO LET YOU HAVE MY PLACE BY HER SIDE AS HER PARTNER... AND YOU DO *THIS?*
GIVE ME MY PLACE BACK! LET ME BE CECILY'S **PARTNER** AGAIN!
I REFUSE. THAT DUTY BELONGS TO ME.
THEN ACT LIKE IT ***MEANS*** SOMETHING TO YOU!

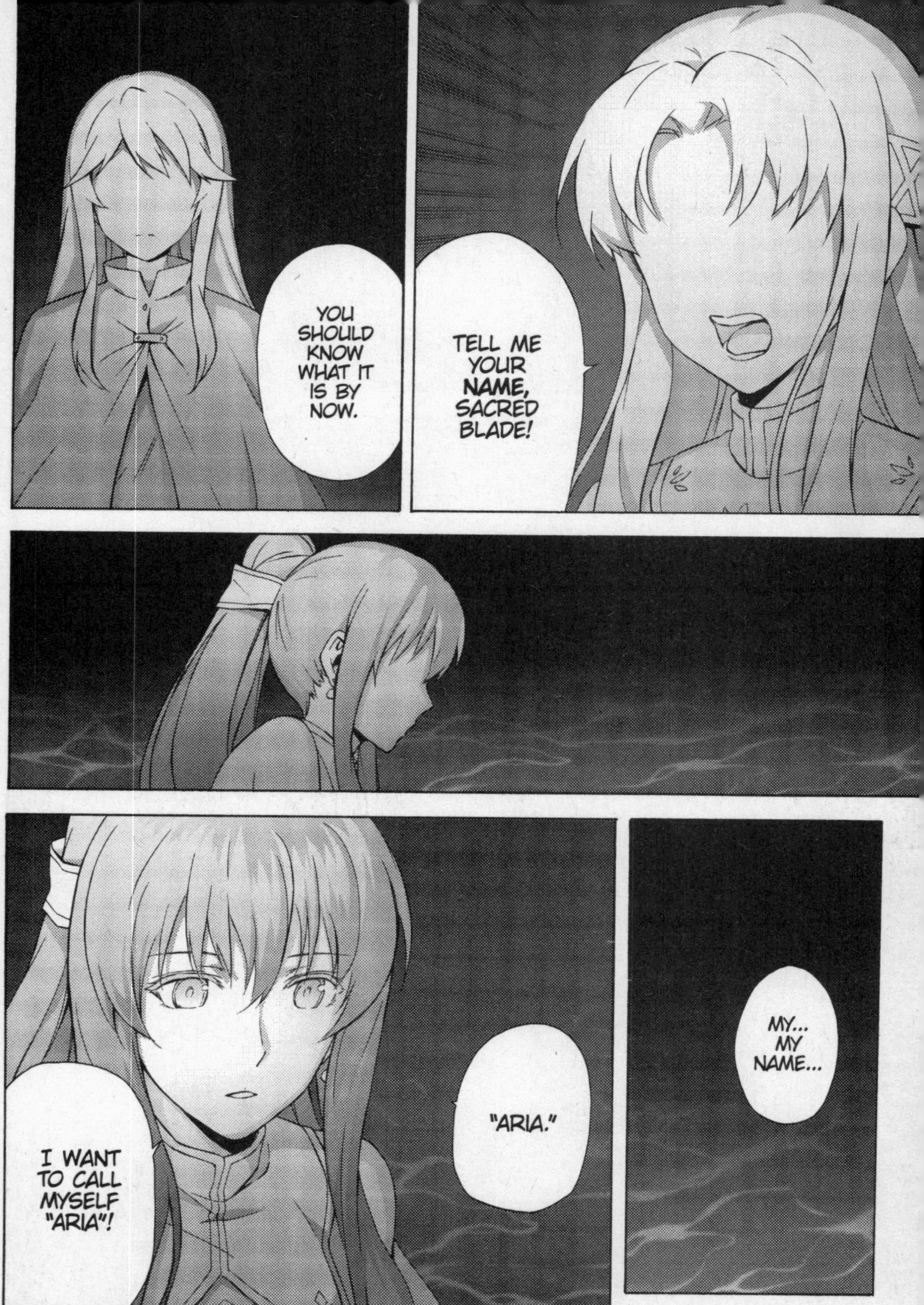
TELL ME YOUR NAME, SACRED BLADE!
YOU SHOULD KNOW WHAT IT IS BY NOW.
MY... MY NAME...
"ARIA."
I WANT TO CALL MYSELF "ARIA"!

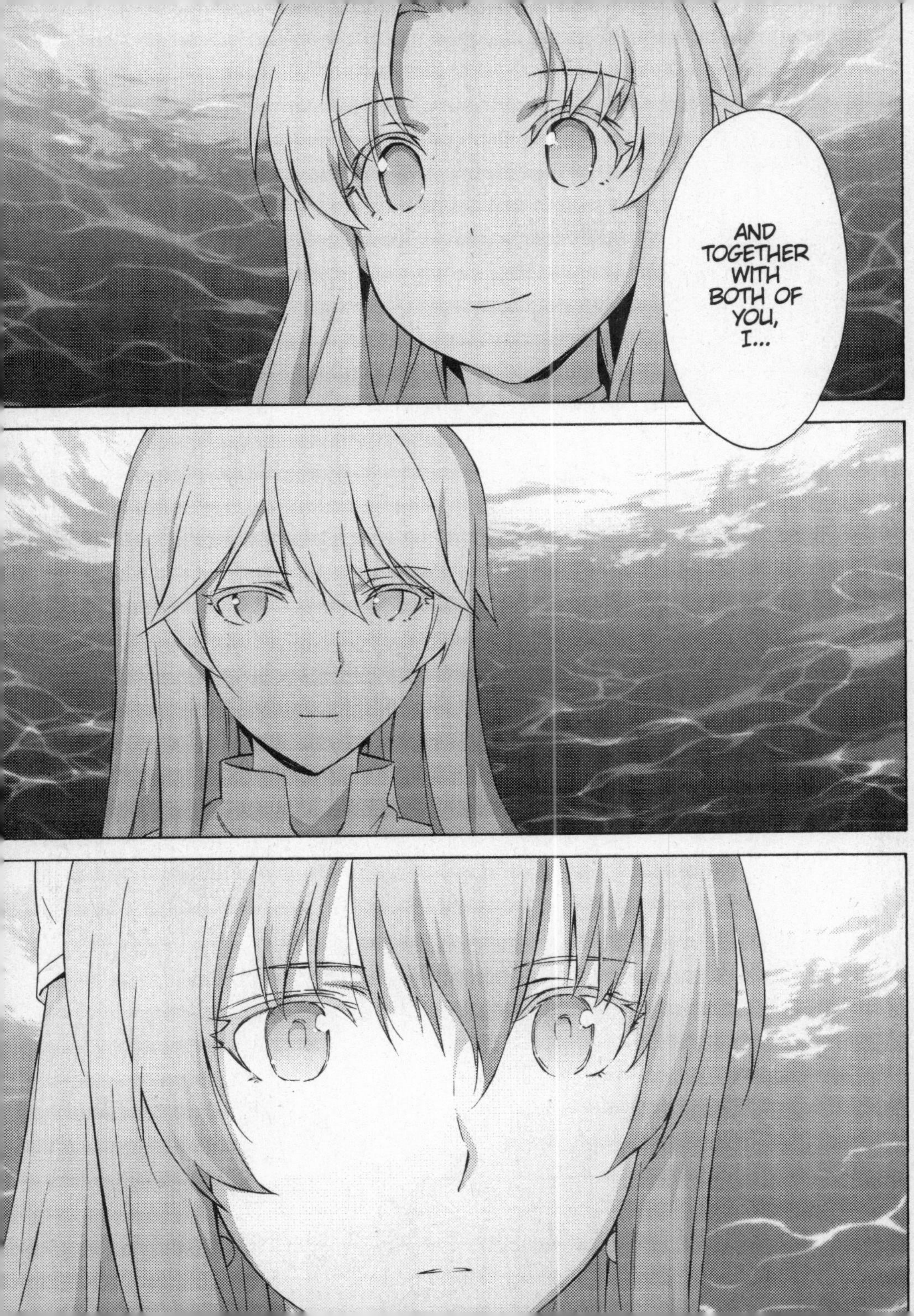
AND TOGETHER WITH BOTH OF YOU, I...

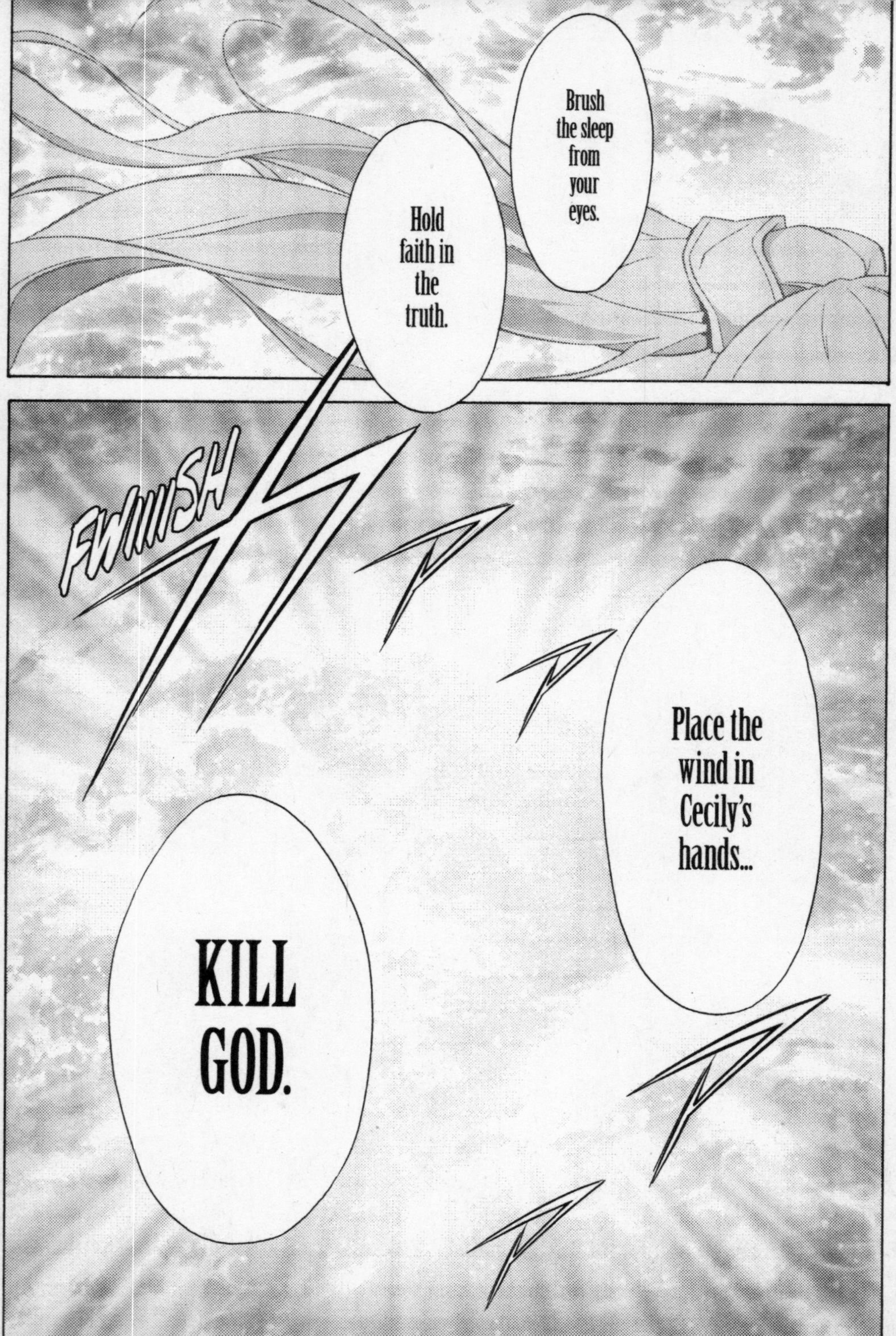
Brush the sleep from your eyes.
Hold faith in the truth.
FWIIISH
Place the wind in Cecily's hands...
KILL GOD.

The Sacred Blacksmith

聖剣の刀鍛治

The Sacred Blacksmith

聖剣の刀鍛治

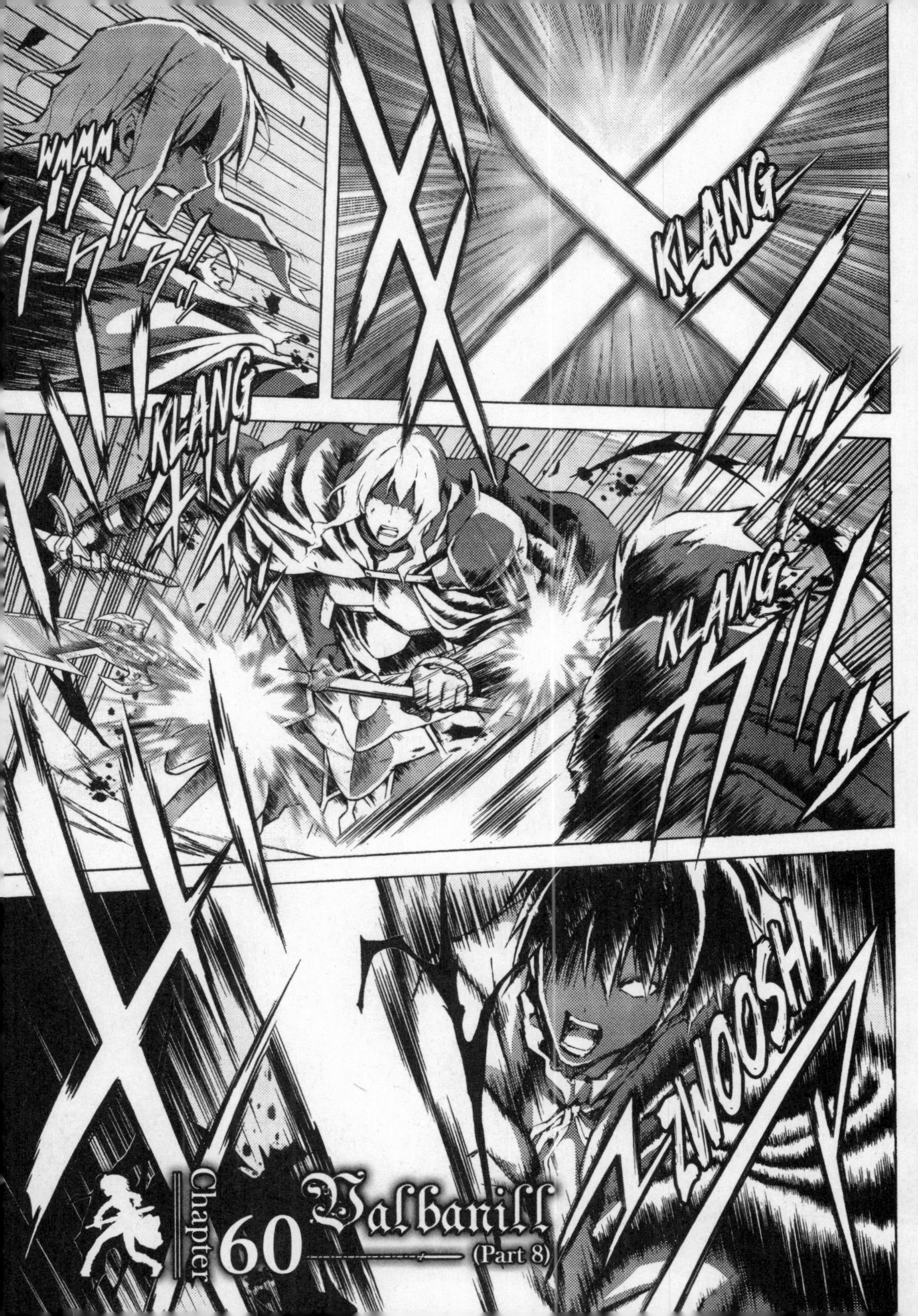
KLANG
WMMM
KLANG
KLANG
WOOSH
Chapter 60 Valbanill (Part 8)

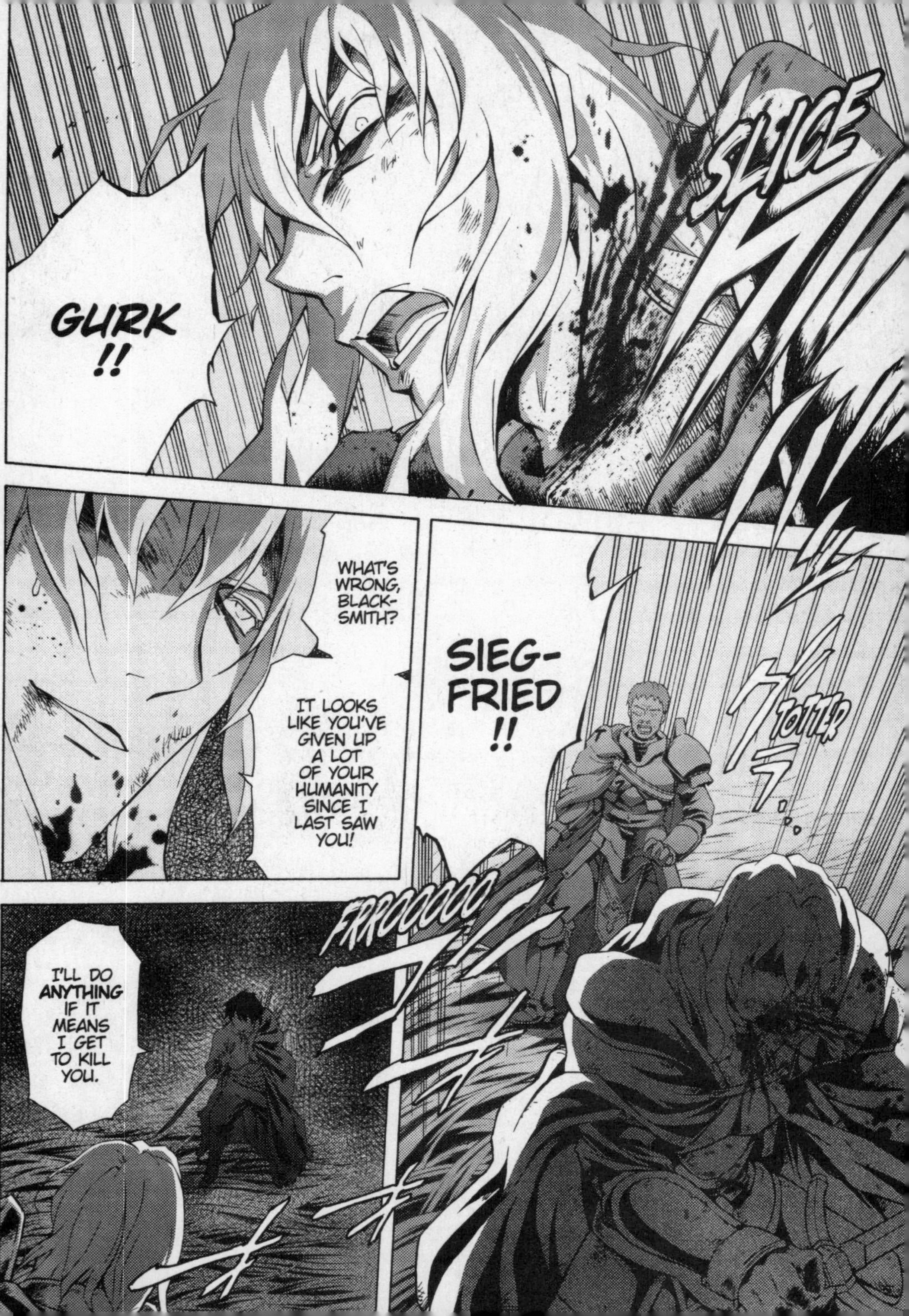
SLICE
GURK!!
SIEG-FRIED!!
TOTTER
WHAT'S WRONG, BLACK-SMITH?
IT LOOKS LIKE YOU'VE GIVEN UP A LOT OF YOUR HUMANITY SINCE I LAST SAW YOU!
FRROOOOOO
I'LL DO ANYTHING IF IT MEANS I GET TO KILL YOU.

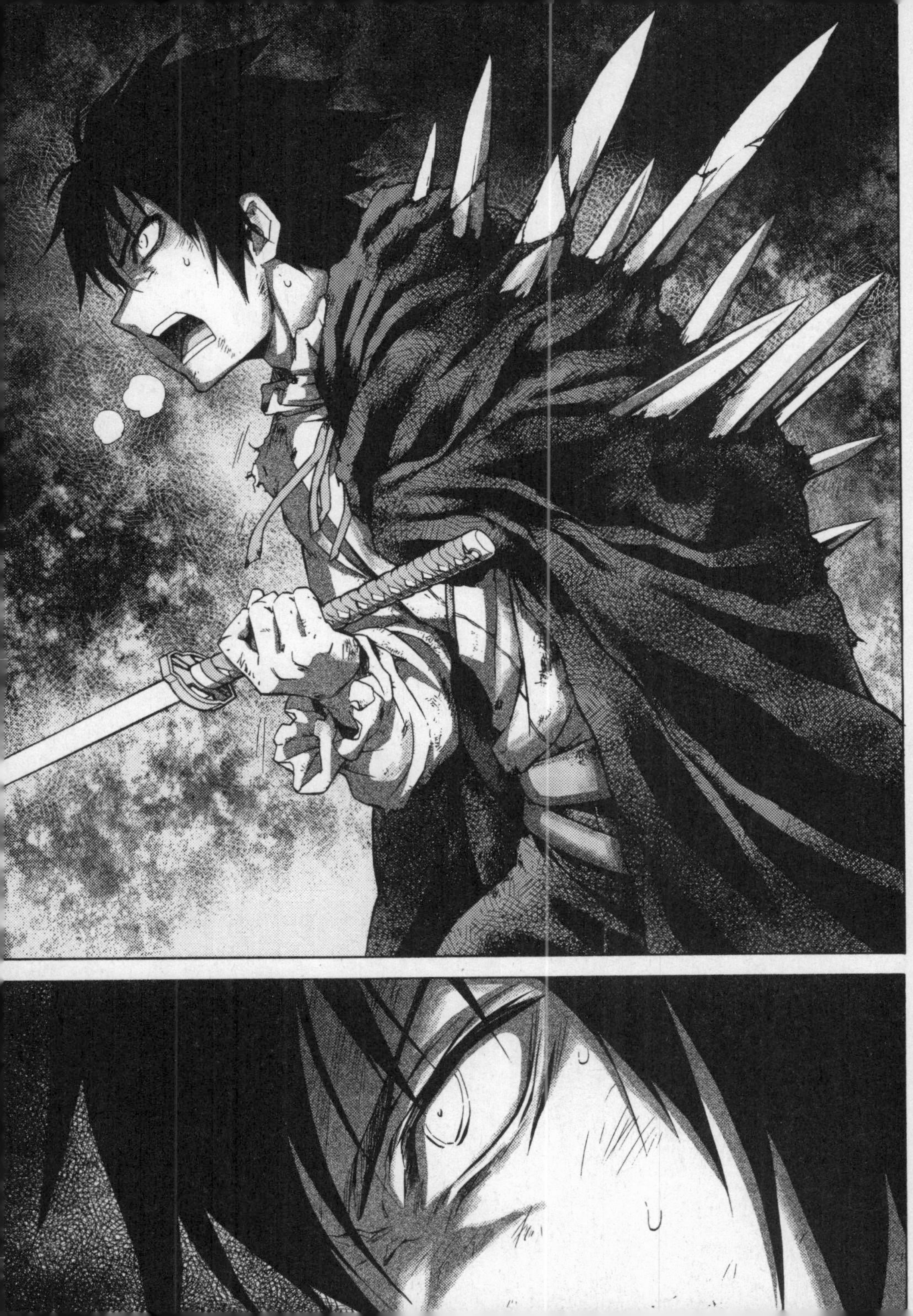

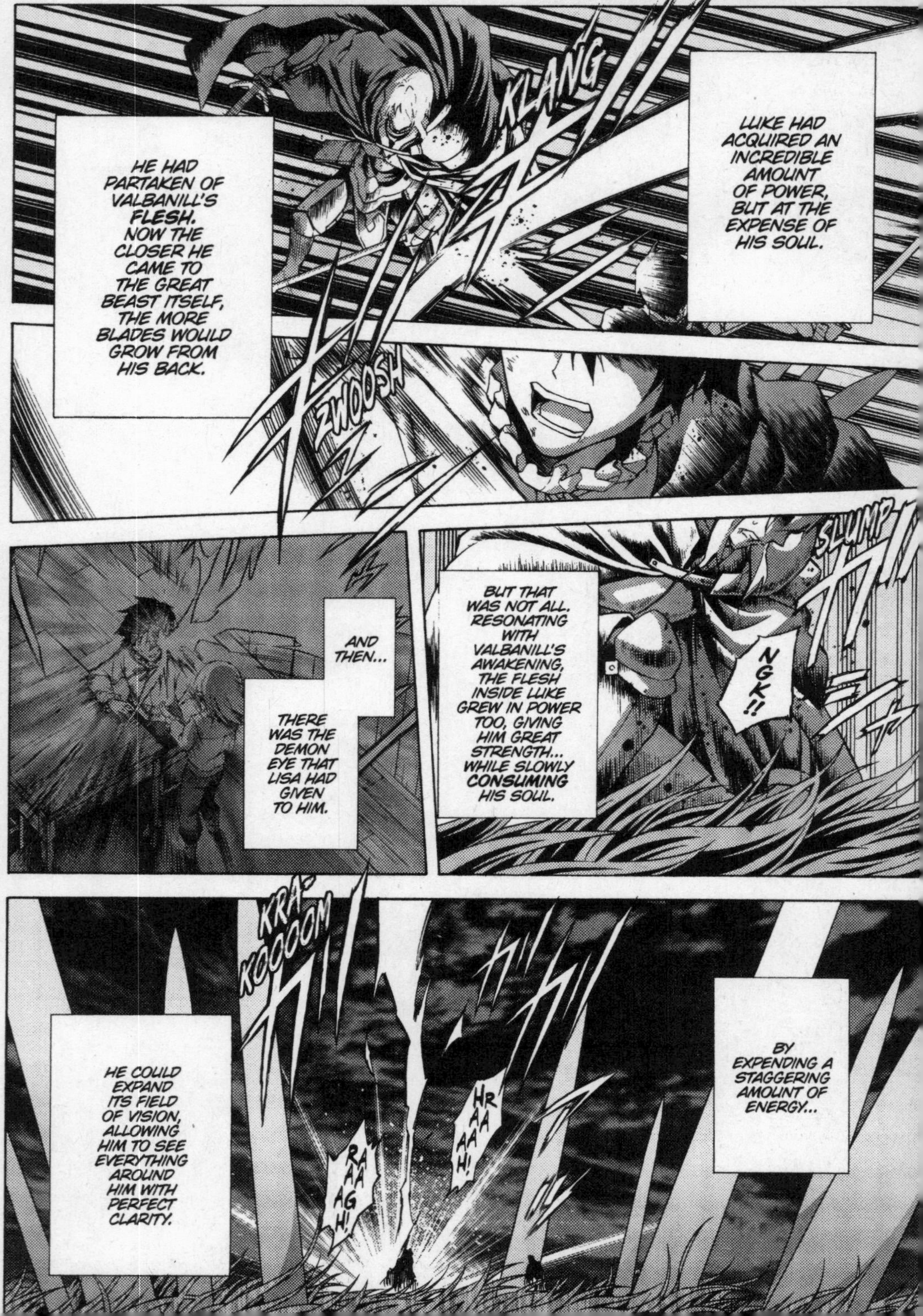
LUKE HAD ACQUIRED AN INCREDIBLE AMOUNT OF POWER, BUT AT THE EXPENSE OF HIS SOUL.
KLANG
HE HAD PARTAKEN OF VALBANILL'S FLESH. NOW THE CLOSER HE CAME TO THE GREAT BEAST ITSELF, THE MORE BLADES WOULD GROW FROM HIS BACK.
ZWOOSH
SLUMP
BUT THAT WAS NOT ALL. RESONATING WITH VALBANILL'S AWAKENING, THE FLESH INSIDE LUKE GREW IN POWER TOO, GIVING HIM GREAT STRENGTH... WHILE SLOWLY CONSUMING HIS SOUL.
NGK!!
AND THEN...
THERE WAS THE DEMON EYE THAT LISA HAD GIVEN TO HIM.
BY EXPENDING A STAGGERING AMOUNT OF ENERGY...
KRA-KOOOOM
HRAAAAH!
RAAAAGH!
HE COULD EXPAND ITS FIELD OF VISION, ALLOWING HIM TO SEE EVERYTHING AROUND HIM WITH PERFECT CLARITY.

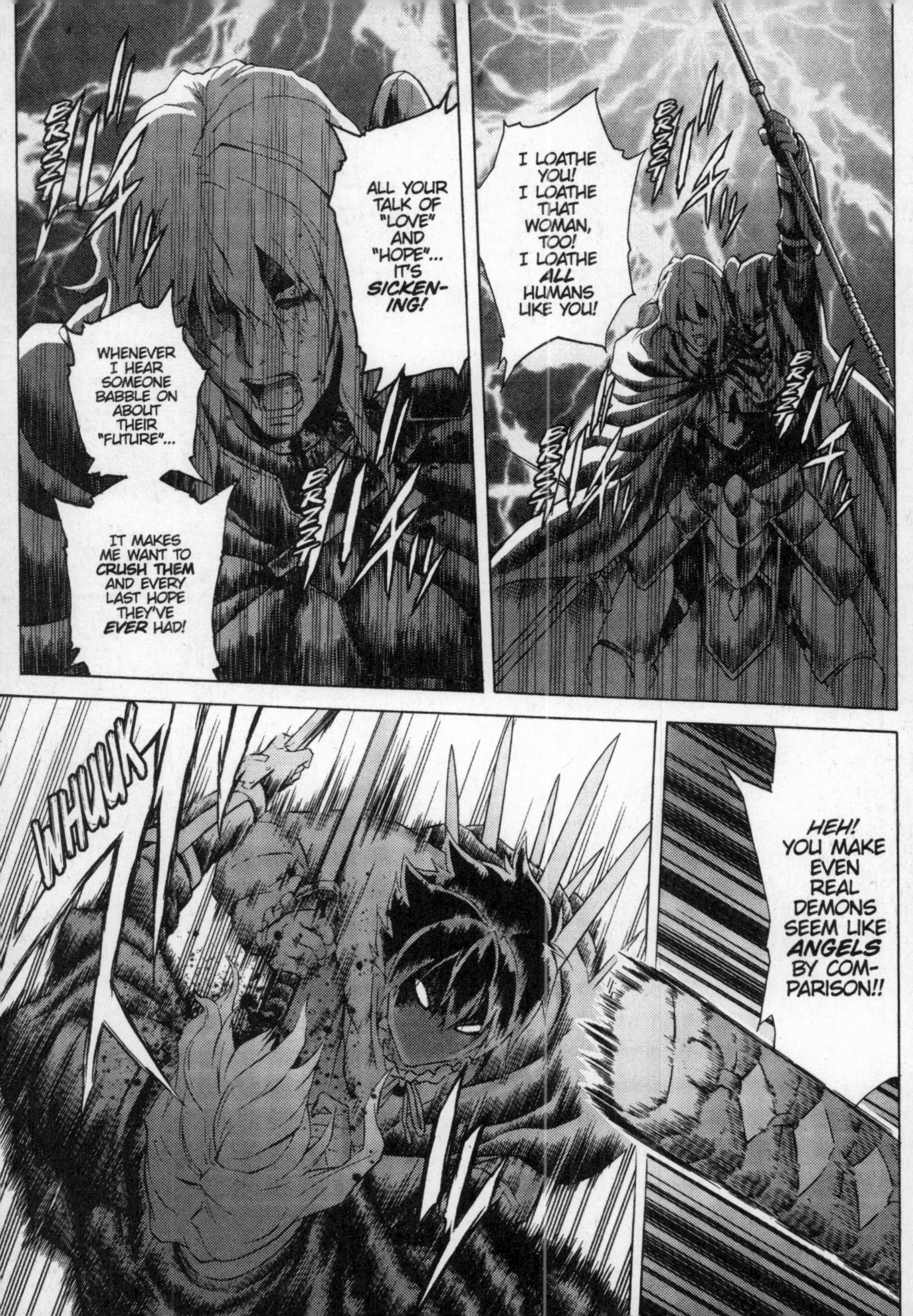
BRZZT
I LOATHE YOU! I LOATHE THAT WOMAN, TOO! I LOATHE ***ALL*** HUMANS LIKE YOU!
BRZZT
BRZZT
ALL YOUR TALK OF "LOVE" AND "HOPE"... IT'S ***SICKEN-ING!***
BRZZT
WHENEVER I HEAR SOMEONE BABBLE ON ABOUT THEIR "FUTURE"...
BRZZT
IT MAKES ME WANT TO **CRUSH THEM** AND EVERY LAST HOPE THEY'VE ***EVER*** HAD!
HEH! YOU MAKE EVEN REAL DEMONS SEEM LIKE ***ANGELS*** BY COM-PARISON!!
WHUCK

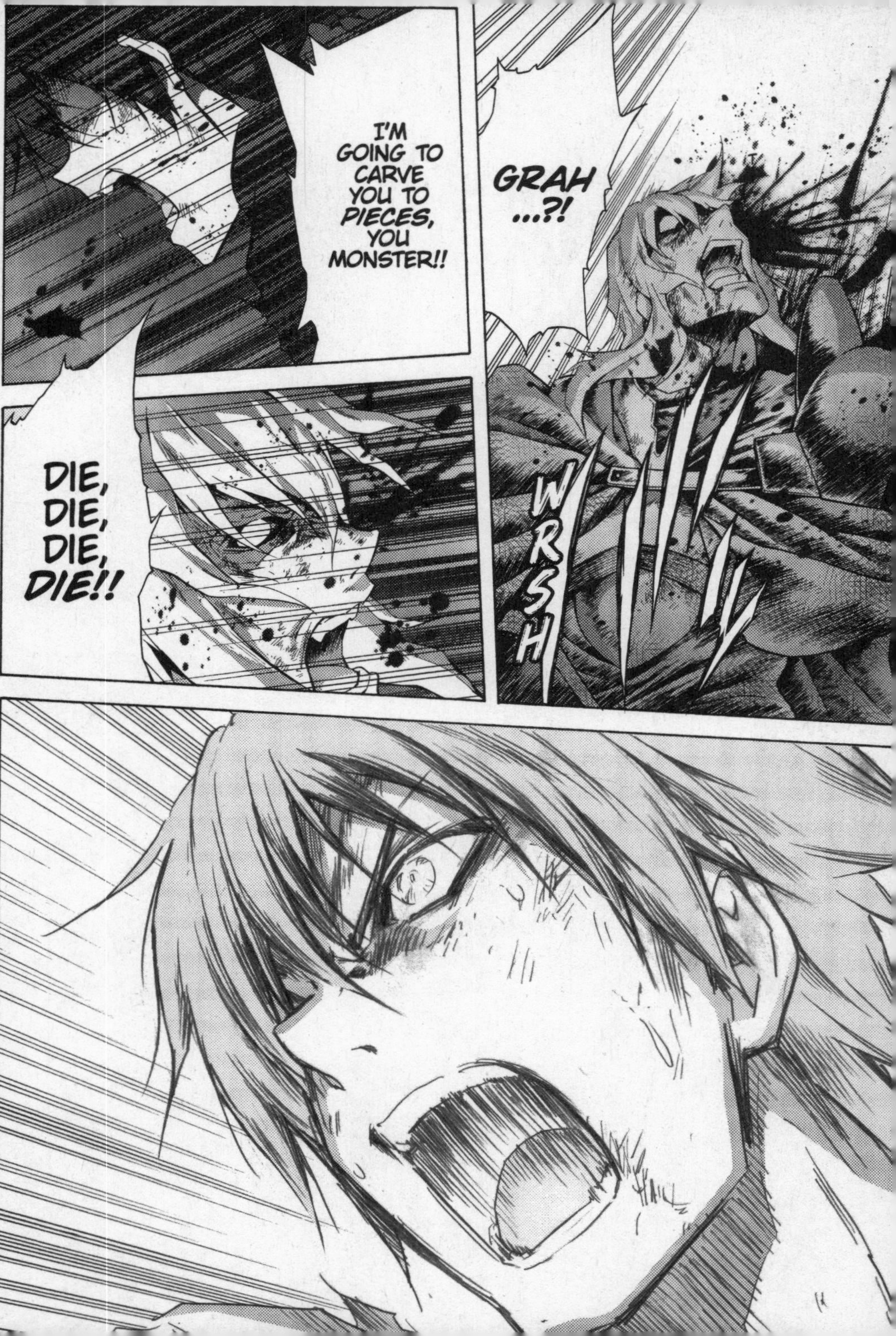
GRAH ...?!
WRSH
I'M GOING TO CARVE YOU TO PIECES, YOU MONSTER!!
DIE, DIE, DIE, DIE!!

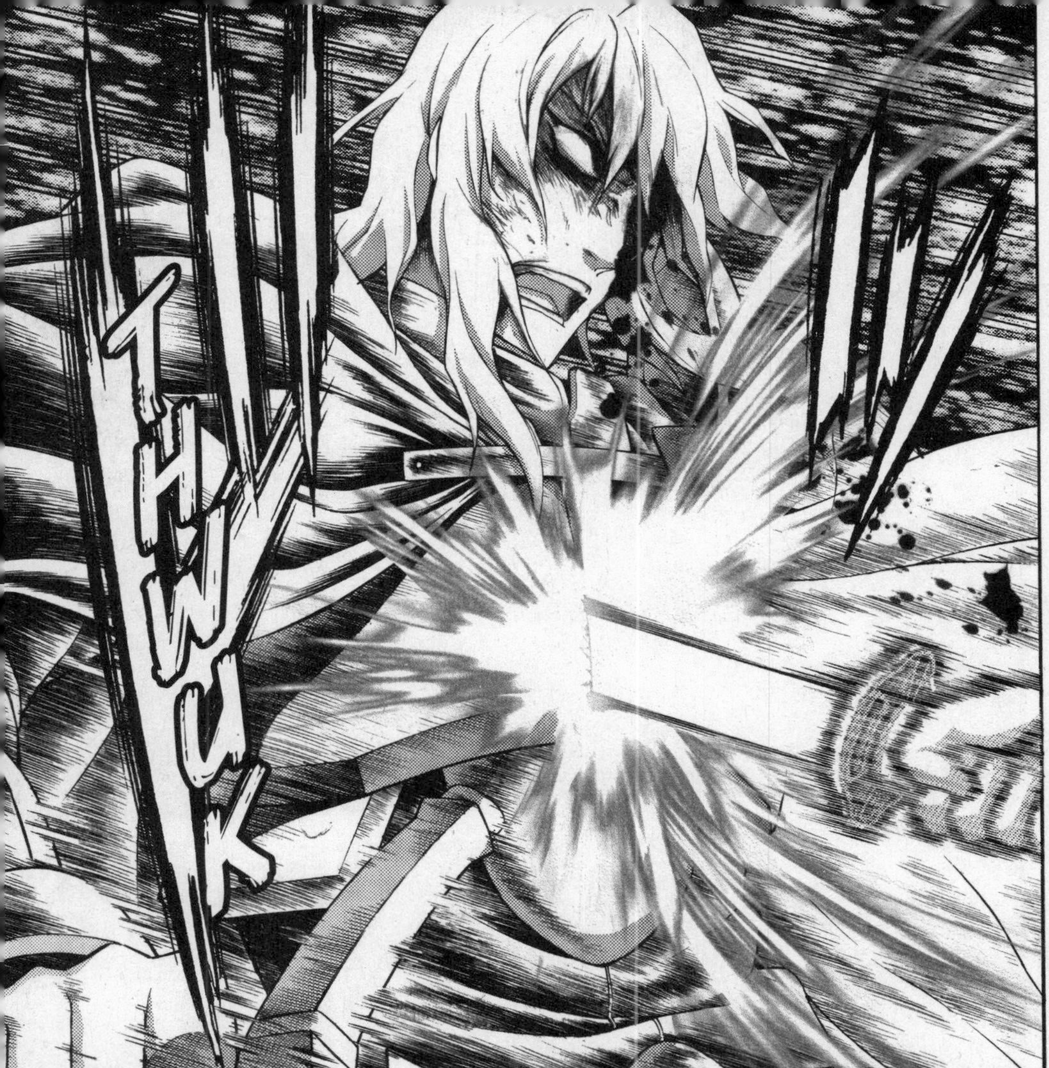
THWUK
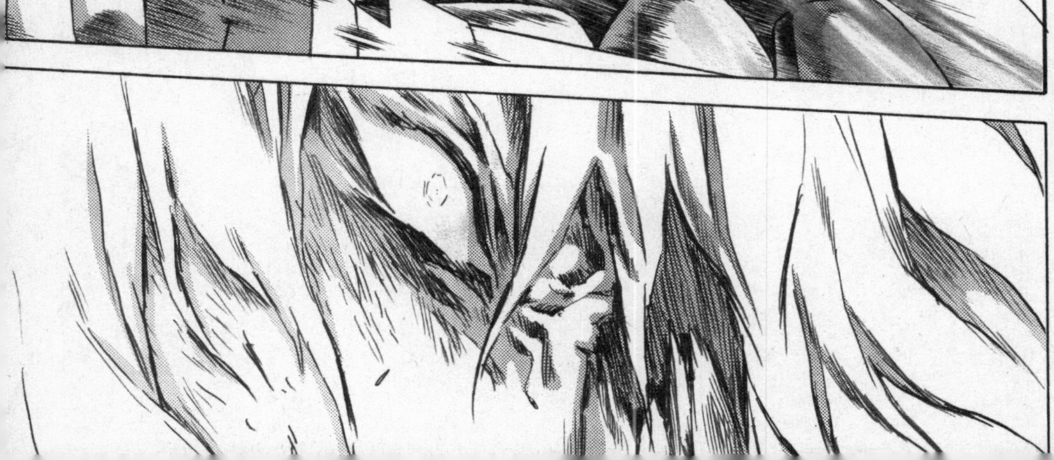

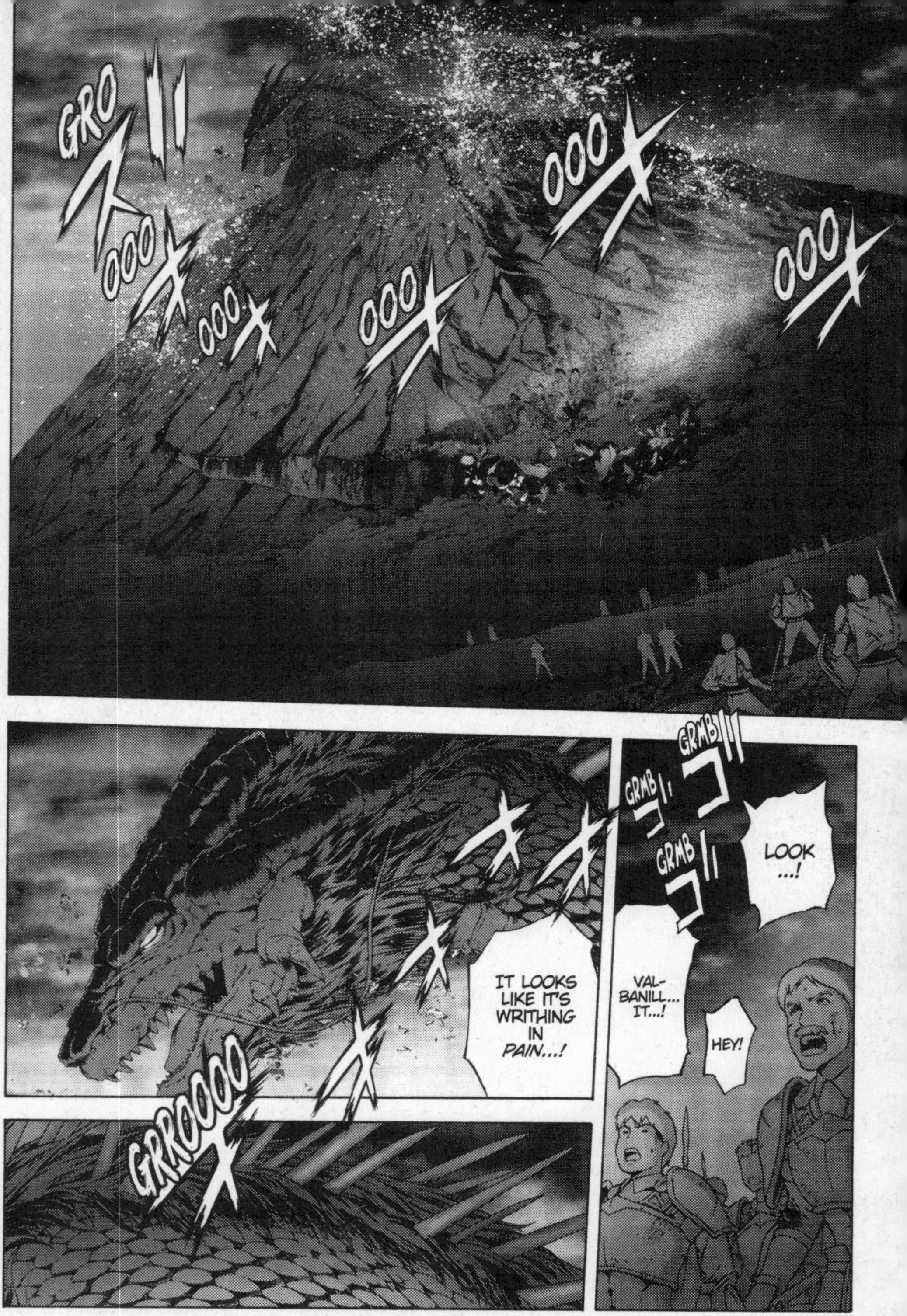
GRO
OOO
OOO
OOO
OOO
OOO
GRMB
GRMB
GRMB
LOOK ...!
VAL-BANILL... IT...!
HEY!
IT LOOKS LIKE IT'S WRITHING IN *PAIN*...!
GRROOOO

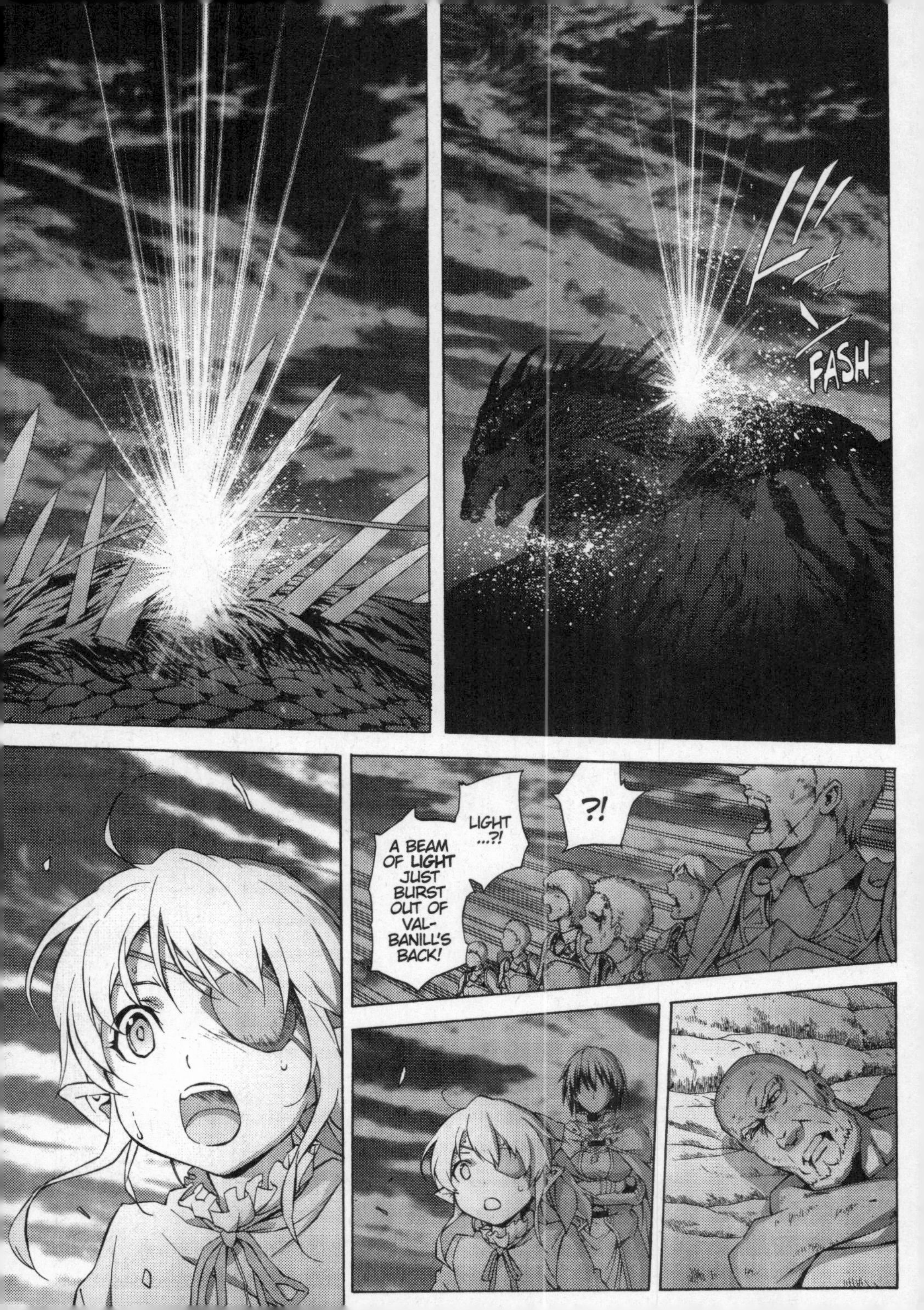
FASH
?!
LIGHT ...?!
A BEAM OF LIGHT JUST BURST OUT OF VAL-BANILL'S BACK!

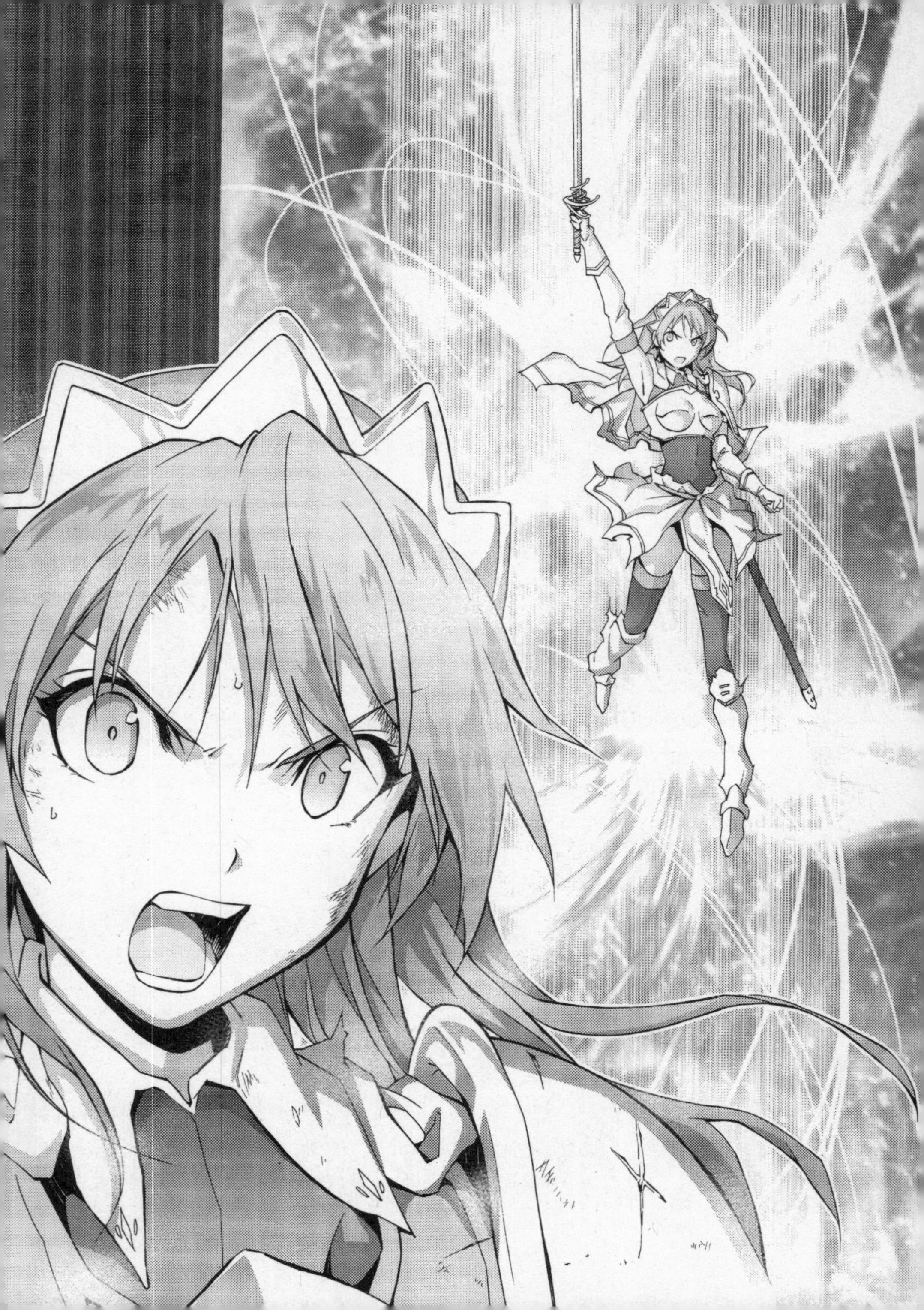

The Sacred Blacksmith

聖剣の刀鍛治

The Sacred Blacksmith

聖剣の刀鍛冶

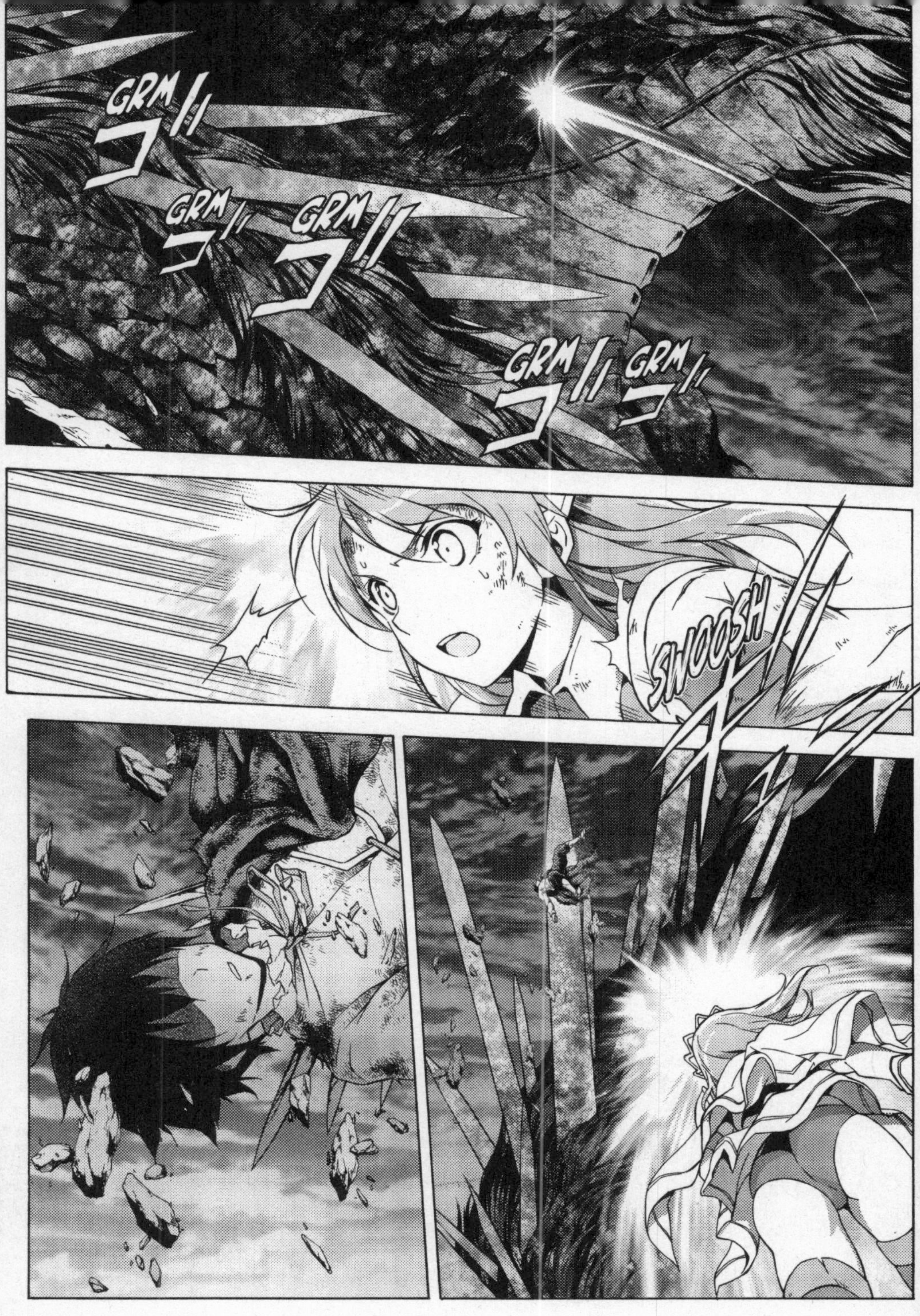
GRM
GRM
GRM
GRM
GRM
SWOOSH

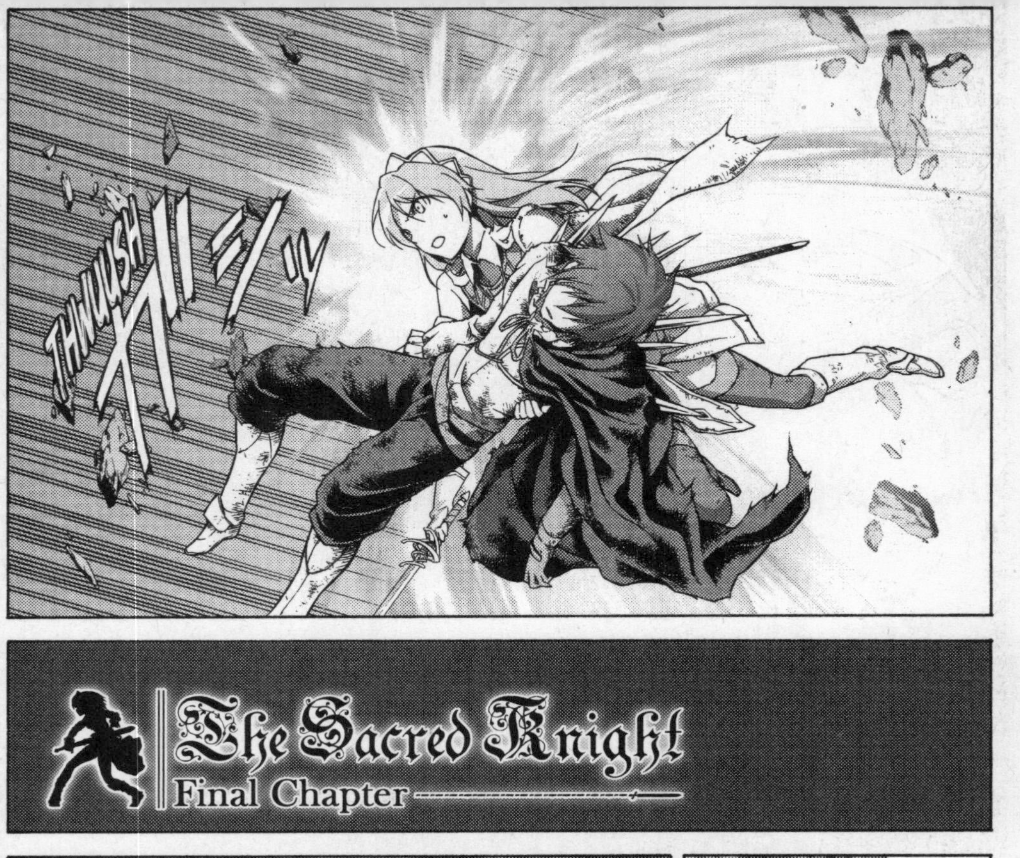
THWUUSH

The Sacred Knight

Final Chapter

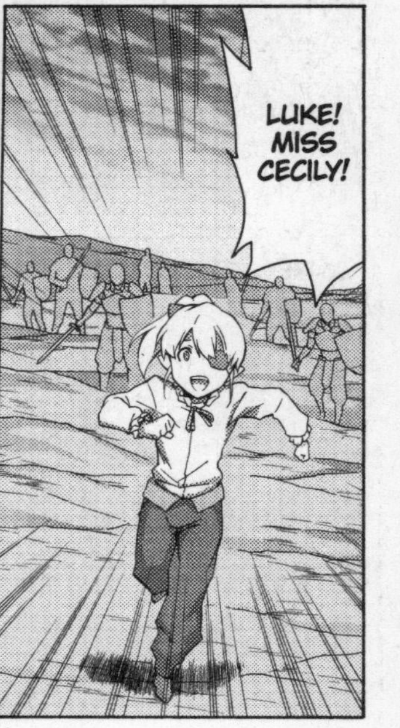
LUKE! MISS CECILY!

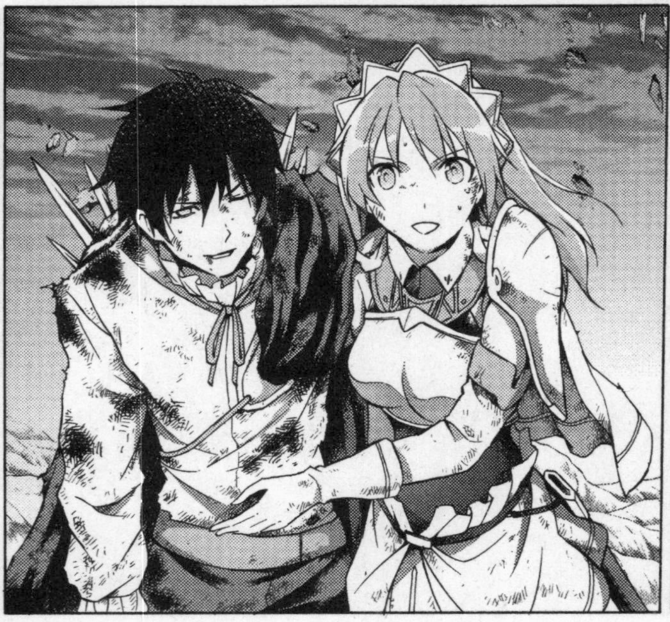

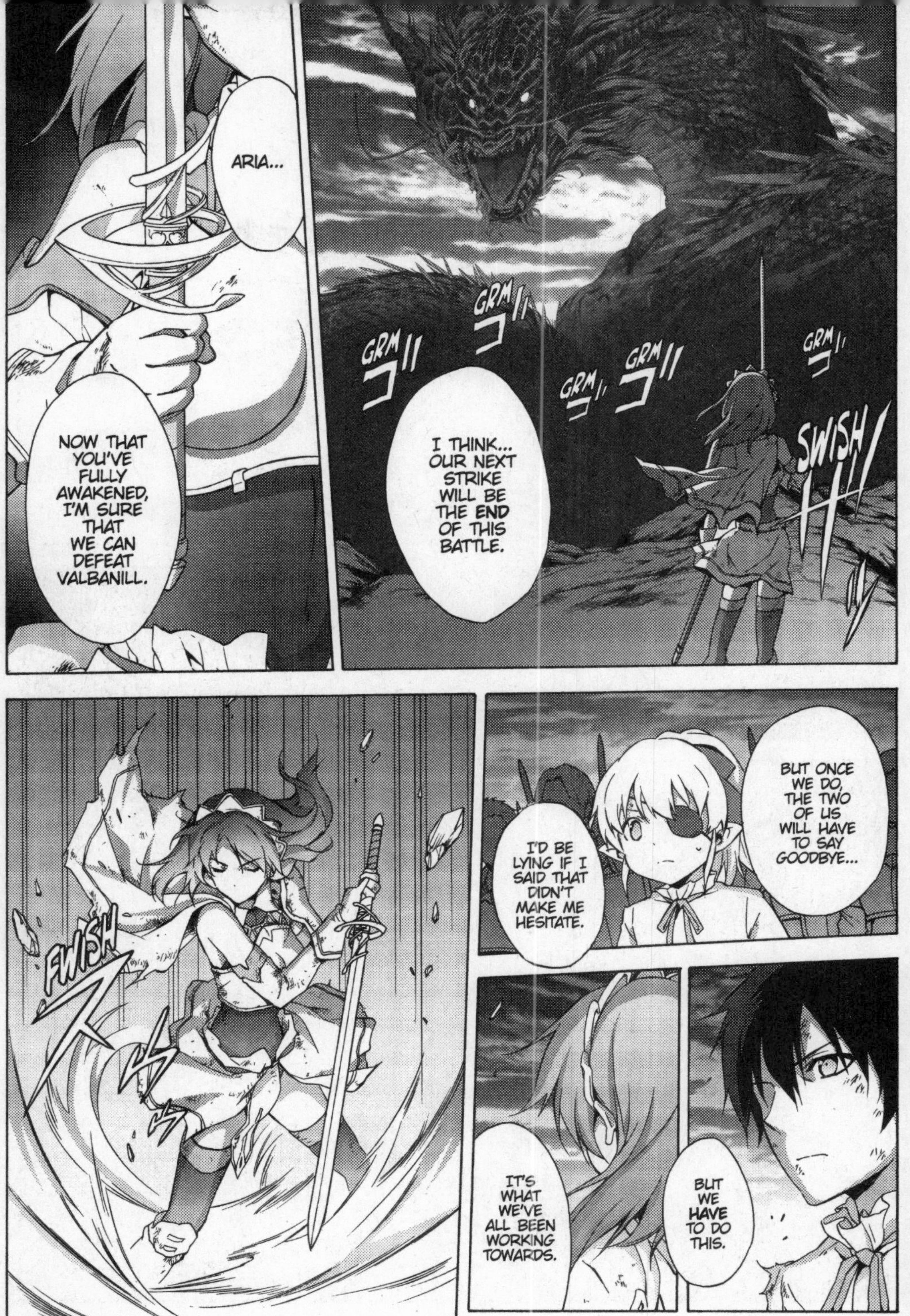
GRM
ゴ
SWISH
GRM
ゴ
GRM
ゴ
GRM
ゴ
GRM
ゴ
I THINK... OUR NEXT STRIKE WILL BE THE END OF THIS BATTLE.
ARIA...
NOW THAT YOU'VE FULLY AWAKENED, I'M SURE THAT WE CAN DEFEAT VALBANILL.
BUT ONCE WE DO, THE TWO OF US WILL HAVE TO SAY GOODBYE...
I'D BE LYING IF I SAID THAT DIDN'T MAKE ME HESITATE.
BUT WE HAVE TO DO THIS.
IT'S WHAT WE'VE ALL BEEN WORKING TOWARDS.
FWISH

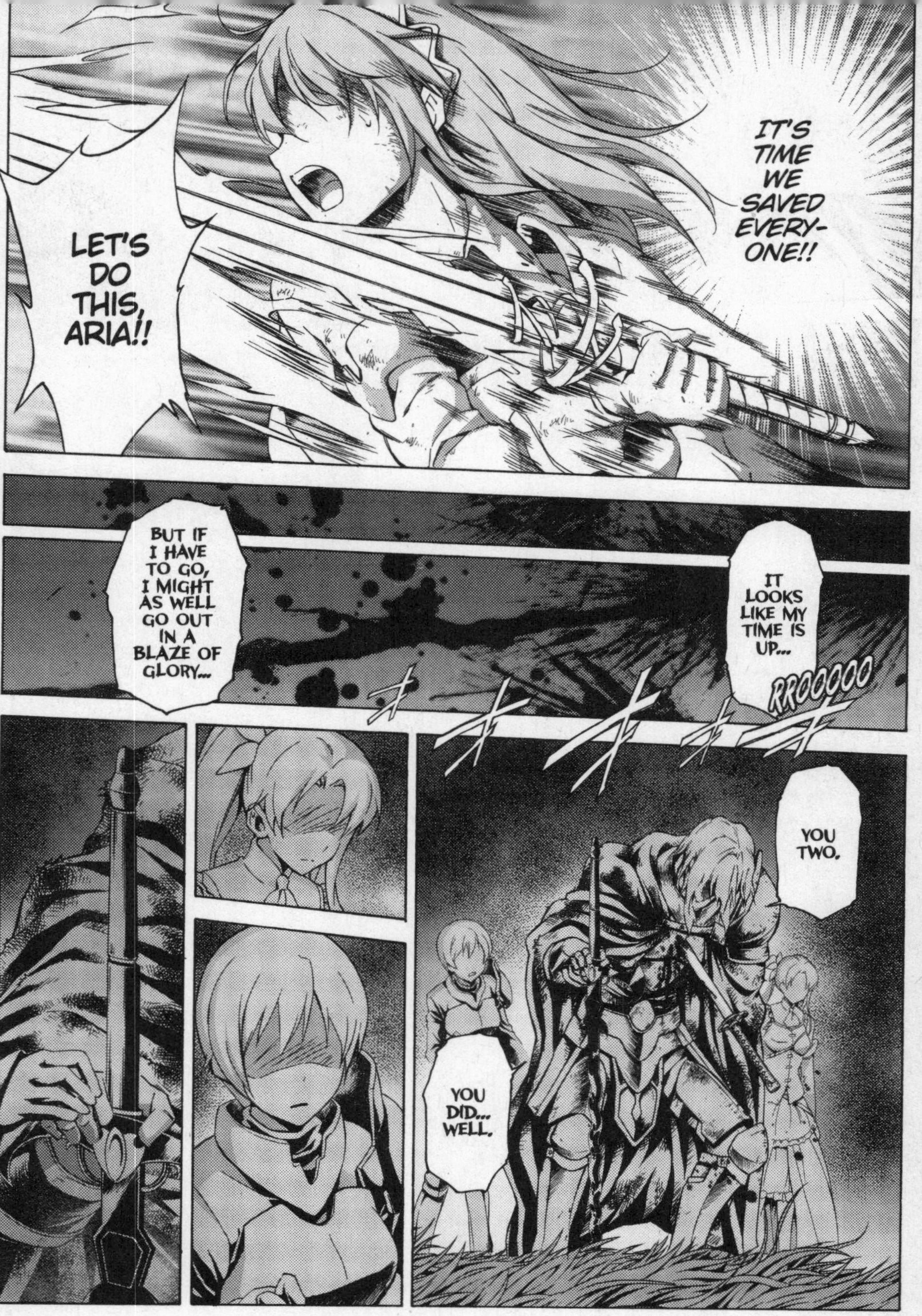
IT'S TIME WE SAVED EVERY-ONE!!
LET'S DO THIS, ARIA!!
IT LOOKS LIKE MY TIME IS UP...
BUT IF I HAVE TO GO, I MIGHT AS WELL GO OUT IN A BLAZE OF GLORY...
RROOOOO
YOU TWO,
YOU DID... WELL.

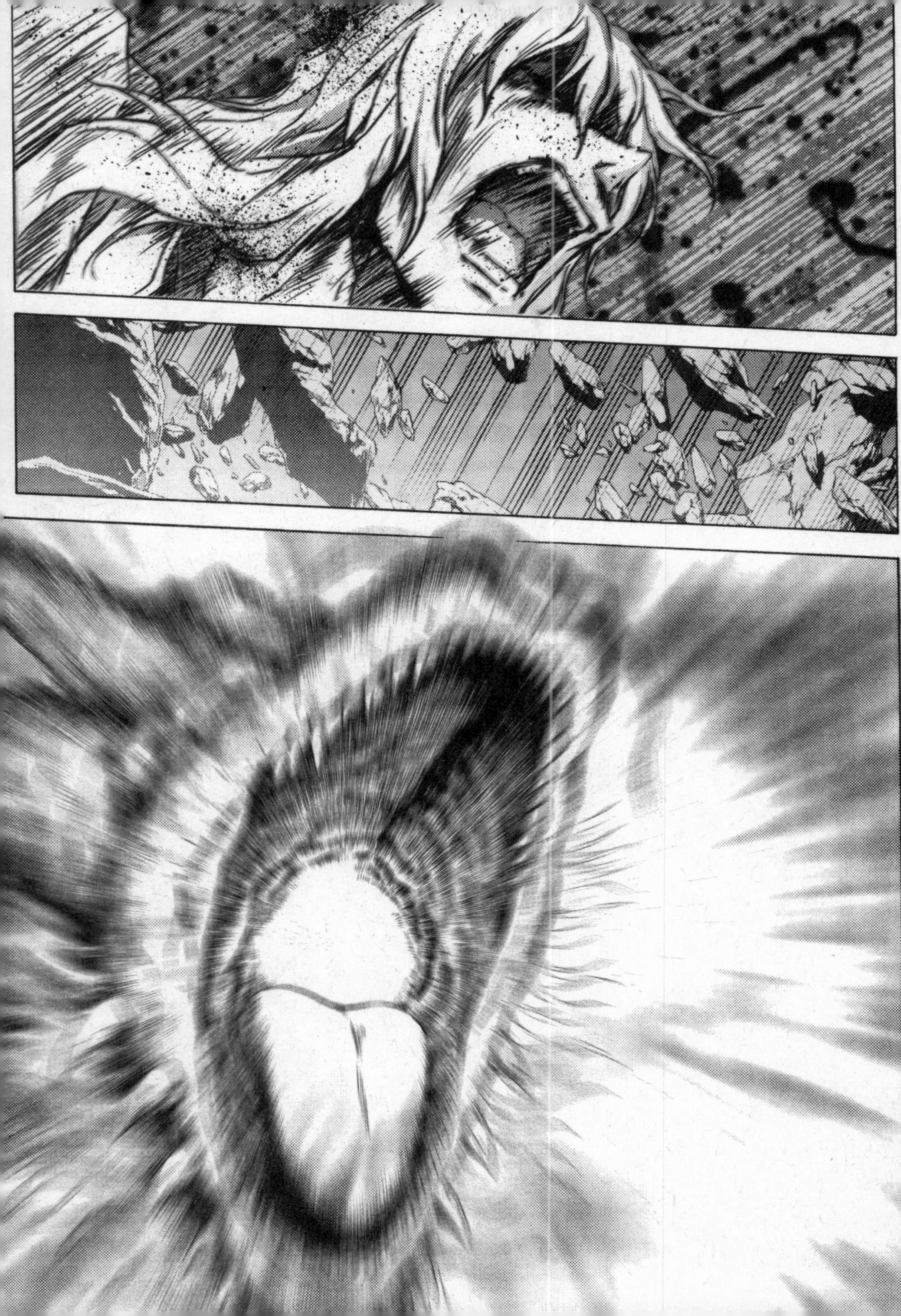

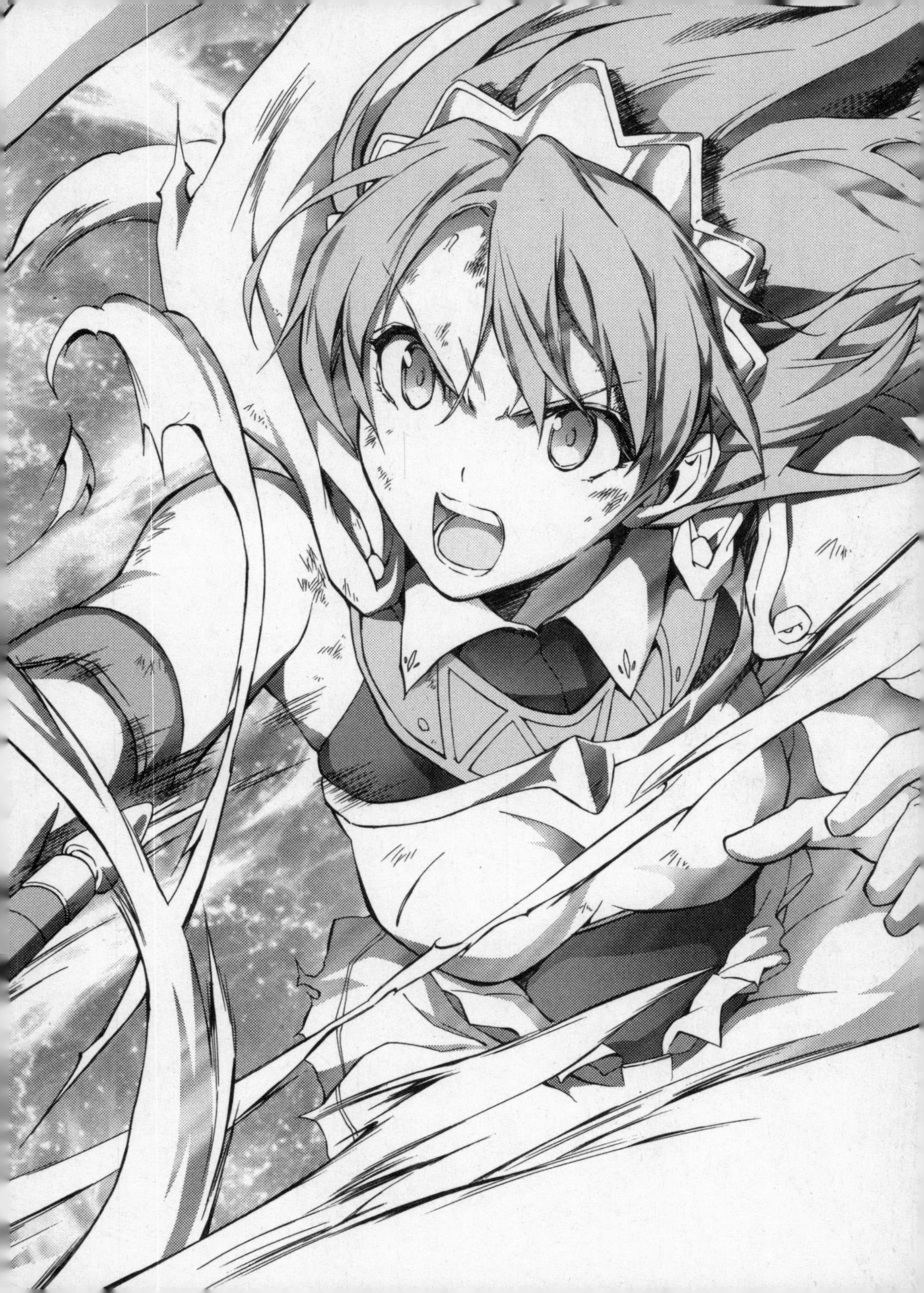

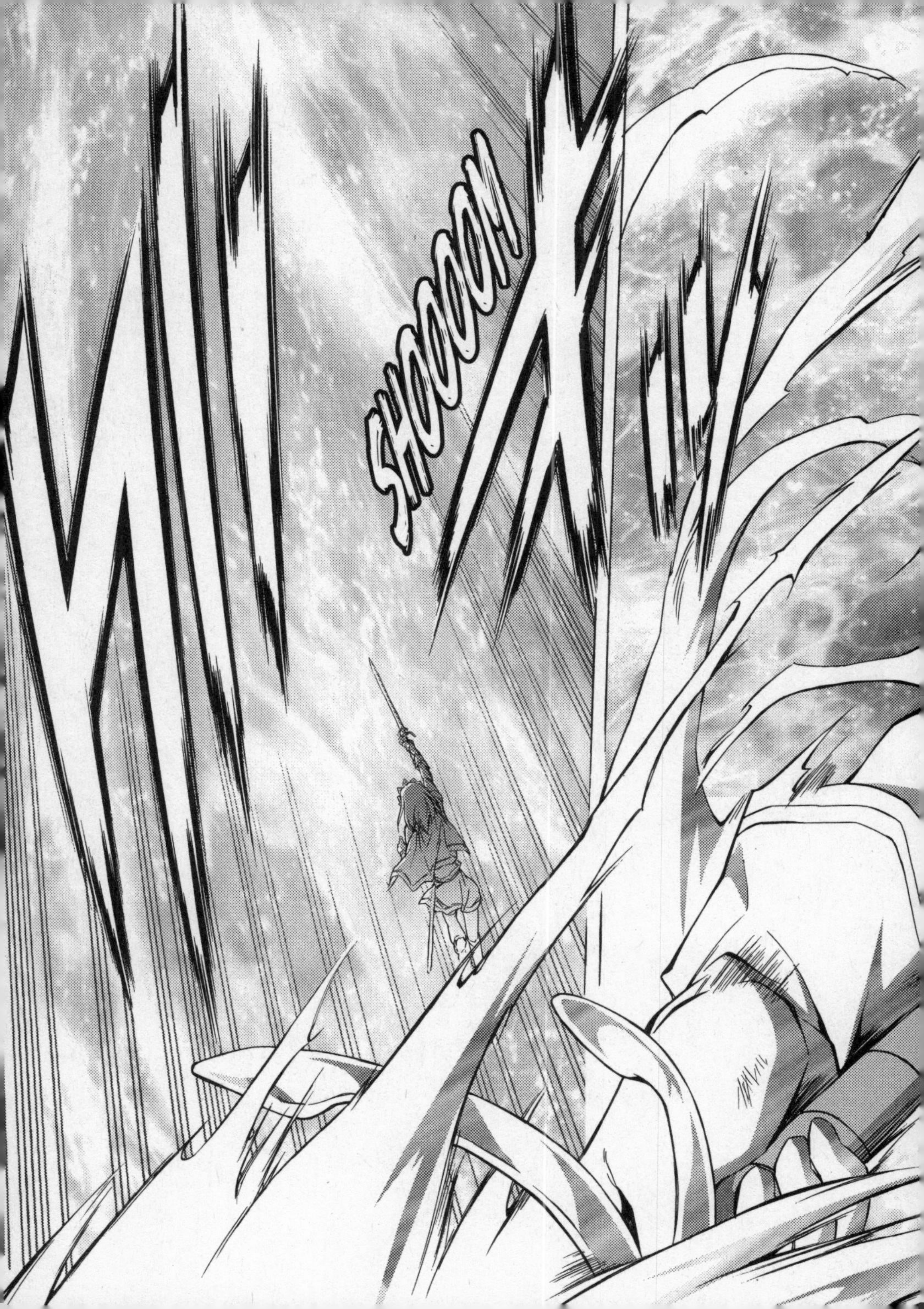
SHOOOM

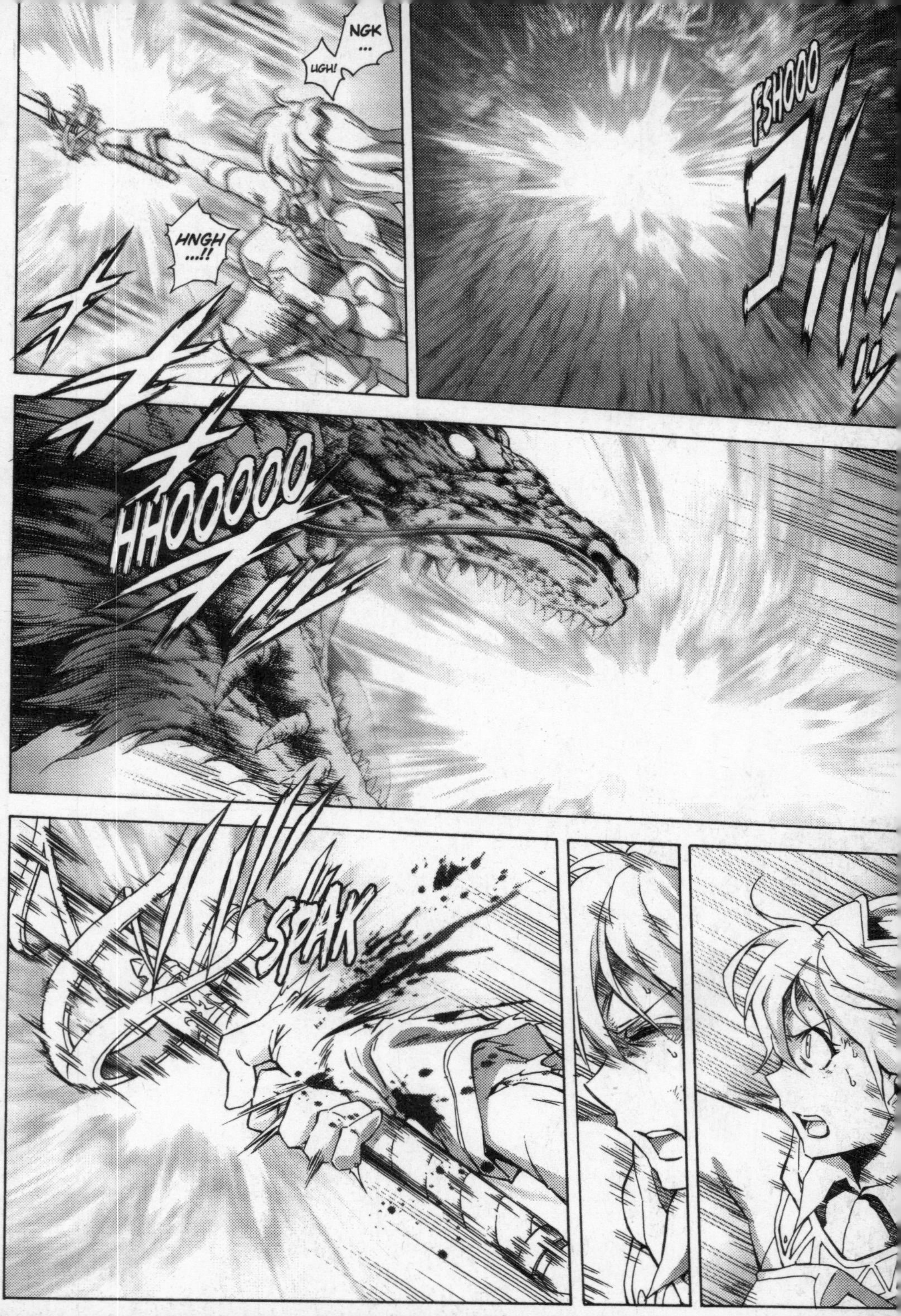
FSHOOO
NGK ...
UGH!
HNGH ...!!
HHOOOOO
SPAK

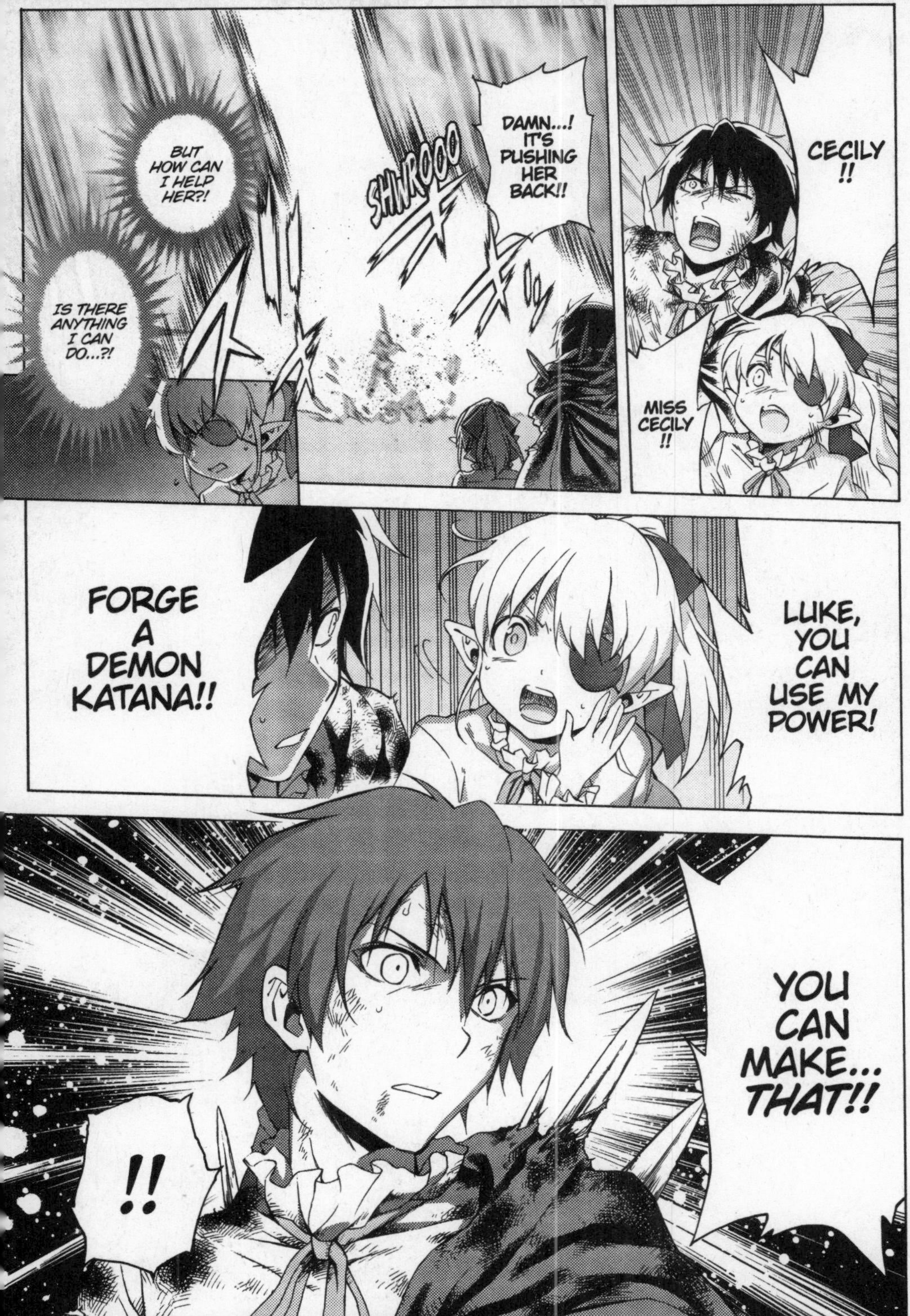
CECILY !!
MISS CECILY !!
DAMN...! IT'S PUSHING HER BACK!!
SHWROOO
BUT HOW CAN I HELP HER?!
IS THERE ANYTHING I CAN DO...?!
LUKE, YOU CAN USE MY POWER!
FORGE A DEMON KATANA!!
YOU CAN MAKE... THAT!!
!!

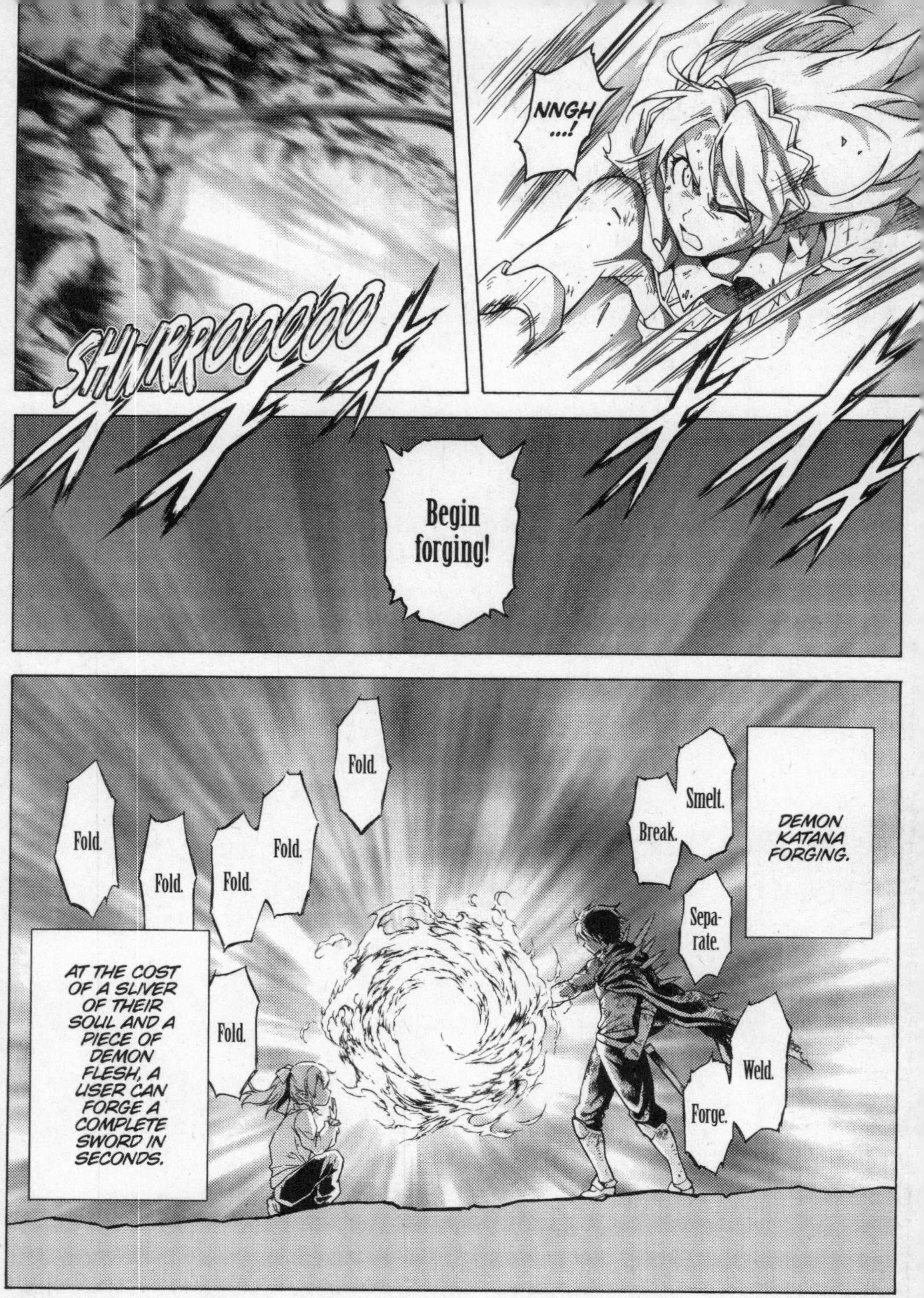
NNGH ...!
SHWRROOOOOO
Begin forging!
DEMON KATANA FORGING.
Smelt.
Break.
Separate.
Weld.
Forge.
Fold.
Fold.
Fold.
Fold.
Fold.
Fold.
AT THE COST OF A SLIVER OF THEIR SOUL AND A PIECE OF DEMON FLESH, A USER CAN FORGE A COMPLETE SWORD IN SECONDS.

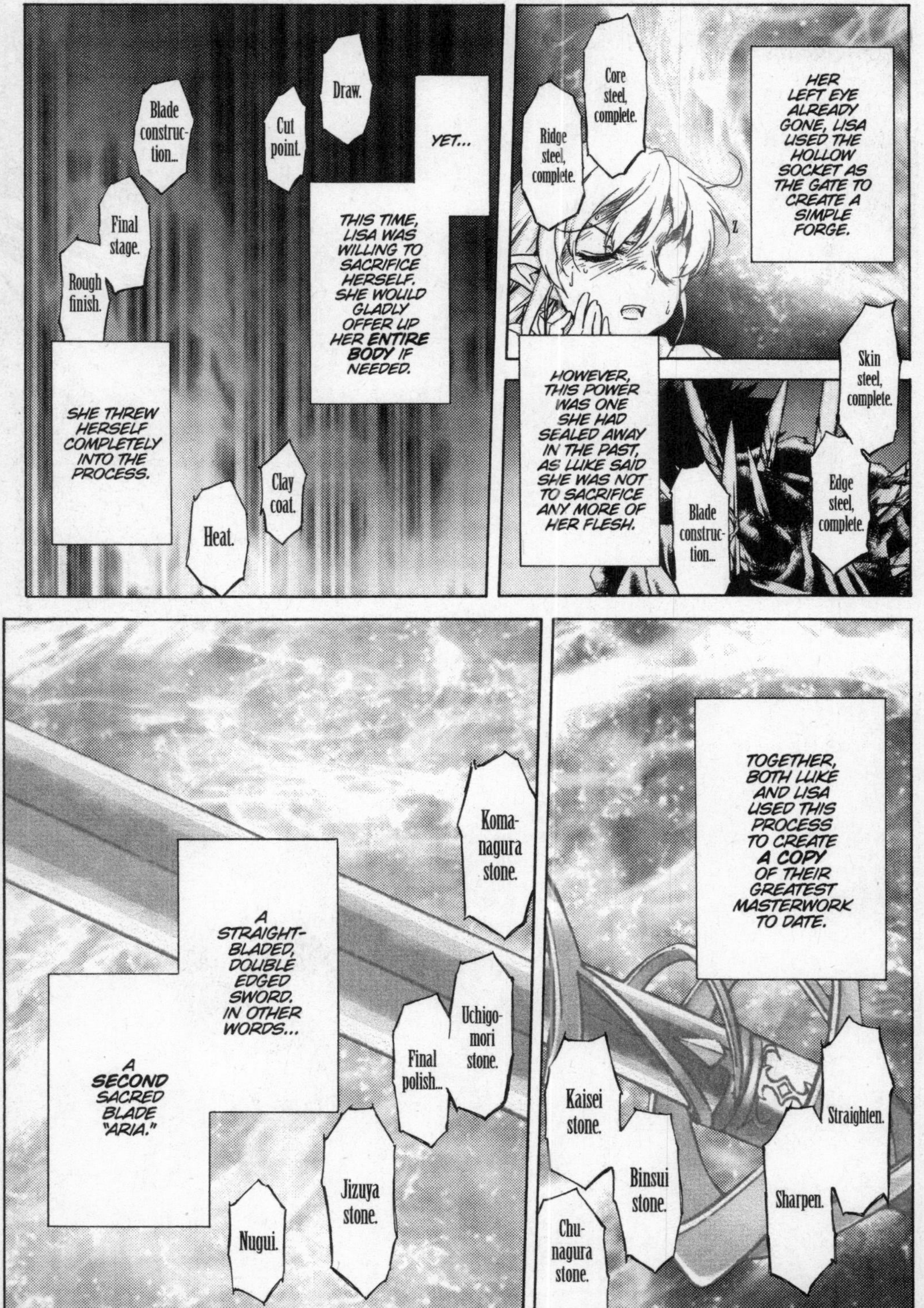
HER LEFT EYE ALREADY GONE, LISA USED THE HOLLOW SOCKET AS THE GATE TO CREATE A SIMPLE FORGE.
Core steel, complete.
Ridge steel, complete.
Skin steel, complete.
Edge steel, complete.
HOWEVER, THIS POWER WAS ONE SHE HAD SEALED AWAY IN THE PAST, AS LUKE SAID SHE WAS NOT TO SACRIFICE ANY MORE OF HER FLESH.
Blade construc-tion...
YET...
Draw.
THIS TIME, LISA WAS WILLING TO SACRIFICE HERSELF. SHE WOULD GLADLY OFFER UP HER ENTIRE BODY IF NEEDED.
Cut point.
Blade construc-tion...
Final stage.
Rough finish.
Clay coat.
Heat.
SHE THREW HERSELF COMPLETELY INTO THE PROCESS.
TOGETHER, BOTH LUKE AND LISA USED THIS PROCESS TO CREATE A COPY OF THEIR GREATEST MASTERWORK TO DATE.
Straighten.
Sharpen.
Kaisei stone.
Binsui stone.
Chu-nagura stone.
Koma-nagura stone.
A STRAIGHT-BLADED, DOUBLE EDGED SWORD. IN OTHER WORDS...
Uchigo-mori stone.
Final polish...
A SECOND SACRED BLADE "ARIA."
Jizuya stone.
Nugui.

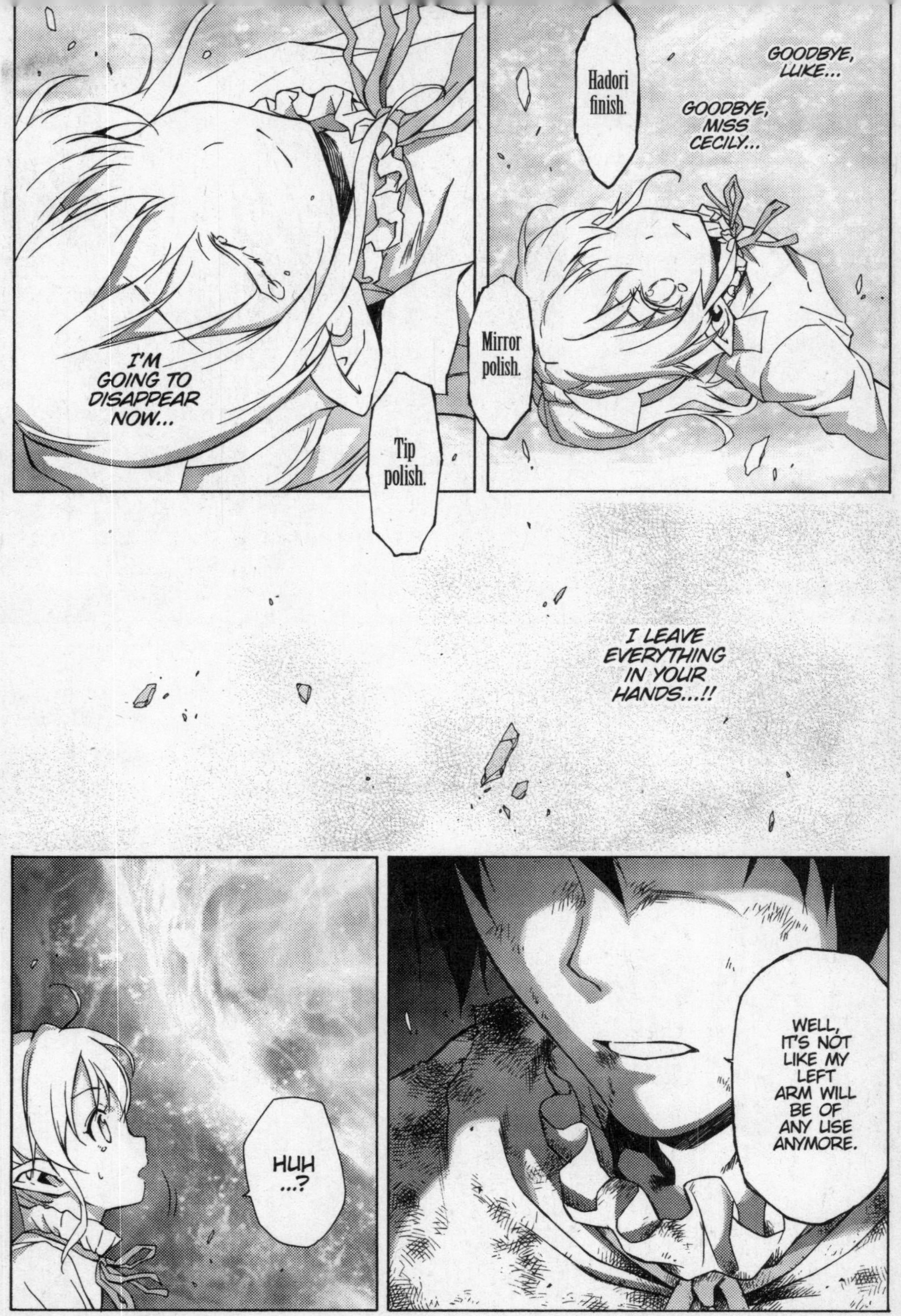
GOODBYE, LUKE...
GOODBYE, MISS CECILY...
Hadori finish.
Mirror polish.
I'M GOING TO DISAPPEAR NOW...
Tip polish.
I LEAVE EVERYTHING IN YOUR HANDS...!!
WELL, IT'S NOT LIKE MY LEFT ARM WILL BE OF ANY USE ANYMORE.
HUH ...?

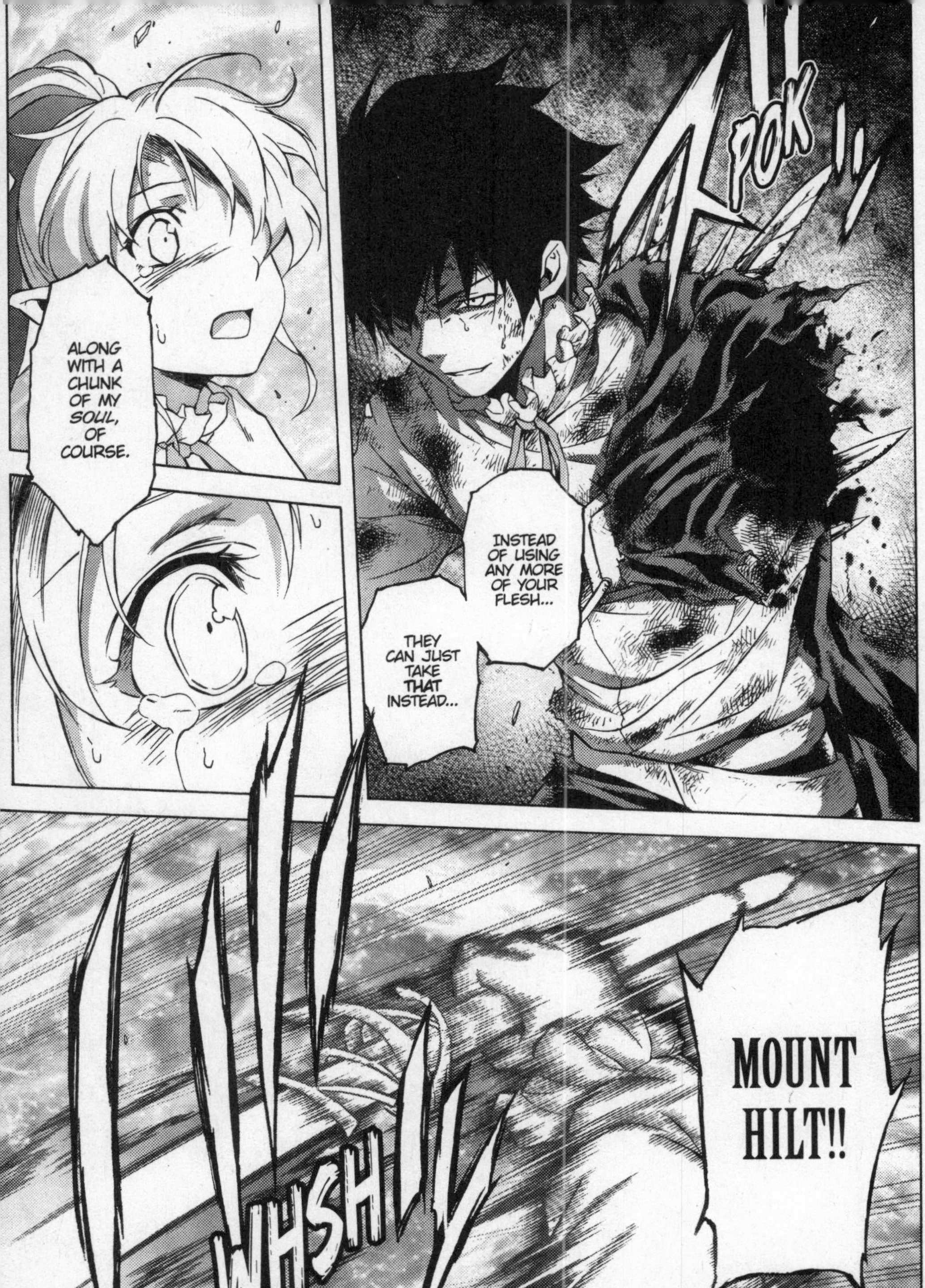
POK
INSTEAD OF USING ANY MORE OF YOUR FLESH...
THEY CAN JUST TAKE THAT INSTEAD...
ALONG WITH A CHUNK OF MY SOUL, OF COURSE.
MOUNT HILT!!
WHSH

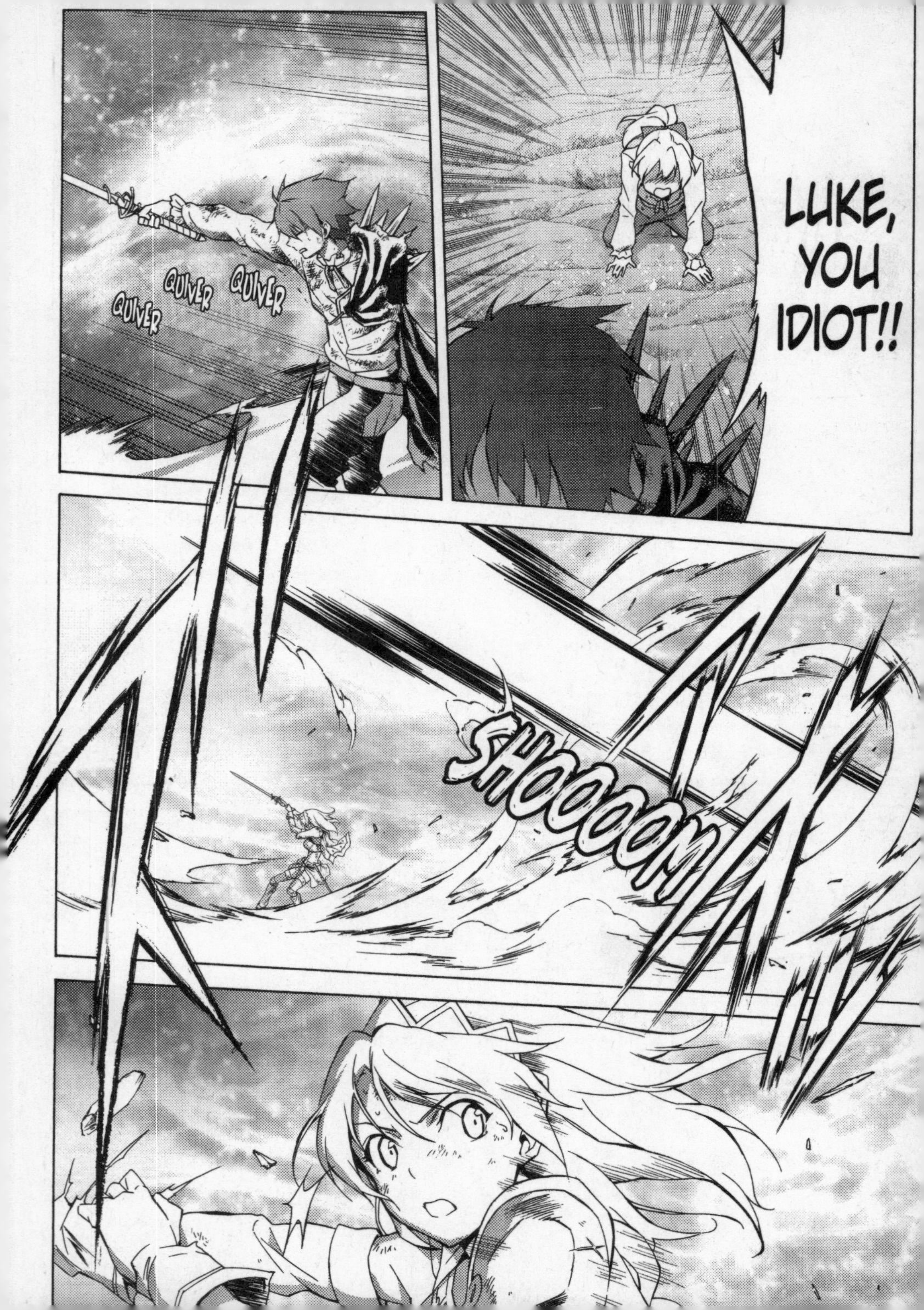
LUKE, YOU IDIOT!!
QUIVER
QUIVER
QUIVER
SHOOOOM

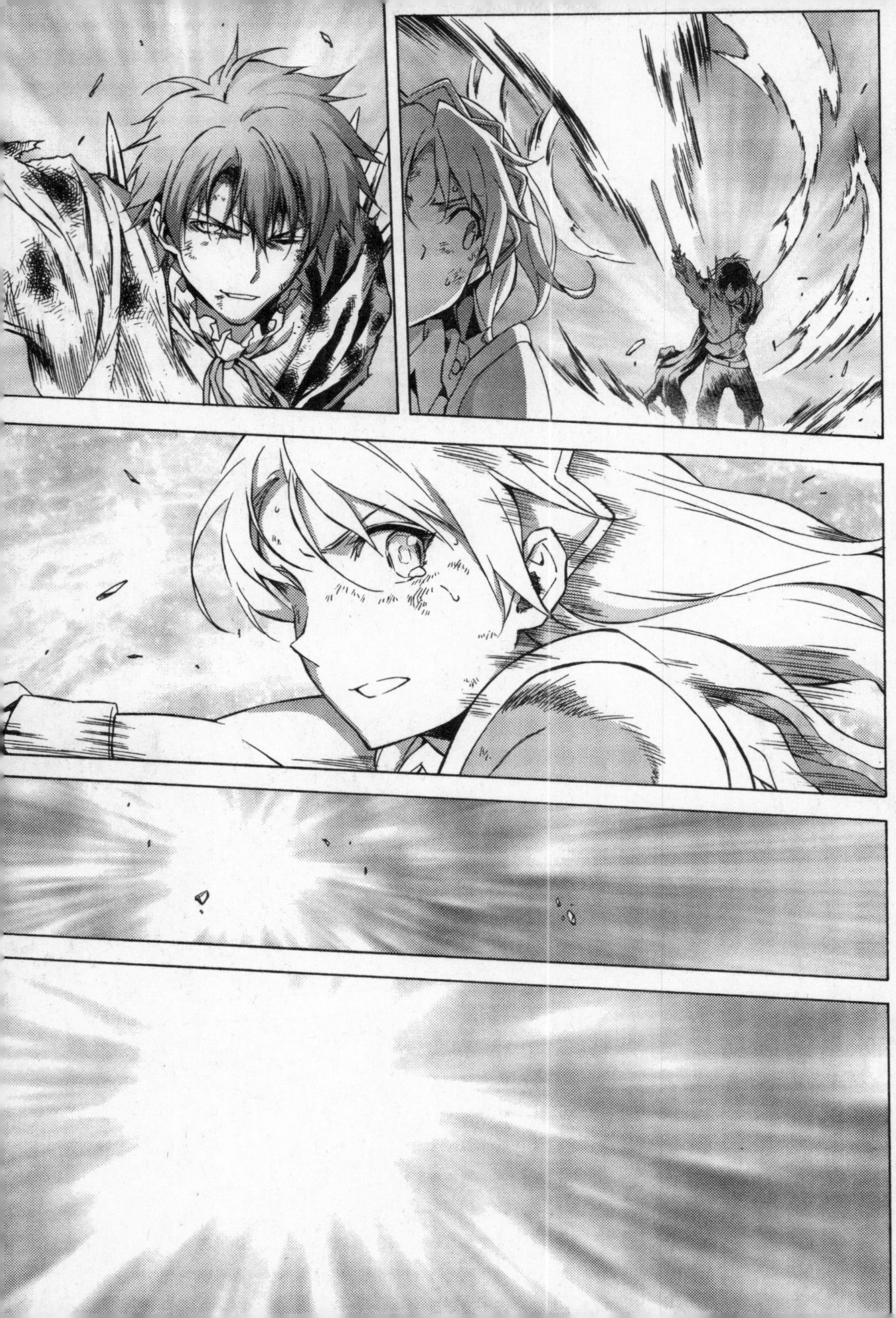

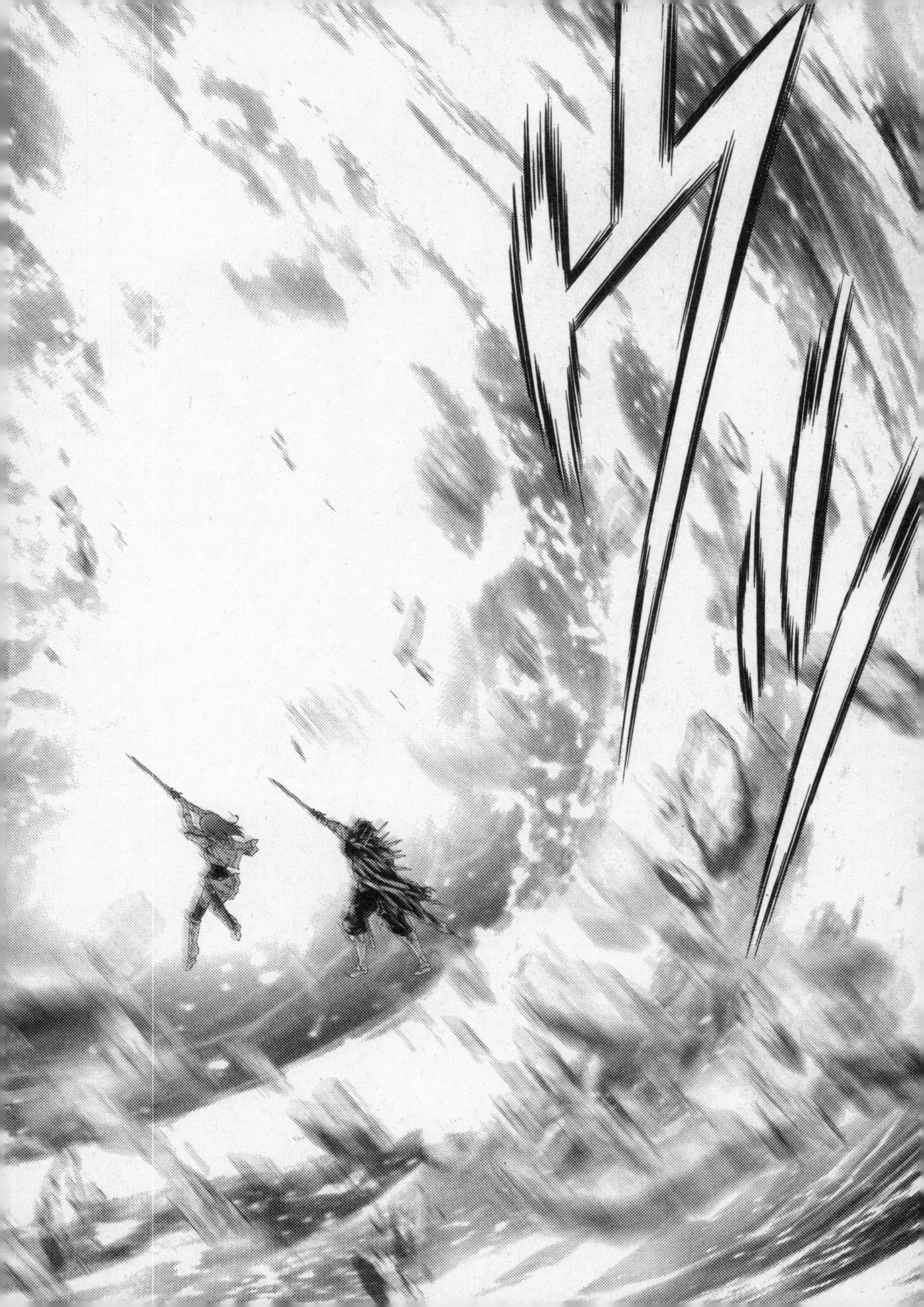

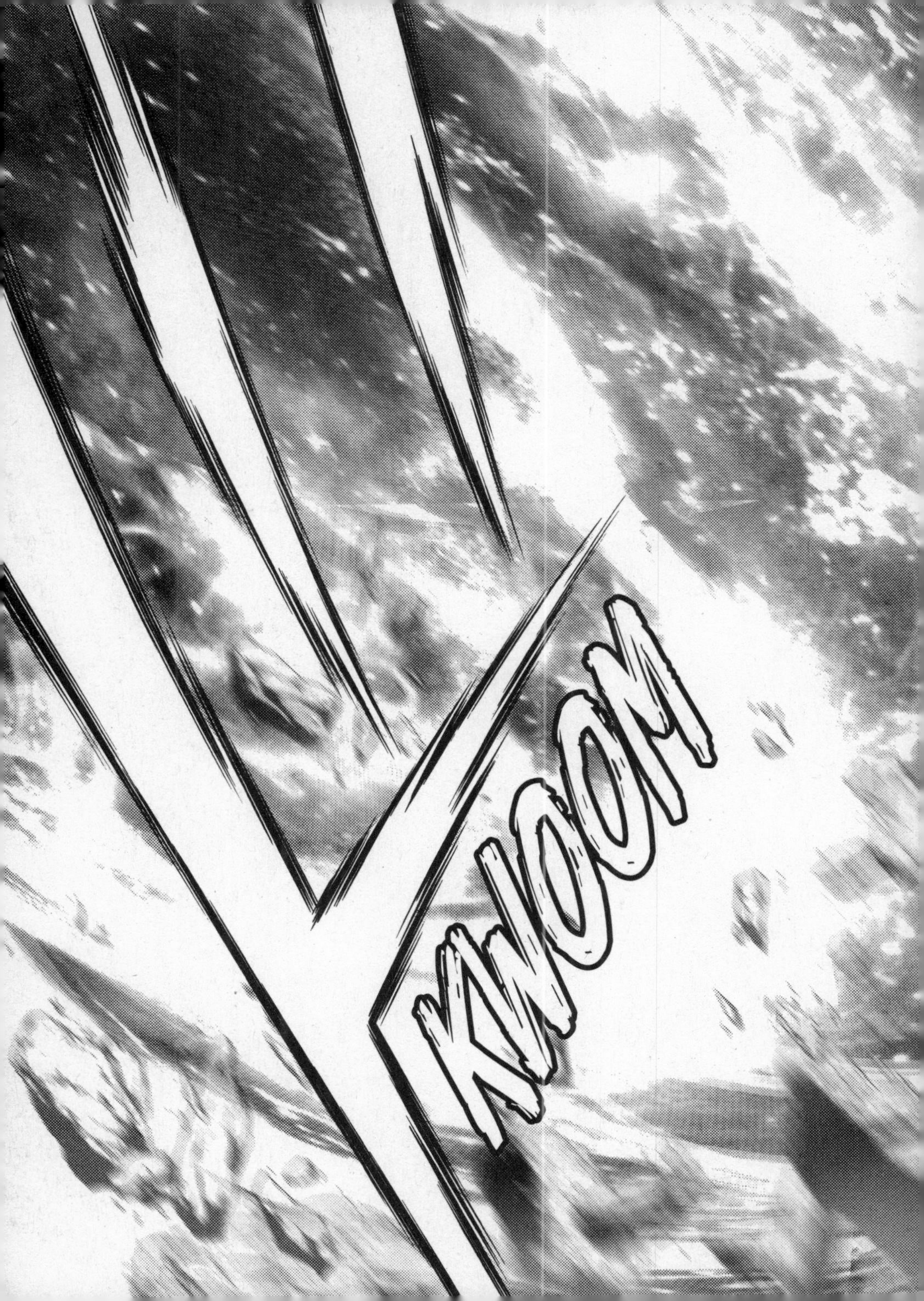
KWOOM

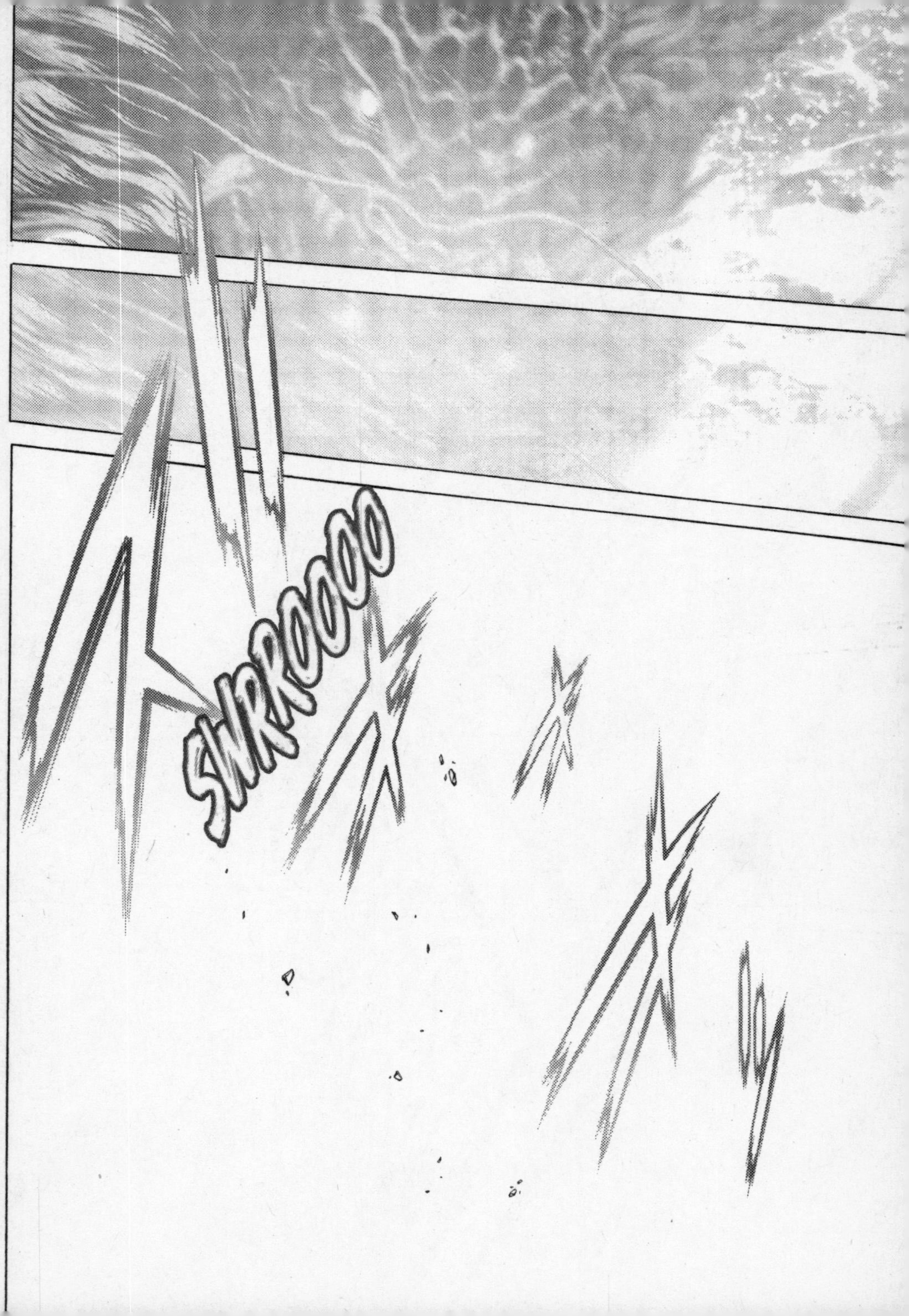
SWROOOO

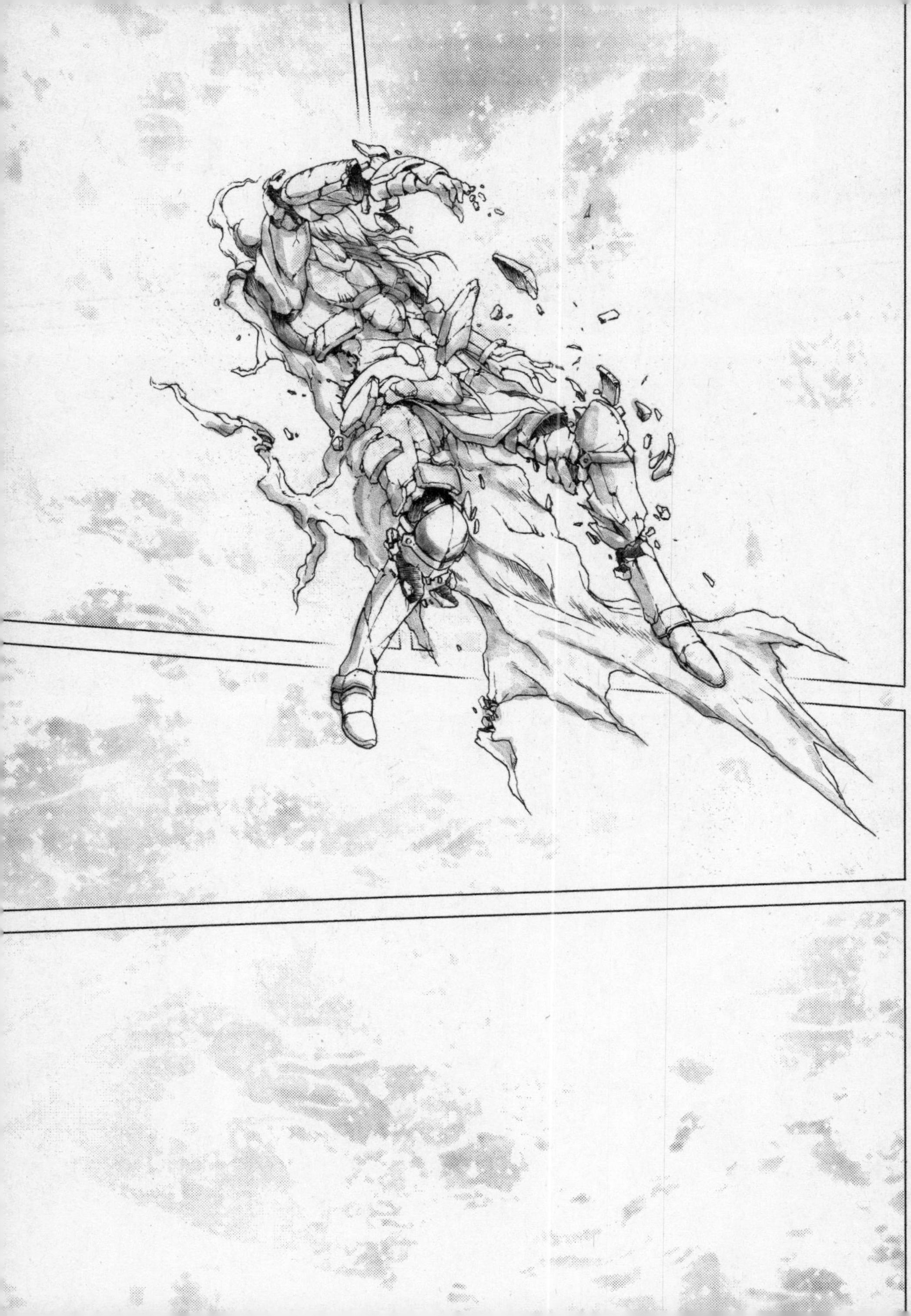

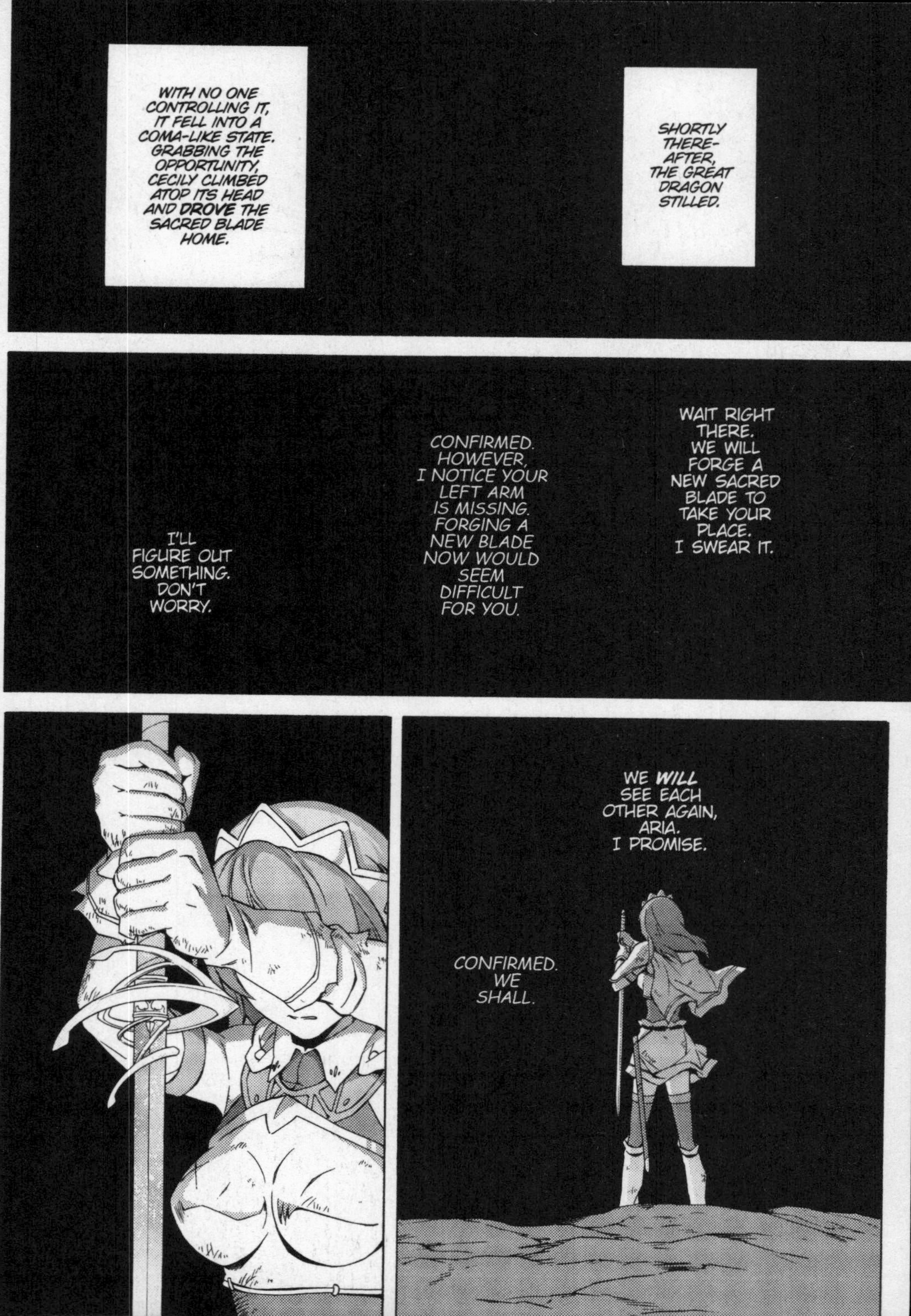
WITH NO ONE CONTROLLING IT, IT FELL INTO A COMA-LIKE STATE. GRABBING THE OPPORTUNITY, CECILY CLIMBED ATOP ITS HEAD AND **DROVE** THE SACRED BLADE HOME.
SHORTLY THERE-AFTER, THE GREAT DRAGON STILLED.
WAIT RIGHT THERE. WE WILL FORGE A NEW SACRED BLADE TO TAKE YOUR PLACE. I SWEAR IT.
CONFIRMED. HOWEVER, I NOTICE YOUR LEFT ARM IS MISSING. FORGING A NEW BLADE NOW WOULD SEEM DIFFICULT FOR YOU.
I'LL FIGURE OUT SOMETHING. DON'T WORRY.
WE ***WILL*** SEE EACH OTHER AGAIN, ARIA. I PROMISE.
CONFIRMED. WE SHALL.

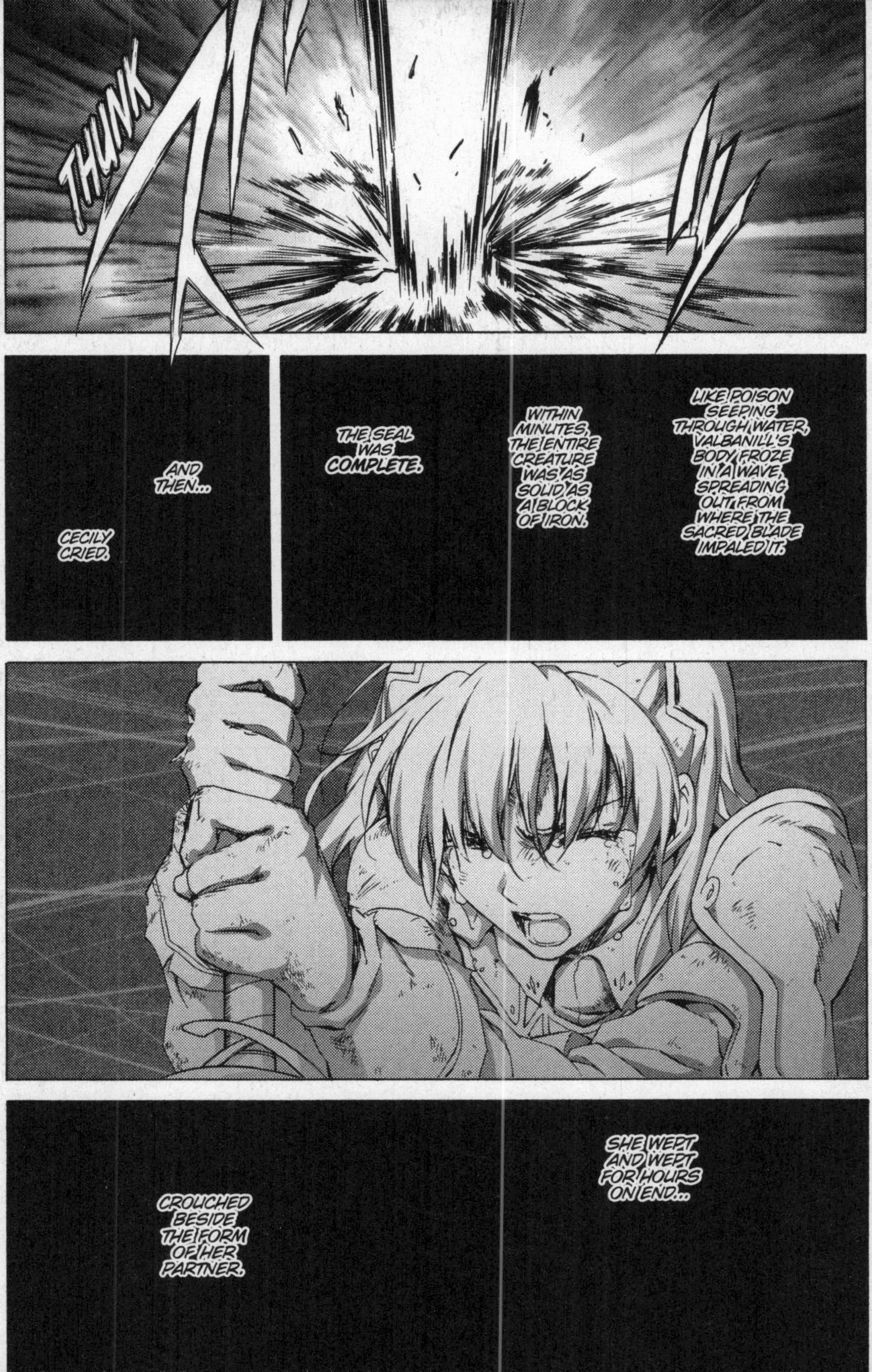
THUNK
LIKE POISON SEEPING THROUGH WATER, VALBANILL'S BODY FROZE IN A WAVE, SPREADING OUT FROM WHERE THE SACRED BLADE IMPALED IT.
WITHIN MINUTES, THE ENTIRE CREATURE WAS AS SOLID AS A BLOCK OF IRON.
THE SEAL WAS COMPLETE.
AND THEN...
CECILY CRIED.
SHE WEPT AND WEPT FOR HOURS ON END...
CROUCHED BESIDE THE FORM OF HER PARTNER.

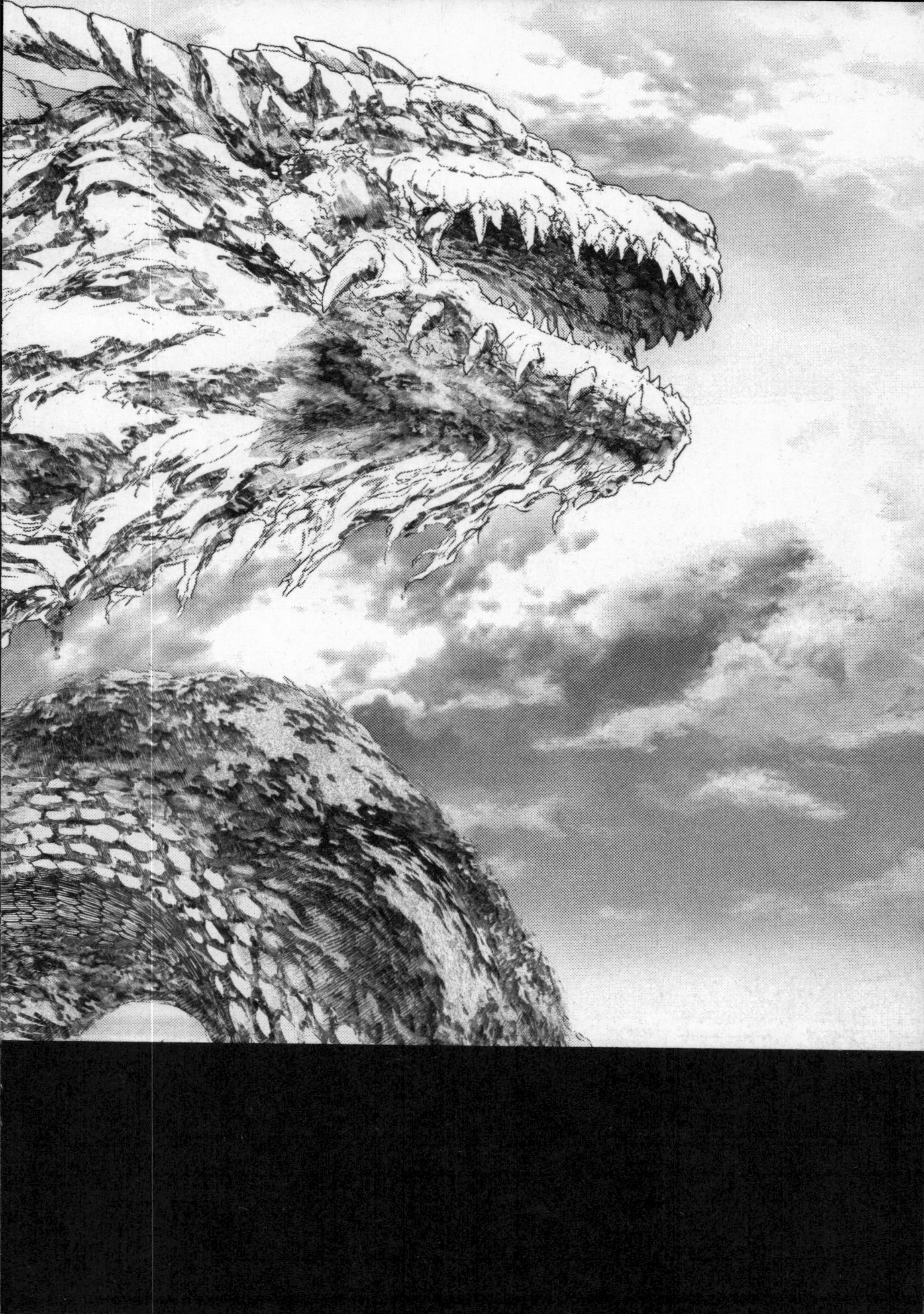

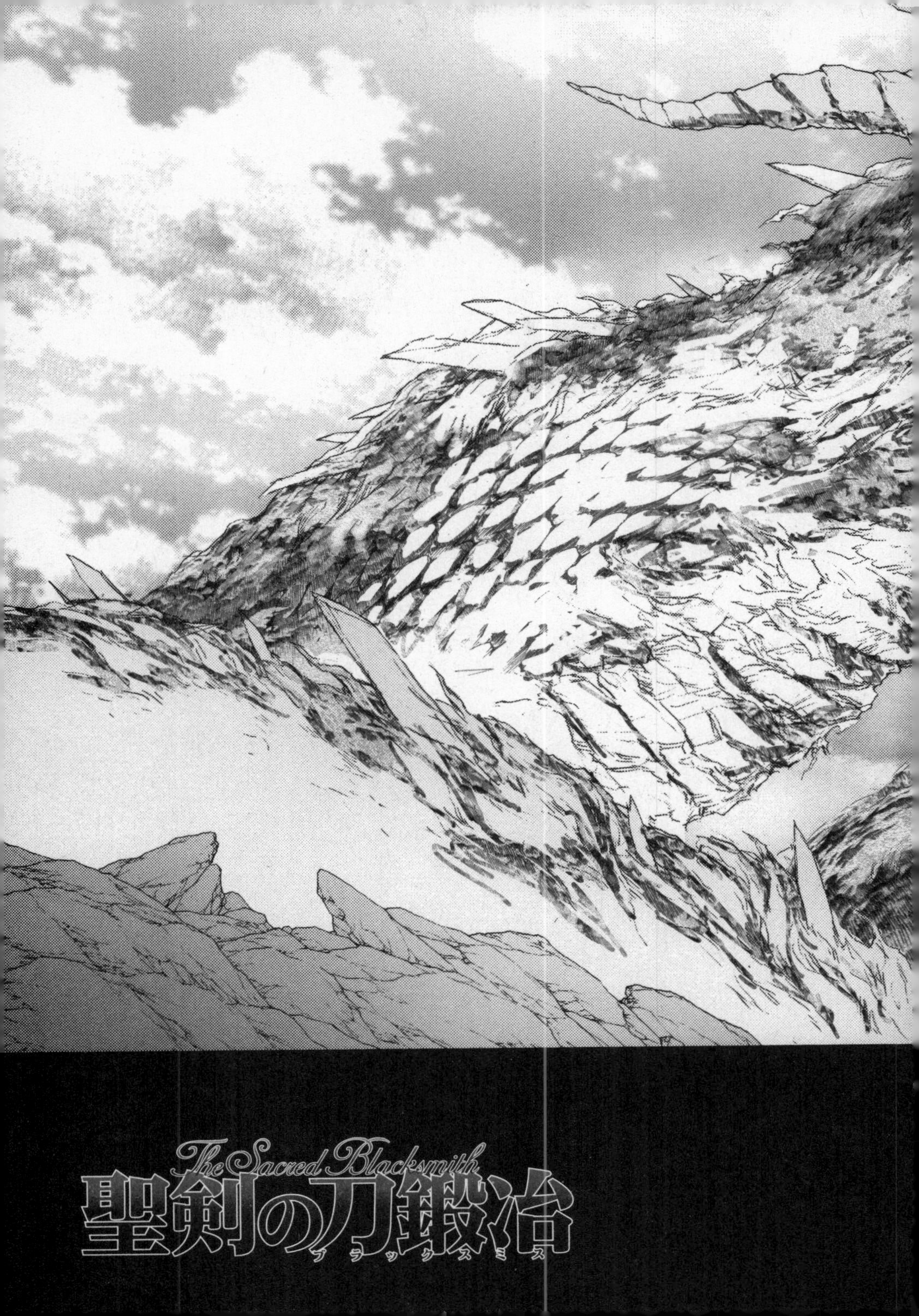
The Sacred Blacksmith
聖剣の刀鍛冶
ブラックスミス

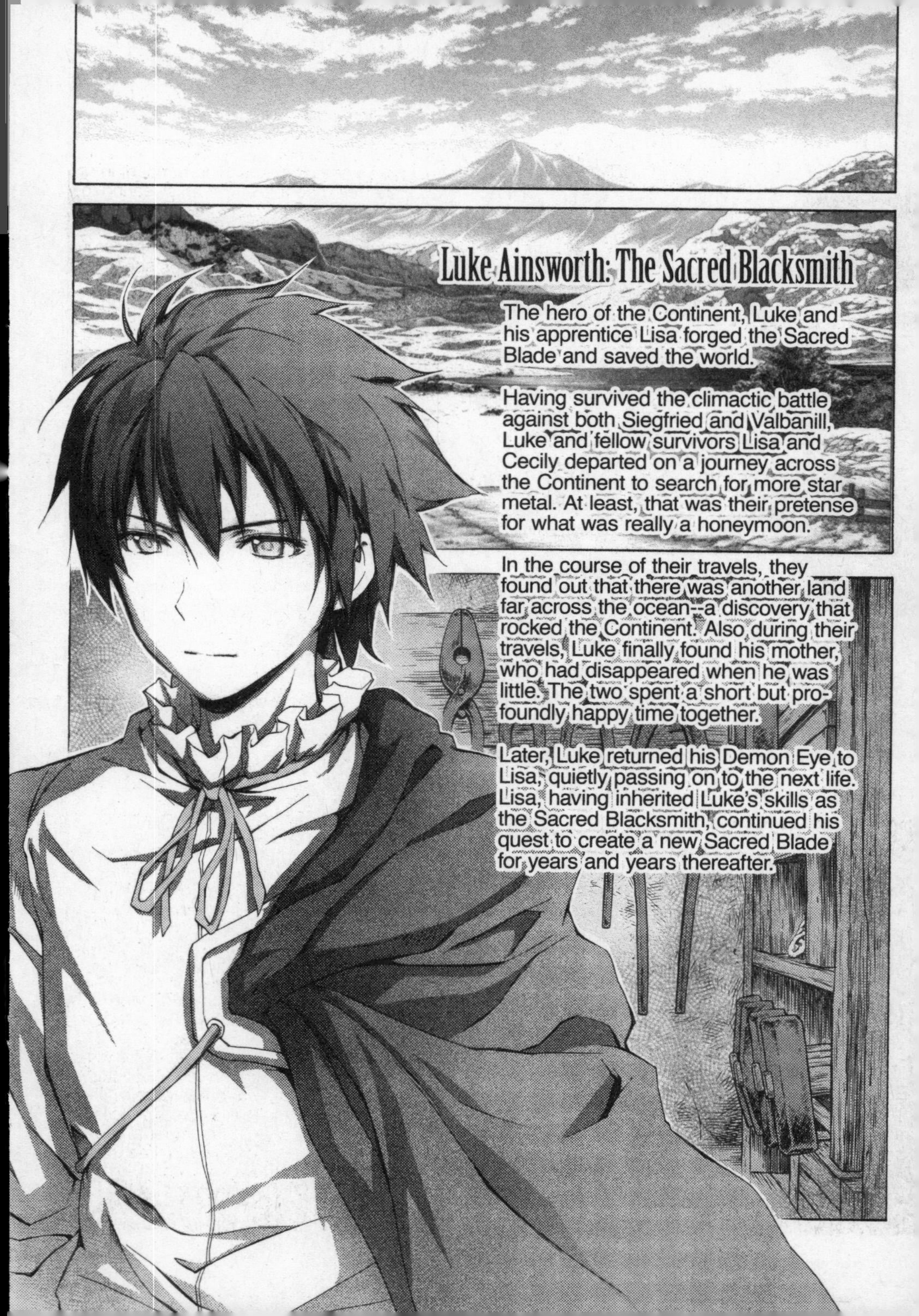

Luke Ainsworth: The Sacred Blacksmith
The hero of the Continent, Luke and his apprentice Lisa forged the Sacred Blade and saved the world.
Having survived the climactic battle against both Siegfried and Valbanill, Luke and fellow survivors Lisa and Cecily departed on a journey across the Continent to search for more star metal. At least, that was their pretense for what was really a honeymoon.
In the course of their travels, they found out that there was another land far across the ocean--a discovery that rocked the Continent. Also during their travels, Luke finally found his mother, who had disappeared when he was little. The two spent a short but profoundly happy time together.
Later, Luke returned his Demon Eye to Lisa, quietly passing on to the next life. Lisa, having inherited Luke's skills as the Sacred Blacksmith, continued his quest to create a new Sacred Blade for years and years thereafter.

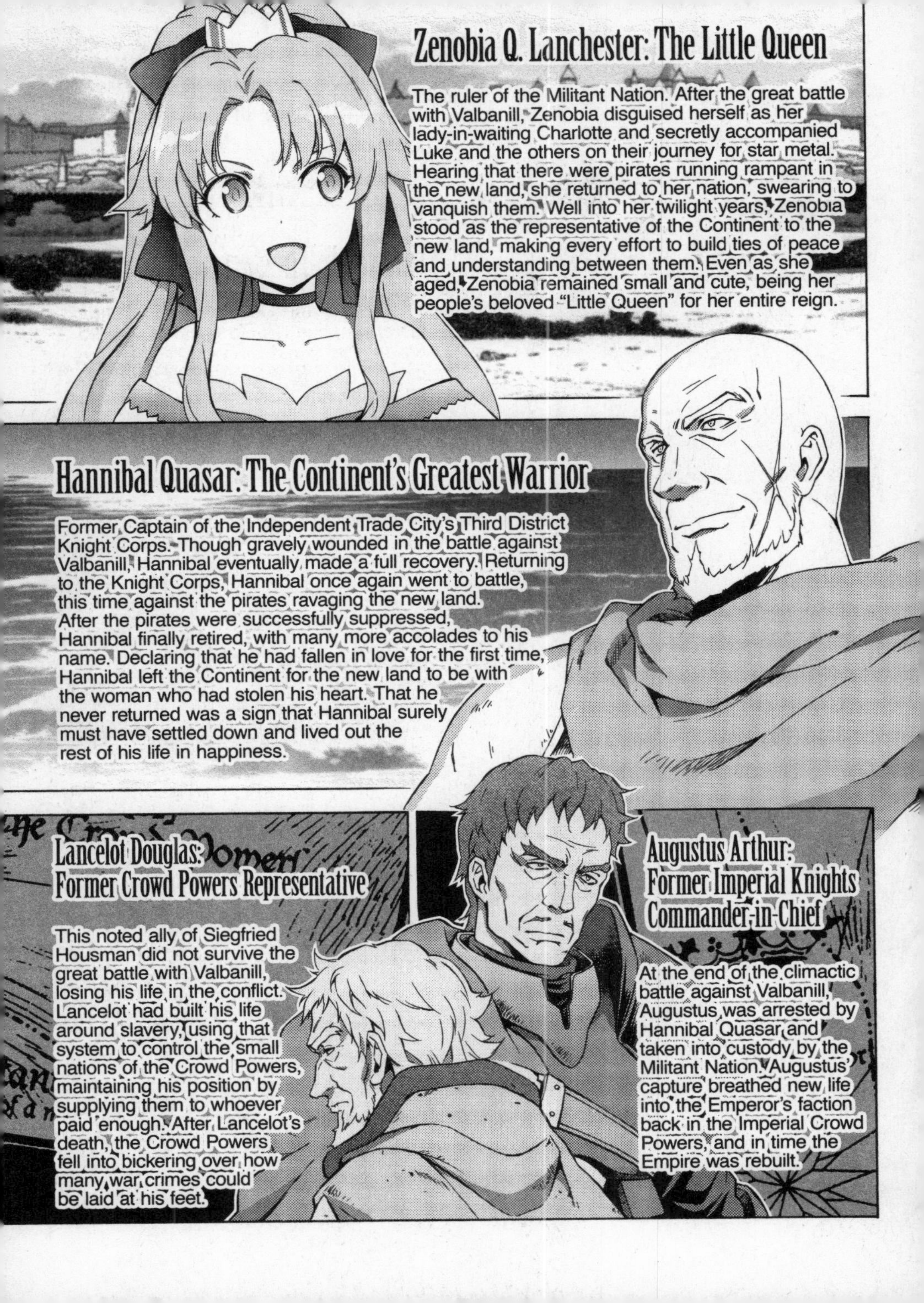

Zenobia Q. Lanchester: The Little Queen

The ruler of the Militant Nation. After the great battle with Valbanill, Zenobia disguised herself as her lady-in-waiting Charlotte and secretly accompanied Luke and the others on their journey for star metal. Hearing that there were pirates running rampant in the new land, she returned to her nation, swearing to vanquish them. Well into her twilight years, Zenobia stood as the representative of the Continent to the new land, making every effort to build ties of peace and understanding between them. Even as she aged, Zenobia remained small and cute, being her people's beloved "Little Queen" for her entire reign.

Hannibal Quasar: The Continent's Greatest Warrior

Former Captain of the Independent Trade City's Third District Knight Corps. Though gravely wounded in the battle against Valbanill, Hannibal eventually made a full recovery. Returning to the Knight Corps, Hannibal once again went to battle, this time against the pirates ravaging the new land. After the pirates were successfully suppressed, Hannibal finally retired, with many more accolades to his name. Declaring that he had fallen in love for the first time, Hannibal left the Continent for the new land to be with the woman who had stolen his heart. That he never returned was a sign that Hannibal surely must have settled down and lived out the rest of his life in happiness.

Lancelot Douglas: Former Crowd Powers Representative

This noted ally of Siegfried Housman did not survive the great battle with Valbanill, losing his life in the conflict. Lancelot had built his life around slavery, using that system to control the small nations of the Crowd Powers, maintaining his position by supplying them to whoever paid enough. After Lancelot's death, the Crowd Powers fell into bickering over how many war crimes could be laid at his feet.

Augustus Arthur: Former Imperial Knights Commander-in-Chief

At the end of the climactic battle against Valbanill, Augustus was arrested by Hannibal Quasar and taken into custody by the Militant Nation. Augustus' capture breathed new life into the Emperor's faction back in the Imperial Crowd Powers, and in time the Empire was rebuilt.

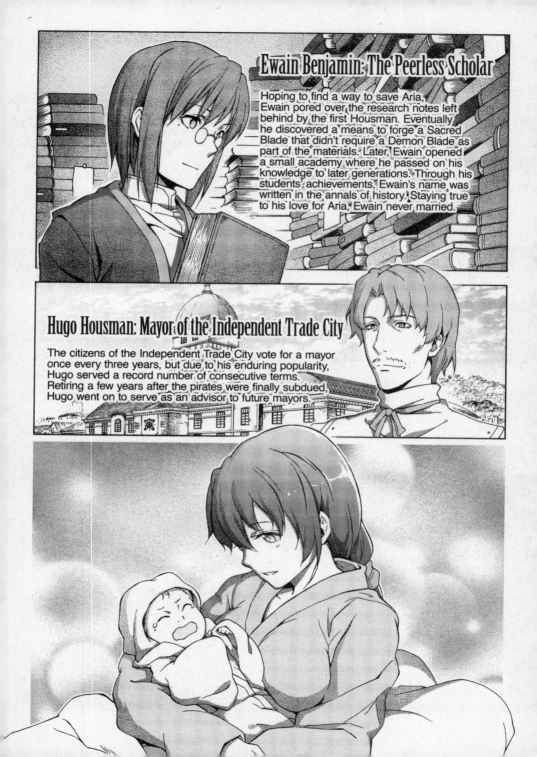

Ewain Benjamin: The Peerless Scholar

Hoping to find a way to save Aria, Ewain pored over the research notes left behind by the first Housman. Eventually he discovered a means to forge a Sacred Blade that didn't require a Demon Blade as part of the materials. Later, Ewain opened a small academy where he passed on his knowledge to later generations. Through his students' achievements, Ewain's name was written in the annals of history. Staying true to his love for Aria, Ewain never married.

Hugo Housman: Mayor of the Independent Trade City

The citizens of the Independent Trade City vote for a mayor once every three years, but due to his enduring popularity, Hugo served a record number of consecutive terms.
Retiring a few years after the pirates were finally subdued, Hugo went on to serve as an advisor to future mayors.

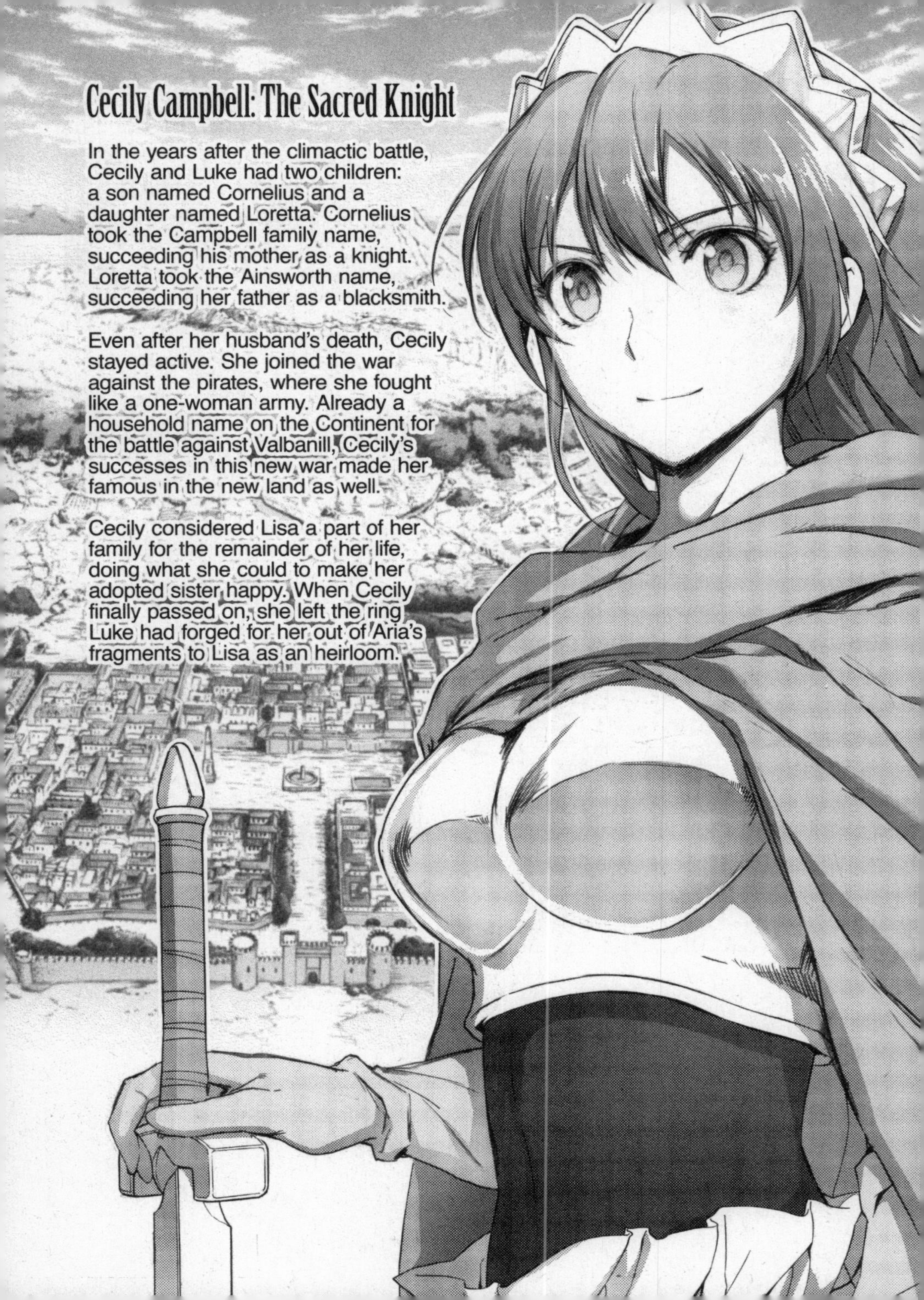

Cecily Campbell: The Sacred Knight

In the years after the climactic battle, Cecily and Luke had two children: a son named Cornelius and a daughter named Loretta. Cornelius took the Campbell family name, succeeding his mother as a knight. Loretta took the Ainsworth name, succeeding her father as a blacksmith.

Even after her husband's death, Cecily stayed active. She joined the war against the pirates, where she fought like a one-woman army. Already a household name on the Continent for the battle against Valbanill, Cecily's successes in this new war made her famous in the new land as well.

Cecily considered Lisa a part of her family for the remainder of her life, doing what she could to make her adopted sister happy. When Cecily finally passed on, she left the ring Luke had forged for her out of Aria's fragments to Lisa as an heirloom.

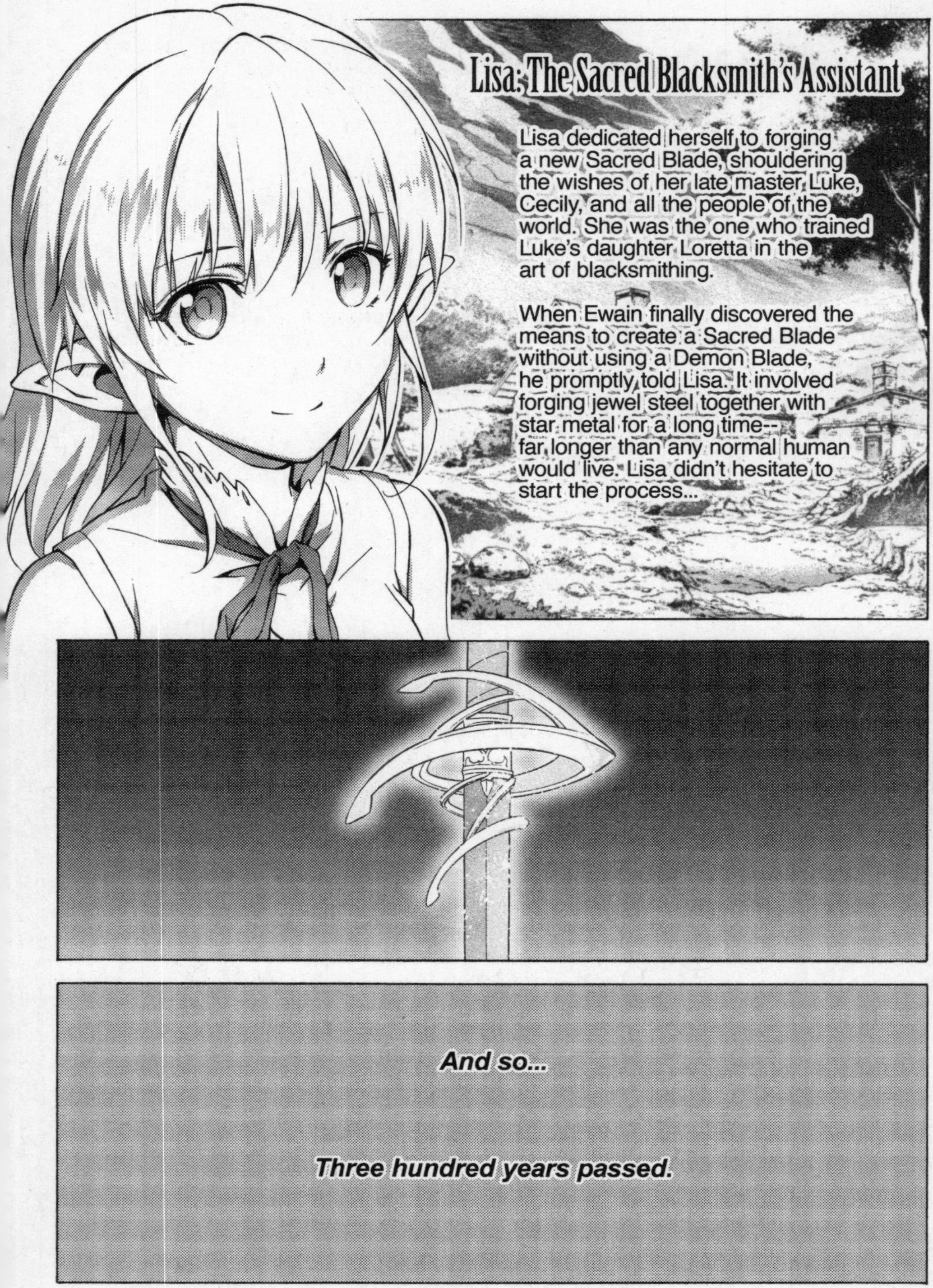
Lisa: The Sacred Blacksmith's Assistant
Lisa dedicated herself to forging a new Sacred Blade, shouldering the wishes of her late master Luke, Cecily, and all the people of the world. She was the one who trained Luke's daughter Loretta in the art of blacksmithing.
When Ewain finally discovered the means to create a Sacred Blade without using a Demon Blade, he promptly told Lisa. It involved forging jewel steel together with star metal for a long time--far longer than any normal human would live. Lisa didn't hesitate to start the process...
And so...
Three hundred years passed.

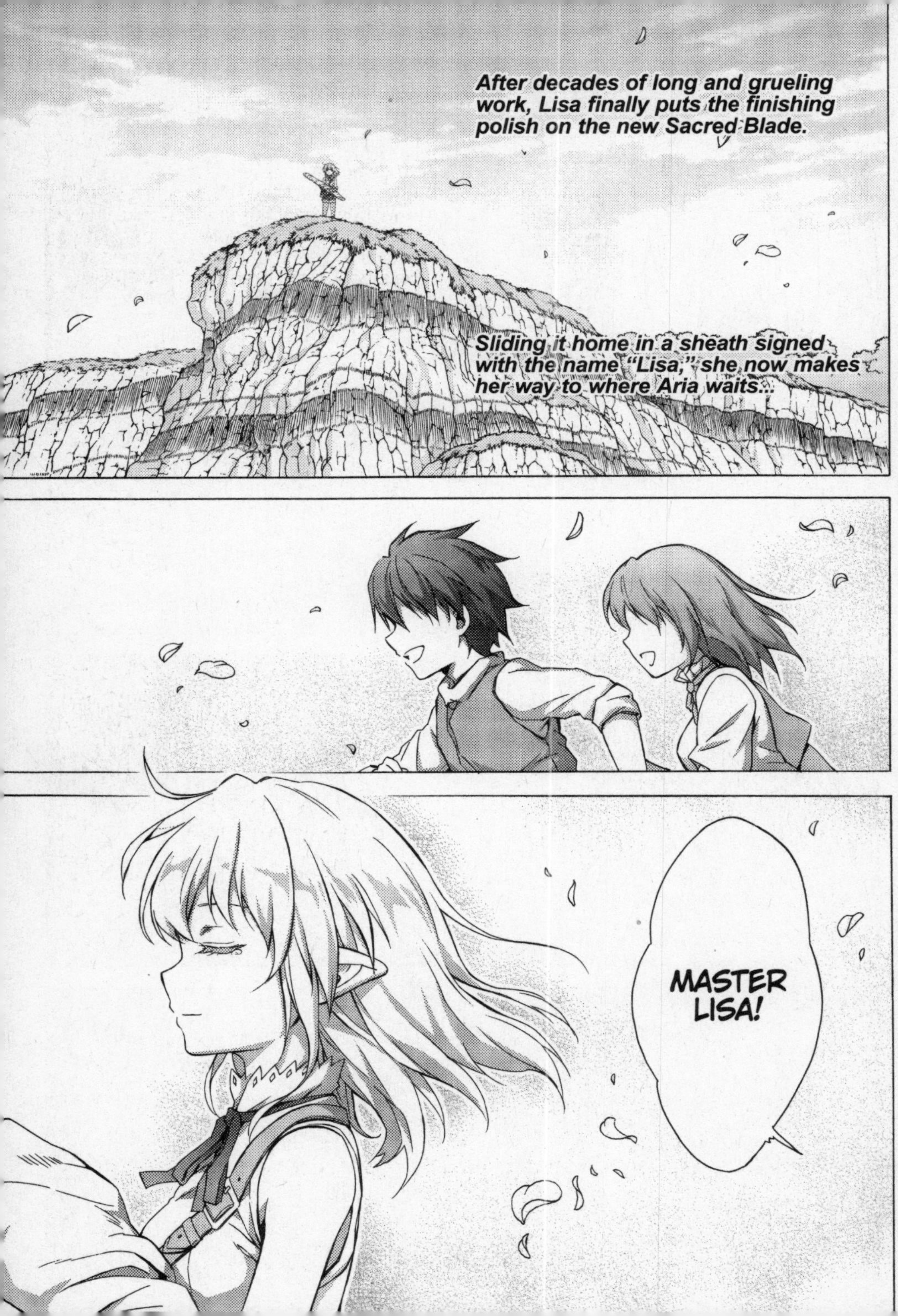
After decades of long and grueling work, Lisa finally puts the finishing polish on the new Sacred Blade.
Sliding it home in a sheath signed with the name "Lisa," she now makes her way to where Aria waits...
MASTER LISA!

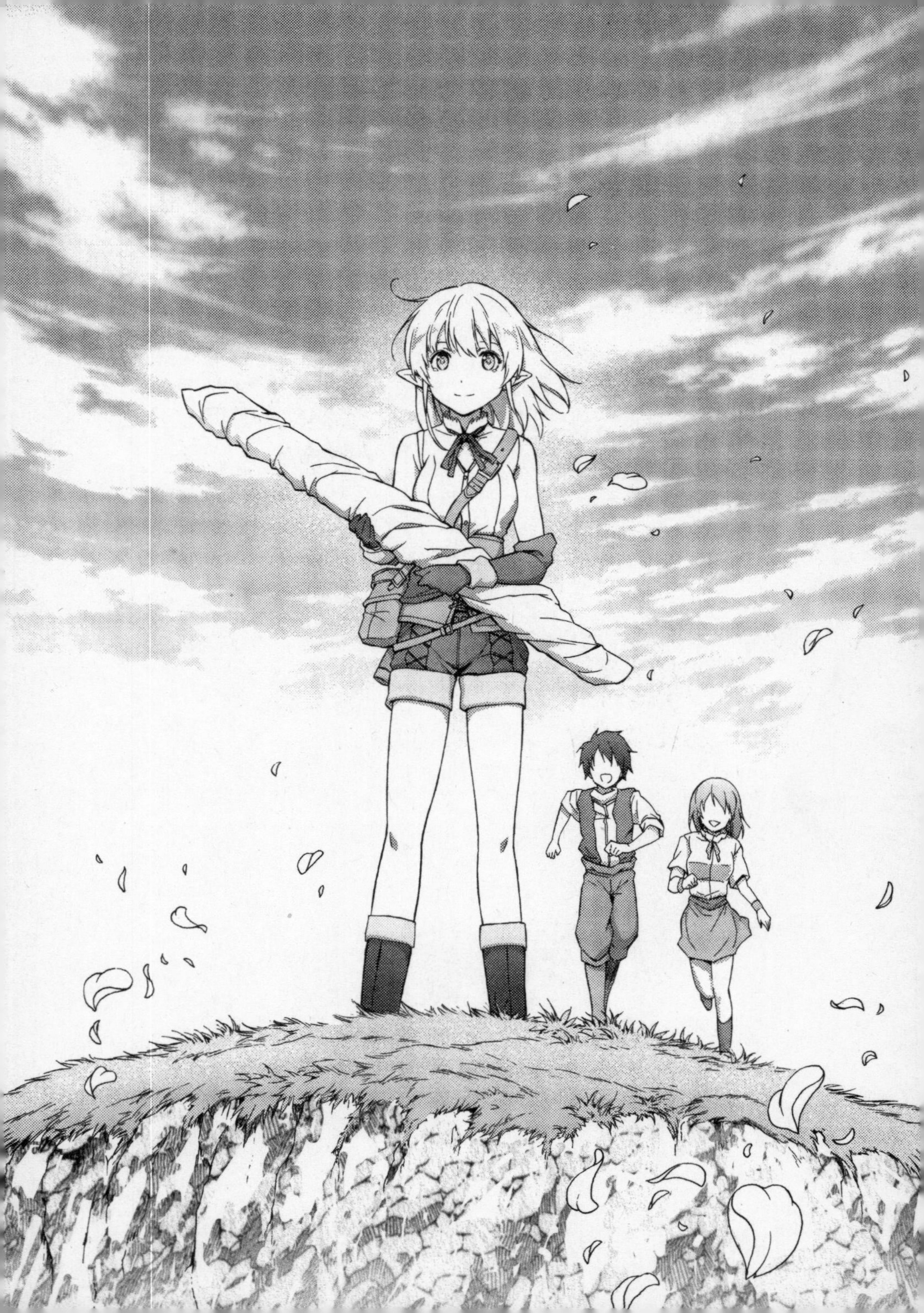

THANK YOU.
THOSE ARE
THE ONLY
WORDS I
CAN SAY...
THANK YOU.

THAT IS
MORE
THAN
ENOUGH.

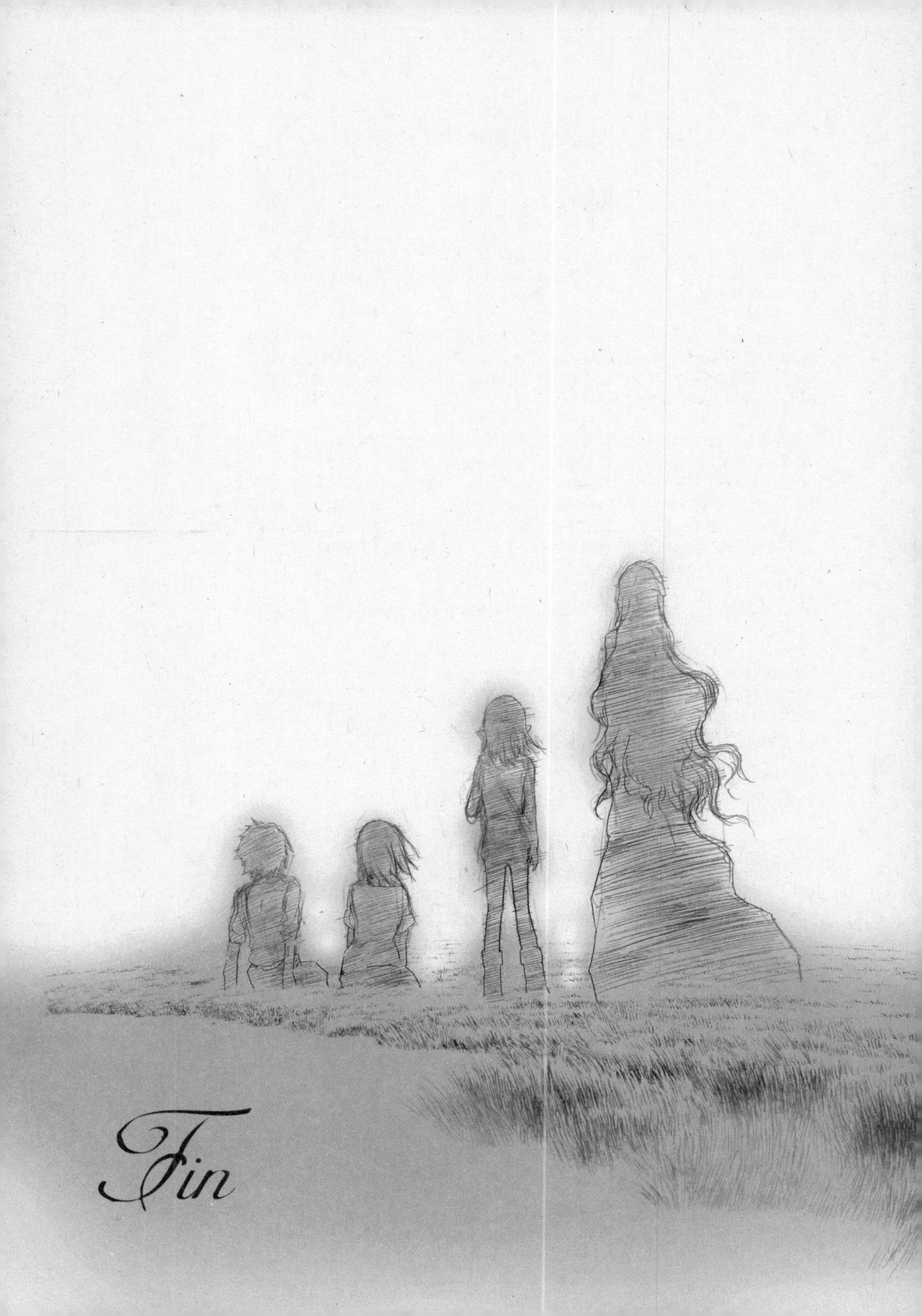
Fin

— A Word from the Artist —

I'm sorry to have made you wait so long, but here is the final volume. With this, the manga version of *The Sacred Blacksmith* is now complete.

Looking back, when I first began working on this title, it was an unsettled time in my life. I wasn't sure what I wanted to do with myself. Discovering this work and getting to serialize it opened my eyes to so many things.

This was such an honest and sincere work. Its fantasy world was one I adored so much it made me want to draw it. But even more than the world, I loved the characters. It felt like, more than once, Cecily's spontaneity influenced me, giving me the push I needed in real life. Luke and Lisa and Aria all resonated with me, too, teaching me that yes, it's okay to feel that way. I think I will carry all of these characters in my heart for the rest of my life.

For so long, I have walked down the road of life side by side with this work.

Now, after seeing everything that I wanted to see, we've reached the end. I can look back on our journey with pride, and say goodbye to it with happiness.

Miura-sensei, thank you for creating *The Sacred Blacksmith*.

Luna-sensei, thank you for bringing it to life.

To all my assistants, my editors, and most of all, to all you readers out there, you have my deepest gratitude. Thank you very much!

 Kotaro Yamada

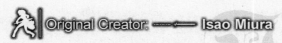

— A Word from the Creators —

 Original Creator: ———✦——— Isao Miura

Hello. I'm Isao Miura, the original author for *The Sacred Blacksmith*.

First, let me say thank you to Kotaro Yamada-sensei for taking time out of his busy schedule to draw the manga version of this story. *The Sacred Blacksmith* manga version began serialization in the January 2009 issue of the *Comic Alive* magazine. That means it was ongoing for a full eight years--that's longer than it took me to write the entire novel series! (shocked)

That one scene in Volume 3, you know the one, was really impactful. I was pretty depressed at the time, so much so it even made the news, but then I suddenly noticed I was getting way more hits on my blog. "I'm stubborn!!" she yelled. Her expression was perfect. The two-page spread during her confession was beautiful, too. I couldn't help but grin! Seeing the scene where the old Sacred Blade takes Lisa's eye in the manga made me glad I added it into the novels.

And wow, Valbanill sure was scary!

I can say with absolute certainty that I was very glad to have this story adapted as it was. Yamada-sensei, thank you so much for all your hard work!

Character Designer: ———✦——— Luna

Yamada-sensei's work on this manga has been a great inspiration for me in my current work.

While the manga and the original novels were being published alongside of each other, I tried to live up to Yamada-sensei's work, but that one pinup of the grand maid march is still a goal of mine.

Please take good care of yourself, and keep up the good work. I'll be cheering you on from the shadows!

CONGRATS ON COMPLETING THE MANGA!

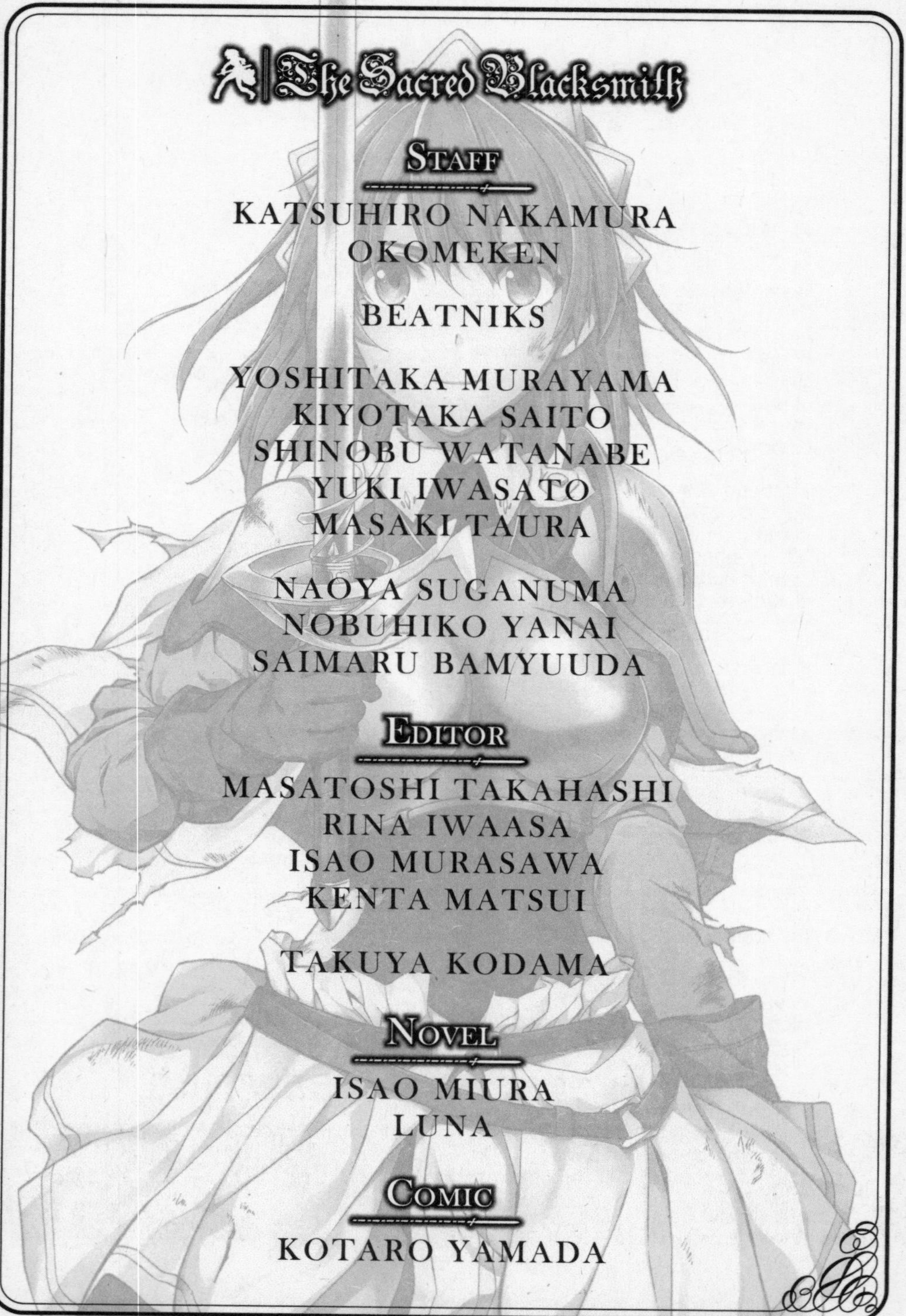

The Sacred Blacksmith

Staff

KATSUHIRO NAKAMURA
OKOMEKEN

BEATNIKS

YOSHITAKA MURAYAMA
KIYOTAKA SAITO
SHINOBU WATANABE
YUKI IWASATO
MASAKI TAURA

NAOYA SUGANUMA
NOBUHIKO YANAI
SAIMARU BAMYUUDA

Editor

MASATOSHI TAKAHASHI
RINA IWAASA
ISAO MURASAWA
KENTA MATSUI

TAKUYA KODAMA

Novel

ISAO MIURA
LUNA

Comic

KOTARO YAMADA

The Sacred Blacksmith

聖剣の刀鍛治

The complete
series available
now in print &
digital editions
from Seven Seas
Entertainment